NTSB/PAR-12/01
PB2012-916501
Notation 8423
Adopted July 10, 2012

# Pipeline Accident Report

Enbridge Incorporated
Hazardous Liquid Pipeline Rupture and Release
Marshall, Michigan
July 25, 2010

**National
Transportation
Safety Board**

490 L'Enfant Plaza, S.W.
Washington, D.C. 20594

National Transportation Safety Board. 2012. *Enbridge Incorporated Hazardous Liquid Pipeline Rupture and Release, Marshall, Michigan, July 25, 2010.* Pipeline Accident Report NTSB/PAR-12/01. Washington, D.C.

**Abstract:** On Sunday, July 25, 2010, at 5:58 p.m., eastern daylight time, a segment of a 30-inch-diameter pipeline (Line 6B), owned and operated by Enbridge Incorporated (Enbridge) ruptured in a wetland in Marshall, Michigan. The rupture occurred during the last stages of a planned shutdown and was not discovered or addressed for over 17 hours. During the time lapse, Enbridge twice pumped additional oil (81 percent of the total release) into Line 6B during two startups; the total release was estimated to be 843,444 gallons of crude oil. The oil saturated the surrounding wetlands and flowed into the Talmadge Creek and the Kalamazoo River. Local residents self-evacuated from their houses, and the environment was negatively affected. Cleanup efforts continue as of the adoption date of this report, with continuing costs exceeding $767 million. About 320 people reported symptoms consistent with crude oil exposure. No fatalities were reported.

As a result of its investigation of this accident, the National Transportation Safety Board (NTSB) makes recommendations to the U.S. Secretary of Transportation, the Pipeline and Hazardous Materials Safety Administration (PHMSA), Enbridge, the American Petroleum Institute, the Pipeline Research Council International, the International Association of Fire Chiefs, and the National Emergency Number Association. The NTSB also reiterates a previous recommendation to PHMSA.

# Contents

Figures.................................................................................................................................. vii

Tables .................................................................................................................................. ix

Acronyms and Abbreviations .............................................................................................x

Executive Summary ......................................................................................................... xii

1   Factual Information...........................................................................................................1
1.1 Introduction .................................................................................................................1
1.2 Accident Narrative ......................................................................................................8
    1.2.1   Preaccident Events............................................................................................8
    1.2.2   The Rupture—Shift A .......................................................................................8
    1.2.3   First Line 6B Startup—Shift B .......................................................................10
    1.2.4   Second Line 6B Startup—Shift B....................................................................13
    1.2.5   Discovery—Shift C.........................................................................................14
    1.2.6   Enbridge Initial Response ...............................................................................15
1.3 Injuries and Evacuations ...........................................................................................18
    1.3.1   Injuries ............................................................................................................18
    1.3.2   Evacuations.....................................................................................................18
1.4 Damages .....................................................................................................................18
    1.4.1   Pipeline ...........................................................................................................18
    1.4.2   Environment....................................................................................................19
1.5 Environmental Conditions .........................................................................................19
    1.5.1   Meteorological ................................................................................................19
    1.5.2   Kalamazoo River Conditions..........................................................................19
1.6 Pipeline Information ..................................................................................................19
    1.6.1   Pipeline History ..............................................................................................19
    1.6.2   Pipeline Operating Pressure ...........................................................................20
    1.6.3   Site Description................................................................................................20
    1.6.4   Other Enbridge Pipeline Incidents .................................................................20
        1.6.4.1     Cohasset, Minnesota......................................................................21
        1.6.4.2     Glenavon, Saskatchewan...............................................................22
1.7 Examination of the Accident Pipe..............................................................................23
    1.7.1   Coating.............................................................................................................24
    1.7.2   Corrosion..........................................................................................................24
    1.7.3   Microbial Corrosion.........................................................................................24
    1.7.4   The Fracture .....................................................................................................25
    1.7.5   Crack and Corrosion Depth Profile..................................................................28
    1.7.6   Mechanical Testing and Chemical Analysis....................................................29
1.8 PHMSA Integrity Management Regulation ................................................................29
    1.8.1   Pipeline Integrity Management in High Consequence Areas ...........................29
    1.8.2   Elements of Integrity Management and Integration of Threats.........................30

1.8.3   Discovery of Condition...........................................................................30
1.8.4   Immediate and 180-Day Conditions ...........................................................31
1.9   Enbridge Integrity Management Program ............................................................31
1.9.1   Corrosion Management..........................................................................32
1.9.2   Crack Management ..............................................................................32
1.9.3   In-line Inspection Intervals ...................................................................33
1.9.4   Stress Corrosion Cracking ....................................................................34
1.9.5   Coating and Cathodic Protection ...........................................................34
1.9.6   In-line Inspection Tools .......................................................................35
        1.9.6.1   USCD Tool........................................................................35
1.9.7   Enbridge Postaccident Threat Assessment Review .....................................36
1.9.8   Prior In-Line Inspections of Line 6B ......................................................37
        1.9.8.1   2004 Ultrasonic Wall Measurement In-Line Inspection....................37
        1.9.8.2   2005 In-Line Inspection—PII USCD Crack Tool Results...................39
        1.9.8.3   2007 In-Line Inspection—PII High-Resolution MFL Tool Results..........41
        1.9.8.4   2009 In-Line Inspection—PII USWM Tool Results............................41
1.10 Pipeline Public Awareness Programs ..................................................................42
1.10.1 Regulatory Requirements.....................................................................42
1.10.2 API Recommended Practice 1162 ........................................................42
1.10.3 Enbridge's PAP ................................................................................42
1.11 Enbridge Operations .......................................................................................44
1.11.1 Edmonton Control Center ...................................................................44
1.11.2 Control Center Personnel Experience ....................................................45
1.11.3 Toxicology .......................................................................................47
1.11.4 Training and Qualifications .................................................................47
        1.11.4.1   Control Center Operations ...................................................47
        1.11.4.2   MBS Analyst ...................................................................48
1.11.5 MBS Leak Detection...........................................................................49
        1.11.5.1   Federal Regulations............................................................49
        1.11.5.2   API 1130 Computational Pipeline Monitoring for Liquids ...............49
        1.11.5.3   Enbridge's MBS ................................................................50
        1.11.5.4   Column Separation.............................................................51
1.11.6 Procedures........................................................................................52
        1.11.6.1   10-Minute Restriction .........................................................52
        1.11.6.2   Suspected Column Separation................................................52
        1.11.6.3   MBS Alarm ......................................................................53
        1.11.6.4   SCADA Leak Triggers.........................................................53
        1.11.6.5   Suspected Leak—Volume Difference........................................54
        1.11.6.6   Leak and Obstruction Trigger—On Startup from SCADA Data................54
1.11.7 Fatigue Management............................................................................54
1.11.8 Enbridge Health and Safety Management System ......................................55
1.12 Environmental Response ..................................................................................55
1.12.1 Volume Released ................................................................................55
1.12.2 Hazardous Materials Information ..........................................................56
1.12.3 Overview of the Oil Spill Response........................................................56
        1.12.3.1   Notifications......................................................................58

1.12.4 Enbridge Facility Response Plan ............................................................58
1.12.5 EPA Oversight of Spill Response Efforts ................................................61
1.12.6 Environmental Monitoring....................................................................62
    1.12.6.1  Air Quality..............................................................................62
    1.12.6.2  Potable Water .........................................................................62
    1.12.6.3  Surface Water and Sediment ...............................................62
1.12.7 Natural Resources and Wildlife ...........................................................63
1.13 Previous NTSB Investigations and Studies...................................................63
1.13.1 NTSB SCADA 2005 Study ....................................................................63
1.13.2 NTSB 2010 Pipeline Investigation of Pacific Gas and Electric Company .................64
1.13.3 Carmichael, Mississippi .......................................................................65
1.14 Postaccident Actions .......................................................................................65
1.14.1 PHMSA Corrective Action Order..........................................................65
1.14.2 PHMSA's Notice of Probable Violation.................................................66
1.14.3 Enbridge Actions ..................................................................................66
    1.14.3.1  Line 6B Replacement Projects ..........................................66
    1.14.3.2  Enbridge Operator Training ................................................67
    1.14.3.3  Integrity Management ..........................................................67
    1.14.3.4  Enbridge Control Center .....................................................67
1.15 Federal Oversight .............................................................................................68
1.15.1 Canadian and U.S. Regulation...............................................................68
1.15.2 Enbridge 2010 Long-Term Pressure Reduction Notification .................69
1.15.3 PHMSA Inspections..............................................................................69
1.15.4 Pipeline Safety, Regulatory Certainty, and Job Creation Act of 2011 .......71
1.15.5 National Energy Board ..........................................................................71
1.15.6 PHMSA Inspection of Enbridge's PAP.................................................72
1.15.7 PHMSA Facility Response Plan Review and Approval .........................73
1.15.8 PHMSA Facility Response Plan Advisory Bulletin ..............................75
1.15.9 Response Preparedness .........................................................................75
1.15.10    PHMSA Control Center Management .................................................76
1.16 Other Information .............................................................................................78
1.16.1 Oil Spill Response Methods..................................................................78
1.16.2 API Standard 1160—Managing System Integrity for Hazardous Liquid Pipelines ....80

2  Analysis .................................................................................................................81
2.1  Introduction .......................................................................................................81
2.2  Pipeline Failure.................................................................................................82
2.2.1  The Rupture ............................................................................................82
2.2.2  Fracture Mechanism................................................................................82
2.3  Federal Regulations Governing Hazardous Liquid Pipelines .........................84
2.4  Deficiencies in the Integrity Management Program.........................................87
2.4.1  Engineering Assessment of Cracks and Margin of Safety.......................88
2.4.2  In-line Inspection Tool Tolerances .........................................................88
2.4.3  Improper Wall Thickness........................................................................89
2.4.4  Corrosion and Cracking Interactions ......................................................89
2.4.5  Crack Growth Rate Not Considered ........................................................90
2.4.6  Need for Continuous Reassessment.........................................................90

2.4.7  Effect of Integrity Management Deficiencies...............................................91
2.5  Mischaracterization of the Crack Feature .........................................................93
2.6  Control Center .................................................................................................93
    2.6.1  Team Performance ....................................................................................94
    2.6.2  Training.....................................................................................................97
    2.6.3  Procedures.................................................................................................98
    2.6.4  Tolerance for Procedural Deviance .........................................................101
    2.6.5  Alcohol and Drug Testing.......................................................................101
    2.6.6  Work/Sleep/Wake History .....................................................................102
2.7  Pipeline Public Awareness .............................................................................103
2.8  Environmental Response.................................................................................105
    2.8.1  Effectiveness of the Emergency Response to this Accident ....................105
    2.8.2  Facility Response Planning......................................................................108
        2.8.2.1  Regulatory Requirements for Facility Response Planning .........109
        2.8.2.2  Adequacy of Enbridge Facility Response Plan ..........................111
        2.8.2.3  PHMSA Oversight of Facility Response Plans...........................112
2.9  Summary of Enbridge Organizational Deficiencies........................................114

3  Conclusions....................................................................................................118
3.1  Findings..........................................................................................................118
3.2  Probable Cause ...............................................................................................121

4  Recommendations.........................................................................................122
4.1  New Recommendations....................................................................................122
4.2  Reiterated Recommendation ...........................................................................124

5  Appendixes.....................................................................................................126
5.1  Appendix A: Investigation ..............................................................................126
5.2  Appendix B: Enbridge's MBS and Control Center Operations Procedures .......127
5.3  Appendix C: Supervisory Control and Data Acquisition Plots.........................146

# Figures

**Figure 1.** Enbridge's Liquids System and the 1,900-mile Lakehead System (the U.S. portion). Inset shows Line 6B, the 293-mile extension from Griffith to Sarnia installed in 1969. ................................................................................................................................ 2

**Figure 2.** The ruptured segment of Line 6B in the trench following the July 25, 2010, rupture. The fracture face measured about 6 feet 8.25 inches long and was 5.32 inches wide at the widest opening. The fracture ran just below the seam weld that was oriented just below the 3 o'clock position. A red circle shows a location where the coating was wrinkled and had separated from the pipe surface. ................................................................... 3

**Figure 3.** Aerial view of the accident location showing the rupture site to the left and the Talmadge Creek flowing west toward the Kalamazoo River. ....................................... 4

**Figure 4.** Cleanup efforts in an oil-soaked wetland near the rupture site. Saturated soil complicated the cleanup and excavation efforts. An excavator with a vacuum attachment is shown situated on wooden matting near the rupture site. .............................................. 5

**Figure 5.** Key events timeline of the Line 6B rupture in Marshall, Michigan, showing the events from the time of rupture on July 25, 2010, to the time of discovery on July 26, 2010. ...... 6

**Figure 6.** Key Enbridge staff involved in the 17-hour accident sequence. MBS refers to Material Balance System. ........................................................................................................ 7

**Figure 7.** Simplified schematic of Line 6B, showing pump stations and delivery locations......... 9

**Figure 8.** Emergency response and 911 calls from nearby residents. First and last calls are noted.......................................................................................................................................... 11

**Figure 9.** Area between rupture site and the Kalamazoo River where first responders concentrated efforts to contain the released oil........................................................................ 15

**Figure 10.** Underflow dam on Talmadge Creek on July 30, 2010............................................. 17

**Figure 11.** Line 6B ruptured segment showing upstream and downstream sections used for Materials Laboratory examination. Detail B shows tented coating over the longitudinal seam weld.............................................................................................................................. 23

**Figure 12.** The outside surface of the pipe looking at the fracture area cut for lab examination.............................................................................................................................. 25

**Figure 13.** Curving arrest lines of preexisting cracks along the upper fracture face shown after cleaning to remove oxides. White arrows indicate multiple origin areas of preexisting cracks. ...................................................................................................................................... 26

**Figure 14.** Close view of fracture surface area in the area of deepest crack penetration. The solid blue line indicates the extent of the preexisting crack penetration. .................................... 27

**Figure 15.** Transverse section through the top of the fracture showing multiple parallel cracks emanating from corrosion pits on the outside surface. ....................................................... 28

**Figure 16.** Lab measurements of crack and corrosion depths along the fracture face measured from images similar to figure 14 near area of deepest penetration (about 344 inches from upstream girth weld). ................................................................................... 29

**Figure 17.** 2004 corrosion inspection of Line 6B and 16 regions of corrosion identified by the tool on the ruptured pipe segment. The detail view shows the areas of corrosion overlapped with the rupture location. .............................................................................. 38

**Figure 18.** 2005 in-line inspection regions where crack-like characterizations were reported by PII on the ruptured segment of Line 6B. ................................................................ 40

**Figure 19.** Map showing rupture location and affected waterways from Talmadge Creek to Morrow Lake. ................................................................................................................ 57

**Figure 20.** Enbridge PLM emergency response trailer containing the company's Tier 1 oil containment equipment, October 17, 2010. ..................................................................... 60

**Figure 21.** (Left) Enbridge employees install sorbent boom in front of a culvert at Division Drive. (Right) Oil residue marks the level of the oil carried through this culvert following the Enbridge release from Line 6B. ............................................................................... 79

# Tables

**Table 1.** Awareness of pipelines in the community. ........................................................... 43

**Table 2.** Pipeline information received. ............................................................................ 43

**Table 3.** Key control center staff involved in the accident and their years of experience. .......... 46

**Table 4.** Enbridge resources deployed as reported at midnight on July 26, 2010....................... 56

**Table 5.** Title 49 CFR 194.115 response tiers.................................................................... 58

**Table 6.** Volpe's comparative study of response plan review....................................................... 74

**Table 7.** Response resources for on-water recovery that Enbridge would have been required to identify in its facility response plan and have available by contract or other means, had its facilities been regulated by the Coast Guard or the EPA.................................... 110

# Acronyms and Abbreviations

| | |
|---|---|
| API | American Petroleum Institute |
| ASME | American Society of Mechanical Engineers |
| CAO | corrective action order |
| CEPA | Canadian Energy Pipeline Association |
| CFR | *Code of Federal Regulations* |
| CMT | commodity movement and tracking |
| Coast Guard | U.S. Coast Guard |
| CPM | computational pipeline monitoring |
| CRM | crew resource management |
| DOT | U.S. Department of Transportation |
| DSAW | double submerged arc welded |
| Enbridge | Enbridge Incorporated |
| EPA | U.S. Environmental Protection Agency |
| FAA | Federal Aviation Administration |
| FOSC | Federal on-scene coordinator |
| HCA | high consequence area |
| Line 6B | 30-inch-diameter accident pipeline |
| LPM | Line Pressure Management |
| MBS | Material Balance System |
| MFL | magnetic flux leakage |
| MOP | maximum operating pressure |
| MP | mile point |
| NEB | National Energy Board |

| | |
|---|---|
| NOPV | Notice of Probable Violation |
| NRC | National Response Center |
| NTSB | National Transportation Safety Board |
| PAP | public awareness program |
| PAPERS | Public Awareness Program Effectiveness Research Survey |
| PG&E | Pacific Gas and Electric Company |
| PHMSA | Pipeline and Hazardous Materials Safety Administration |
| PII | PII Pipeline Solutions |
| PIPES | Pipeline Inspection, Protection, Enforcement and Safety |
| PLM | pipeline maintenance |
| PREP | Preparedness for Response Exercise Program |
| PS | pump station |
| psi | pounds per square inch |
| psig | pounds per square inch, gauge |
| RP | recommended practice |
| SCADA | supervisory control and data acquisition |
| SCC | stress corrosion cracking |
| SMS | safety management system |
| SMYS | specified minimum yield strength |
| TSB | Transportation Safety Board of Canada |
| USCD | UltraScan Crack Detection |
| USGS | U.S. Geological Survey |
| USWM | UltraScan Wall Measurement |
| Volpe | Volpe National Transportation Systems Center |

# Executive Summary

On Sunday, July 25, 2010, at 5:58 p.m., eastern daylight time, a segment of a 30-inch-diameter pipeline (Line 6B), owned and operated by Enbridge Incorporated (Enbridge) ruptured in a wetland in Marshall, Michigan. The rupture occurred during the last stages of a planned shutdown and was not discovered or addressed for over 17 hours. During the time lapse, Enbridge twice pumped additional oil (81 percent of the total release) into Line 6B during two startups; the total release was estimated to be 843,444 gallons of crude oil. The oil saturated the surrounding wetlands and flowed into the Talmadge Creek and the Kalamazoo River. Local residents self-evacuated from their houses, and the environment was negatively affected. Cleanup efforts continue as of the adoption date of this report, with continuing costs exceeding $767 million. About 320 people reported symptoms consistent with crude oil exposure. No fatalities were reported.

The National Transportation Safety Board (NTSB) determines that the probable cause of the pipeline rupture was corrosion fatigue cracks that grew and coalesced from crack and corrosion defects under disbonded polyethylene tape coating, producing a substantial crude oil release that went undetected by the control center for over 17 hours. The rupture and prolonged release were made possible by pervasive organizational failures at Enbridge Incorporated (Enbridge) that included the following:

- Deficient integrity management procedures, which allowed well-documented crack defects in corroded areas to propagate until the pipeline failed.

- Inadequate training of control center personnel, which allowed the rupture to remain undetected for 17 hours and through two startups of the pipeline.

- Insufficient public awareness and education, which allowed the release to continue for nearly 14 hours after the first notification of an odor to local emergency response agencies.

Contributing to the accident was the Pipeline and Hazardous Materials Safety Administration's (PHMSA) weak regulation for assessing and repairing crack indications, as well as PHMSA's ineffective oversight of pipeline integrity management programs, control center procedures, and public awareness.

Contributing to the severity of the environmental consequences were (1) Enbridge's failure to identify and ensure the availability of well-trained emergency responders with sufficient response resources, (2) PHMSA's lack of regulatory guidance for pipeline facility response planning, and (3) PHMSA's limited oversight of pipeline emergency preparedness that led to the approval of a deficient facility response plan.

Safety issues identified during this accident investigation include the following:

- **The inadequacy of Enbridge's integrity management program to accurately assess and remediate crack defects.** Enbridge's crack management program relied on a single in-line inspection technology to identify and estimate crack sizes. Enbridge used the resulting inspection reports to perform engineering assessments without accounting for uncertainties associated with the data, tool, or interactions between cracks and corrosion. A 2005 Enbridge engineering assessment and the company's criteria for excavation and repair showed that six crack-like defects ranging in length from 9.3 to 51.6 inches were left in the pipeline, unrepaired, until the July 2010 rupture.

- **The failure of Enbridge's control center staff to recognize abnormal conditions related to ruptures.** Enbridge's leak detection and supervisory control and data acquisition systems generated alarms consistent with a ruptured pipeline on July 25 and July 26, 2010; however, the control center staff failed to recognize that the pipeline had ruptured until notified by an outside caller more than 17 hours later. During the July 25 shutdown, the control center staff attributed the alarms to the shutdown and interpreted them as indications of an incompletely filled pipeline (known as column separation). On July 26, the control center staff pumped additional oil into the rupture pipeline for about 1.5 hours during two startups. The control center staff received many more leak detection alarms and noted large differences between the amount of oil being pumped into the pipeline and the amount being delivered, but the staff continued to attribute these conditions to column separation. An Enbridge supervisor had granted the control center staff permission to start up the pipeline for a third time just before they were notified about the release.

- **The inadequacy of Enbridge's facility response plan to ensure adequate training of the first responders and sufficient emergency response resources allocated to respond to a worst-case release.** The first responders to the oil spill were four Enbridge employees from a local pipeline maintenance shop in Marshall, Michigan. Their efforts were focused downstream along the Talmadge Creek rather than near the immediate area of the rupture. The first responders neglected to use the culverts along the Talmadge Creek as underflow dams to minimize the spread of oil, and they deployed booms unsuitable for the fast-flowing waters. Further, the oil spill response contractors, identified in Enbridge's facility response plan, were unable to immediately deploy to the rupture site and were over 10 hours away.

- **Inadequate regulatory requirements and oversight of crack defects in pipelines.** Title 49 *Code of Federal Regulations* (CFR) 195.452(h) fails to provide clear requirements for performing an engineering assessment and remediation of crack-like defects on a pipeline. In the absence of prescriptive regulatory requirements, Enbridge applied its own methodology and margins of safety. Enbridge chose to use a lower margin of safety for cracks than for corrosion when assessing crack defects. PHMSA expects pipeline operators to excavate all crack features; however, PHMSA did not issue any findings about the methods used by Enbridge in previous inspections.

- **Inadequate regulatory requirements for facility response plans under 49 CFR 194.115, which do not mandate the amount of resources or recovery capacity required for a worst-case discharge.** In the absence of such requirements, Enbridge interpreted the level of oil response resources required under PHMSA's three-tier response time frame, resulting in a lack of adequate oil spill recovery equipment and resources in the early hours of the first response. By contrast, the U.S. Coast Guard (Coast Guard) and the U.S. Environmental Protection Agency (EPA) regulations specify effective daily response capability for each of the three tiers for oil spill response planning.

- **PHMSA's inadequate review and approval of Enbridge's facility response plan that failed to verify that the plan content was accurate and timely for an estimated worst-case discharge of 1,111,152 gallons.** PHMSA's facility response program oversaw 450 facility response plans with 1.5 full-time employees, which is a lower staffing commitment than comparable response plan review programs carried out by the EPA and the Coast Guard. PHMSA and other Federal agencies receive funding from the Oil Spill Liability Trust Fund to cover operational, personnel, enforcement, and other related program costs.

As a result of this investigation, the NTSB makes safety recommendations to the U.S. Secretary of Transportation, PHMSA, Enbridge, the American Petroleum Institute, the Pipeline Research Council International, the International Association of Fire Chiefs, and the National Emergency Number Association. The NTSB also reiterates a previous recommendation to PHMSA.

# 1 Factual Information

## 1.1 Introduction

On Sunday, July 25, 2010, at 5:58 p.m., eastern daylight time,[1] a segment of a 30-inch-diameter pipeline (Line 6B), owned and operated by Enbridge Incorporated (Enbridge) ruptured in a wetland in Marshall, Michigan, about 0.6 mile downstream of the Marshall Pump Station (PS), releasing about 843,444 gallons of crude oil.[2] The accident pipeline was part of Enbridge's liquid pipeline system that originates in Edmonton, Alberta, Canada, and terminates in Sarnia, Ontario, Canada. The 1,900-mile U.S. portion, known as the Lakehead System, consists of pipelines of various diameters and ages operated from a control center in Edmonton. Line 6B is a 293-mile section of the Lakehead System, which crosses the state of Michigan joining Griffith, Indiana, to Sarnia. (See figure 1.)

Line 6B was installed in 1969 and constructed from 30-inch-diameter carbon steel pipe wrapped with a single layer of polyethylene tape. The ruptured pipe segment was manufactured to an American Petroleum Institute (API) Standard 5LX[3] grade X52[4] specification with a 0.25-inch wall thickness and a double submerged arc welded (DSAW) longitudinal seam; it was cathodically protected. Immediately prior to the accident, the highest recorded downstream pressure at the Marshall PS was 486 pounds per square inch, gauge (psig).[5] During 2010, Line 6B transported about 11.9 million gallons of crude oil per day.

The rupture occurred in the final stages of a planned Line 6B shutdown that was scheduled to have the pipeline out of operation for 10 hours. The shutdown, started at 5:55 p.m., was performed in just a few minutes by shutting off pumps from the Griffith PS to the Marshall PS while increasing pressure at a pressure control valve that was downstream of the Marshall PS at the Stockbridge Terminal. (The shutdown, during which oil would not be pumped through the pipeline, had been planned to accommodate the oil delivery schedule at the Griffith Terminal.) About 1 minute after increasing the pressure at the Stockbridge Terminal, the pipeline ruptured downstream of the Marshall PS. Multiple alarms were immediately generated at the Enbridge control center following the rupture, but Enbridge staff believed the alarms

---

[1] All times in this report are eastern daylight time unless otherwise specified.

[2] Line 6B transports multiple grades of heavy bituminous crude oil from the oil sand regions of Western Canada that require dilution with lighter petroleum products to enable the crude to flow easier. For simplicity, this report will refer to the product in Line 6B as crude oil.

[3] The API develops industry-based consensus standards that support oil and gas production and distribution. API 5LX is a specification for line pipe.

[4] Grade X52 signifies that the pipe has a specified minimum yield strength (SMYS) of 52,000 pounds per square inch (psi). Yield strength is a measure of the pipe's material strength and indicates the stress level at which the material will exhibit permanent deformation. Although yield strength is expressed in psi, this value is not equivalent to a pipe's internal pressure.

[5] Psig is a unit of measure for pressure expressed relative to pressure exerted by the surrounding atmosphere. Psi will be used in this report as a unit of measure for stress and is a measure of force acting over a given area.

resulted from a combination of column separation[6] and erratic pressures generated during shutdown rather than a rupture.

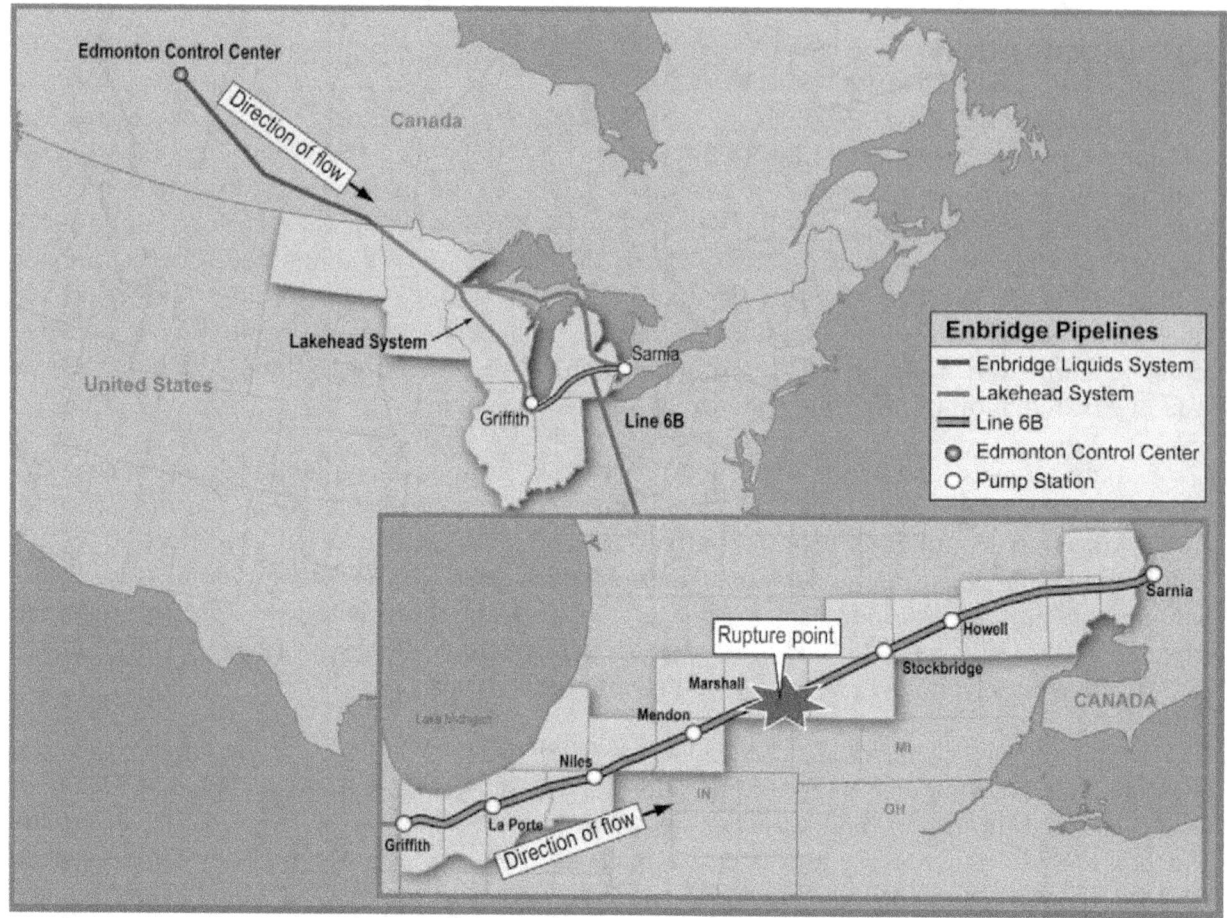

**Figure 1.** Enbridge's Liquids System and the 1,900-mile Lakehead System (the U.S. portion). Inset shows Line 6B, the 293-mile extension from Griffith to Sarnia installed in 1969.

To resume operations following the planned 10-hour shutdown, Enbridge staff started Line 6B once at 4:04 a.m. on July 26 and pumped oil for about 1 hour before shutting down the line. At 7:20 a.m., Enbridge staff started Line 6B again and pumped oil for about 30 minutes before shutting down the line. During the two startups and 1.5 hours of operation, Enbridge staff pumped about 683,436 gallons of oil[7] (81 percent of the total release) into the ruptured pipeline without seeing an increase in the pressure. Leak-detection alarms were generated, but Enbridge staff continued to believe the alarms were the result of column separation, even though the Marshall area was relatively flat, without significant elevation changes. Enbridge staff also

---

[6] *Column separation* is a condition indicating a mixture of liquid and vapor—a vapor bubble—exists in the pipeline. Column separation usually occurs at changes in elevation or where liquid does not completely fill the pipeline. The immediate area around the Marshall PS was relatively flat; however, a 100-foot elevation increase existed about 13 miles downstream. For more information about column separation, see section 1.11.5.4, "Column Separation," of this report.

[7] An NTSB study estimated this amount.

considered operational changes implemented before the startups, including a Niles PS shutdown and valve closure (due to an in-line crack inspection) and the possibility that large volumes of oil had settled into lower elevations and delivery locations, to be complicating factors.

The Calhoun County 911 dispatch center received the first call about odors associated with the oil release about 9:25 p.m. on July 25 (3.5 hours after the rupture) and dispatched firefighters from Marshall City; however, firefighters were unable to pinpoint a source of the odors. A gas utility worker, responding to the area because of numerous calls about gas odors, notified the Enbridge control center about oil on the ground at 11:17 a.m. on July 26 (more than 17 hours after the rupture). In less than 5 minutes, Enbridge staff began closing remote valves upstream and downstream of the rupture, sealing off the site within a 2.95-mile section.

The fracture in the ruptured segment measured 6 feet 8.25 inches long and up to 5.32 inches wide. (See figure 2.) External corrosion was present along the longitudinal weld seam and in areas where the adhesive bond between the pipe and its protective polyethylene tape coating had deteriorated (disbonded). The coating was wrinkled and had separated from the pipe surface as shown in the red circle in figure 2.

**Figure 2.** The ruptured segment of Line 6B in the trench following the July 25, 2010, rupture. The fracture face measured about 6 feet 8.25 inches long and was 5.32 inches wide at the widest opening. The fracture ran just below the seam weld that was oriented just below the 3 o'clock position. A red circle shows a location where the coating was wrinkled and had separated from the pipe surface.

The crude oil release soaked the rupture site and the surrounding wetlands, eventually spreading to the Talmadge Creek and the Kalamazoo River. Enbridge's early response efforts were focused downstream of the rupture. Recent heavy rainfall had increased the flow of the Talmadge Creek and the Kalamazoo River, which spread the oil faster, hindering the response efforts. (See figure 3.)

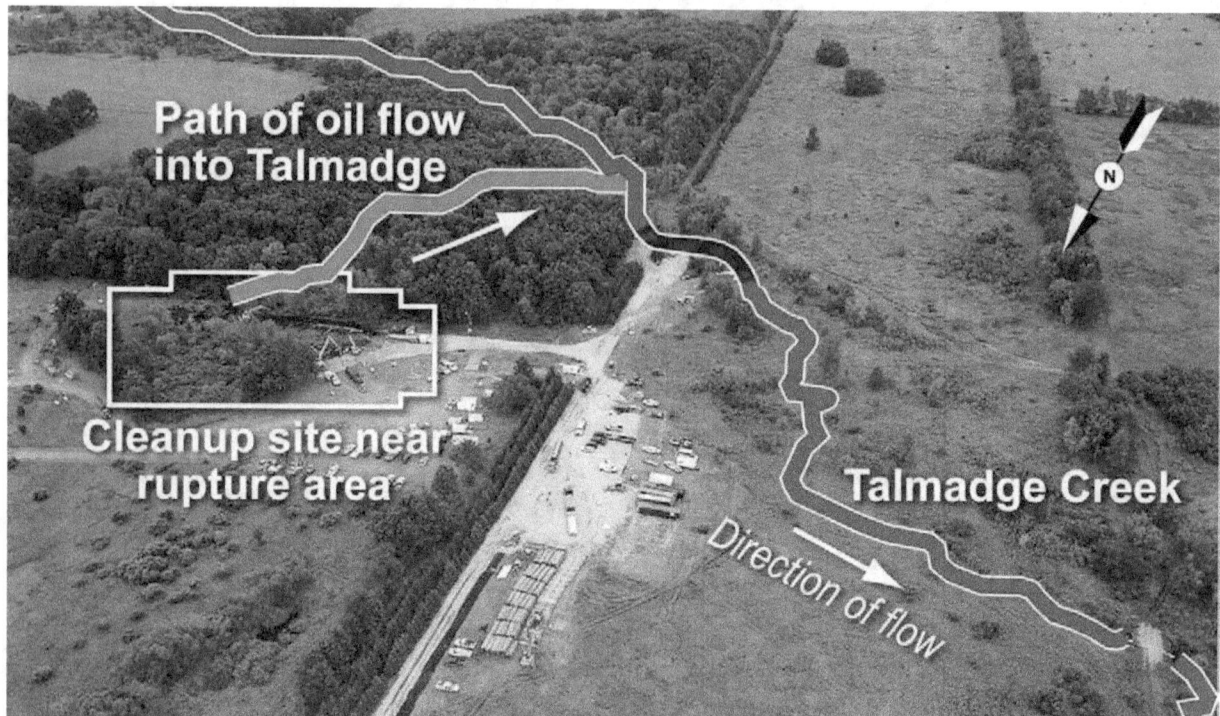

**Figure 3.** Aerial view of the accident location showing the rupture site to the left and the Talmadge Creek flowing west toward the Kalamazoo River.

The wetland conditions in addition to the crude oil release made it difficult for vacuum trucks and excavators to get near the rupture location. Large wooden matting had to be placed around the rupture location to bring heavy equipment close to the release. (See figure 4.) The conditions at the accident site also delayed efforts to extract the pipe and to contain the oil near the rupture source.

**Figure 4.** Cleanup efforts in an oil-soaked wetland near the rupture site. Saturated soil complicated the cleanup and excavation efforts. An excavator with a vacuum attachment is shown situated on wooden matting near the rupture site.

Figure 5 shows a timeline highlighting the accident events that spanned over 17 hours from the time of the rupture until the Enbridge control center was made aware of it. Figure 6 shows the key Enbridge staff involved.

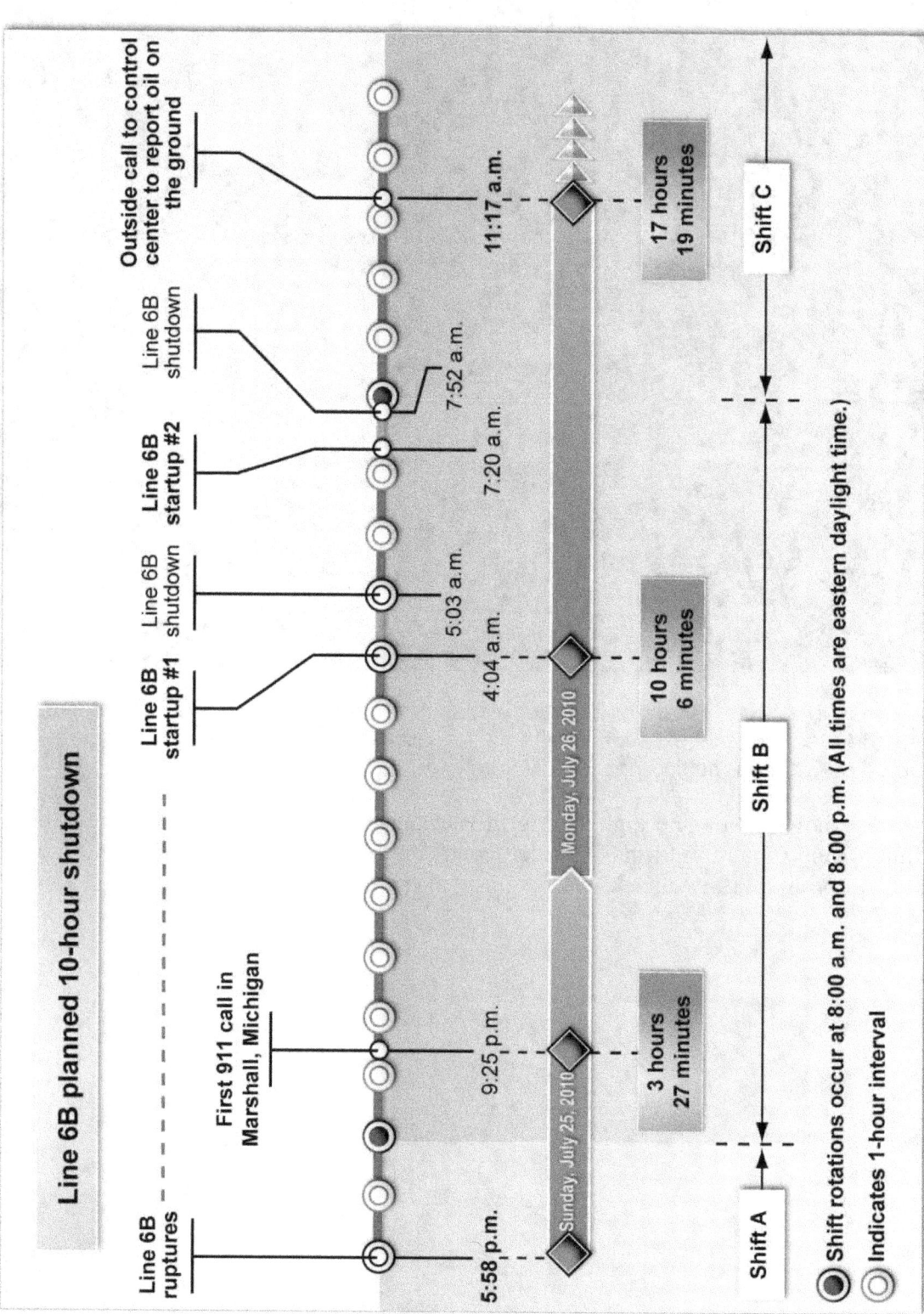

**Figure 5.** Key events timeline of the Line 6B rupture in Marshall, Michigan, showing the events from the time of rupture on July 25, 2010, to the time of discovery on July 26, 2010.

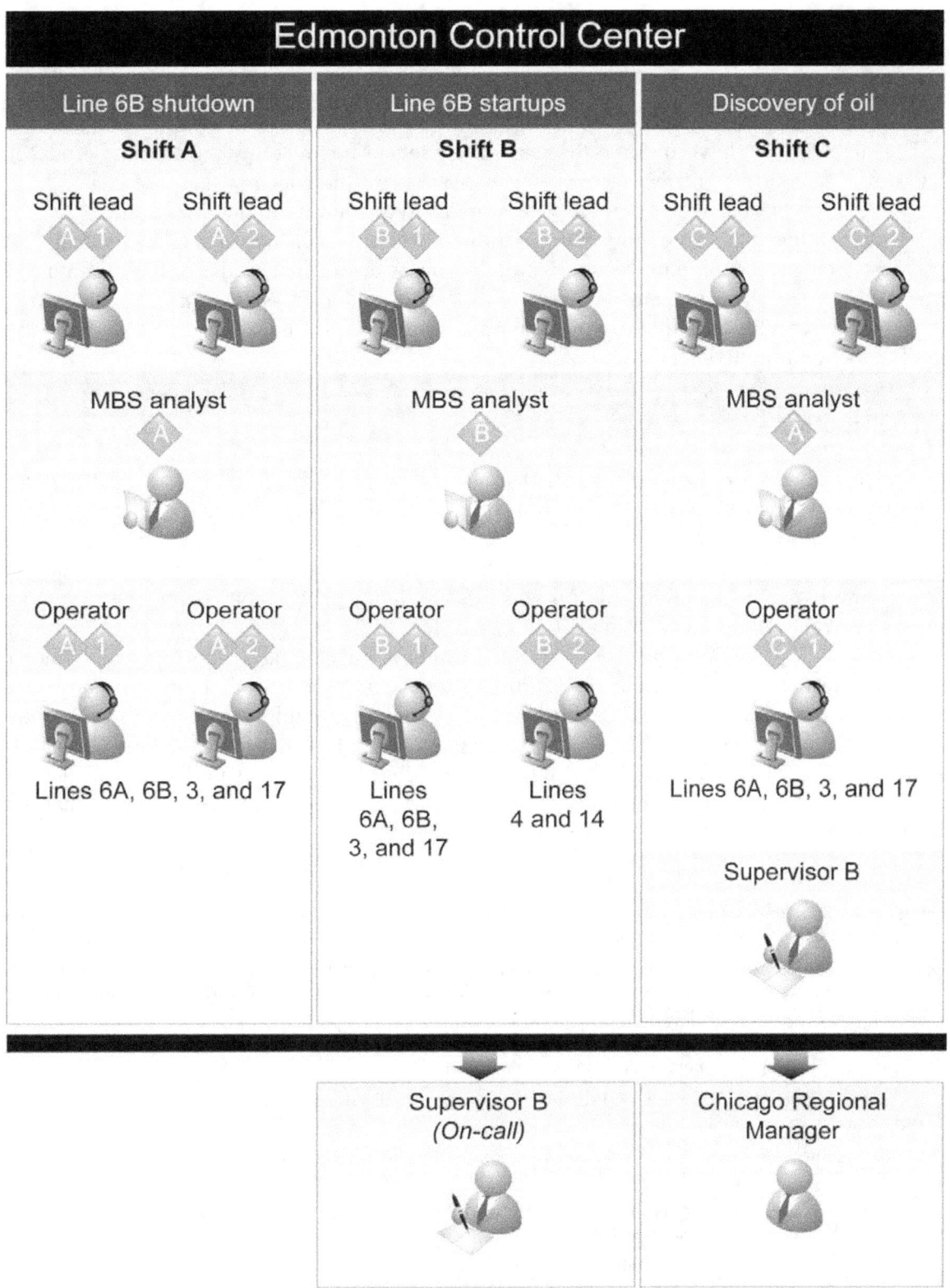

**Figure 6.** Key Enbridge staff involved in the 17-hour accident sequence. MBS refers to Material Balance System.

## 1.2  Accident Narrative

### 1.2.1  Preaccident Events

The planned shutdown of Line 6B was scheduled to begin following the last crude oil delivery to the Stockbridge Terminal, located downstream of the Marshall PS (see figure 7). A shutdown was to be performed by pipeline operator A1, sequentially, in the direction of flow, by turning off the pumps at the following PSs: Griffith, La Porte, Niles, Mendon, and Marshall. The shutdown was started at 5:55 p.m. by stopping two pumps at the Griffith PS and a pump at the La Porte PS. At 5:57 p.m., operator A1 increased the upstream pressure at a pressure control valve[8] at the Stockbridge Terminal before stopping a pump at the Niles PS and a pump at the Mendon PS about 1 minute later.

### 1.2.2  The Rupture—Shift A

The rupture occurred on July 25, 2010, at 5:58 p.m. in the final minute of a planned Line 6B shutdown, about 45 seconds after operator A1[9,10] increased upstream pressure (toward the Marshall PS) at a pressure control valve located at the Stockbridge Terminal and had stopped pumps at the Niles and the Mendon PSs. When the pipeline segment ruptured, the Marshall PS shut down automatically and three alarms almost simultaneously appeared on operator A1's supervisory control and data acquisition (SCADA) system display: an invalid-pressure[11] alarm (a severe alarm),[12] a low-suction-pressure alarm (a warning alarm),[13] and a station local shutdown alarm[14] (a warning alarm). The first two alarms cleared within 5 seconds but then reappeared because of the pressure changes resulting from the rupture. Within the same few seconds, operator A1 stopped the Marshall PS as part of the planned shutdown; he later told investigators that he had not recognized that a rupture had occurred. After the pipeline shut down, valves were closed at the Niles PS (see figure 7) to accommodate a Line 6B in-line inspection tool[15] that had been launched the previous day.

---

[8] Operator A1 increased the holding pressure from 50 to 200 psig at the Stockbridge Terminal pressure control valve (see appendix C for more information).

[9] Operator A1 had 29 years of pipeline operator experience but was requalifying after a 6-month-long disability leave from the control center. During his requalification, a mentor was overseeing his work. The mentor (operator A2) had an equivalent amount of experience.

[10] Control center operators were responsible for the operation of multiple pipelines and sometimes pipelines and terminals. The Line 6B operator (operator A1) was also responsible for Lines 3, 17, and 6A.

[11] This alarm was generated by the Line Pressure Management (LPM) system, which is designed to protect the pipeline from being overpressured.

[12] Enbridge defined a "severe alarm" as requiring the control center operator to notify the shift lead, advise the on-site/on-call staff, and create an entry in the facility maintenance database system.

[13] Enbridge defined a "warning alarm" as discretionary operator response dependent on operating conditions. Multiple alarms can result in an increased severity.

[14] These latter two alarms were generated by the Marshall PS.

[15] A cleaning tool and an in-line crack inspection tool were launched on July 24 at the Griffith Terminal, separated by about 5 miles. They remained upstream of the Niles PS even after the oil release was identified. The tools remained in the pipeline until the failed section was replaced and Line 6B returned to service in September 2010.

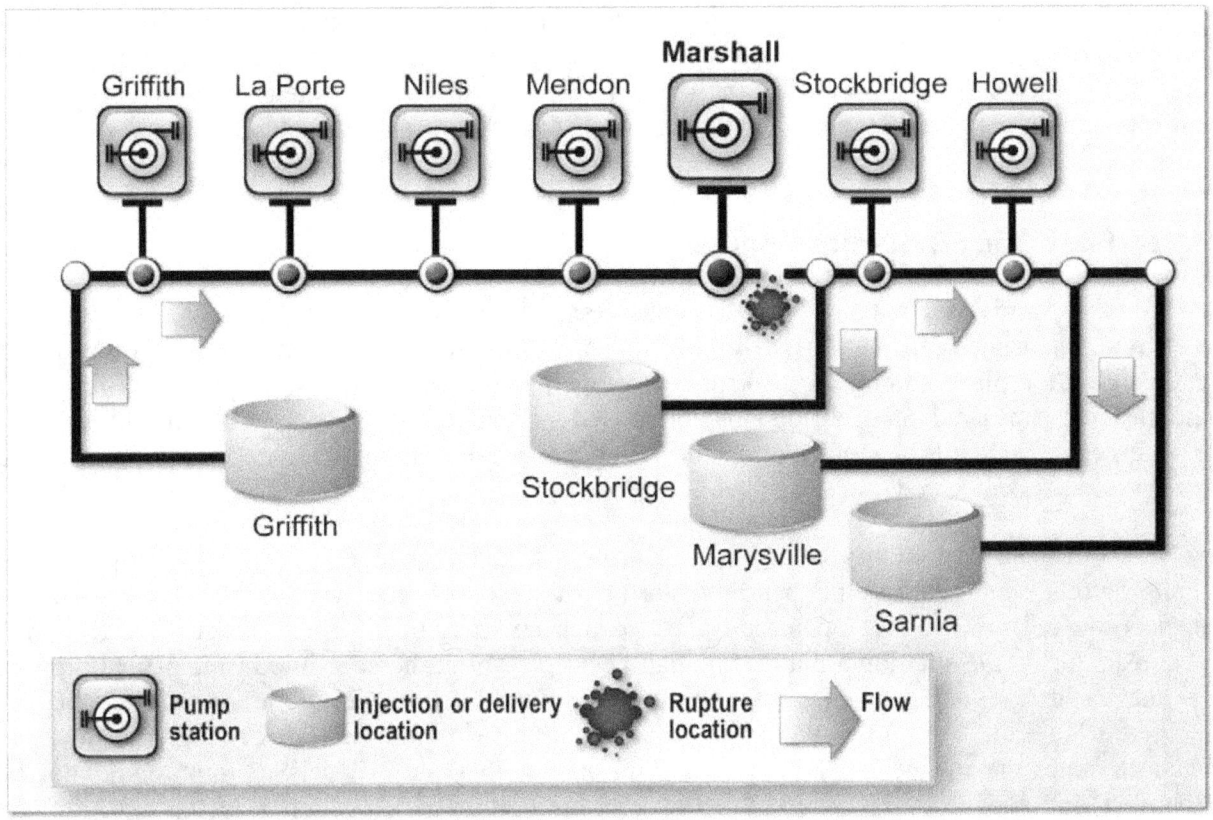

**Figure 7.** Simplified schematic of Line 6B, showing pump stations and delivery locations.

By 6:03 p.m., operator A1 had received several more alarms related to the Line 6B rupture, including a 5-minute Material Balance System (MBS) alarm[16] (a severe leak alarm), another low-suction-pressure alarm, and six additional invalid-pressure alarms. (All of the alarms were indications of the rupture.) The 5-minute MBS alarm indicated that a large oil volume imbalance had been detected in the pipeline. Operator A1 informed shift lead A1 about the MBS alarm, and shift lead A1 contacted MBS analyst A about the MBS alarm.

At 6:05 p.m., MBS analyst A called operator A1 to explain that he had concluded column separation near the Marshall PS had generated the MBS alarm.

Within minutes, the MBS alarm cleared on its own. (MBS alarms clear after a shutdown because the oil flow stops.) About this time, MBS analyst A told shift lead A2 about the alarm, his conclusion about its suspected cause, and its status. There was no further discussion about the MBS alarm during the shift.

---

[16] A single MBS alarm may be associated with multiple instances of column separation. MBS alarms display as 5-minute, 20-minute, or 2-hour alarms, indicating relative leak size. The 5-minute alarm represents the largest leak rate, and the 2-hour alarm represents the smallest leak rate.

Operators A1 and A2[17] independently told National Transportation Safety Board (NTSB) investigators that when the MBS alarm had cleared, they were no longer concerned about the low pressure at the Marshall PS because they believed the alarms were related to column separation and the shutdown. Line 6B remained shut down[18] for 10 hours, as scheduled. The Marshall PS pressures remained at zero.

### 1.2.3  First Line 6B Startup—Shift B

The Sunday second shift control center staff took over operations between 8:00 p.m. and 8:30 p.m.[19] During shift rotations, a verbal exchange of operational information, known as a shift exchange, took place among the control center operators, MBS analysts, and the shift leads. At the time of the accident, Enbridge had a procedure that required specific information to be exchanged during shift changes, but no formal documentation or written record of the exchanged information was required.

Shift lead B1 told investigators that, during the shift exchange, he was not informed about the previous shutdown or the pending startup of Line 6B, the MBS alarm, or the in-line inspection tool in Line 6B. Operator B1[20] said that he was not informed about the alarms that occurred during the shutdown but that he had been told about the scheduled Line 6B startup, the in-line inspection, and the Niles PS valve closure for the in-line inspection. He stated that he expected the Line 6B startup would be difficult because of the Niles PS being shut down to accommodate the in-line inspection tool. This meant that the Niles PS pumps could not be operated and the pressures would be lower coming into the Mendon PS (upstream of the Marshall PS). He did not question the low pressures at the Marshall PS.

At 8:56 p.m., Michigan Gas Utilities dispatched a senior service technician to respond to a residential report of natural gas odor. At 9:25 p.m. on July 25, a local resident called the Calhoun County 911 dispatch center and stated the following:

> I was just at the airport in Marshall and drove south on Old 27 [17 Mile Road] and drove back north again and there's a very, very, very strong odor, either natural gas or maybe crude oil or something, and because the wind's coming out of the north, you can smell it all the way up to the tanks, right across from where the airport's at, and then you can't smell it anymore.

By 9:32 p.m., the Marshall City Fire Department had been dispatched in response to the 9:25 p.m. call to 911. The 911 dispatcher told the responders there was a report of a bad smell of natural gas near the airport.

---

[17] Operator A2 told investigators that she was working on special projects alongside operator A1 when the accident occurred. She said she was aware of the MBS alarm but not directly involved with handling it.

[18] When Line 6B was shut down, valves upstream and downstream of the rupture were closed, isolating a 75-mile span of the line and the rupture site.

[19] The control center work shifts were 12 hours.

[20] Operator B1 had about 3.5 years experience in the Edmonton control center as a pipeline operator. See table 3 for further information about control center staff experience.

Marshall City Fire Department personnel responded to the area near the airport and requested the Marshall Township Fire Department to respond as well. To find the source of the odor, fire department personnel investigated several pipeline facilities and industrial buildings around Division Drive and 17 Mile Road, using a combustible gas indicator[21] to try to locate the origin of the odor. No combustibles were detected. The Michigan Gas Utilities senior service technician crossed paths with some of the fire department personnel also trying to locate the source; he found no evidence of a gas leak. The fire department personnel departed the scene at 10:54 p.m. to return to the station. At 11:33 p.m., an employee at a business called 911 to report a natural gas odor. The 911 dispatcher explained that the fire department had already responded to calls in the area, and no more personnel were dispatched.[22] (See figure 8.)

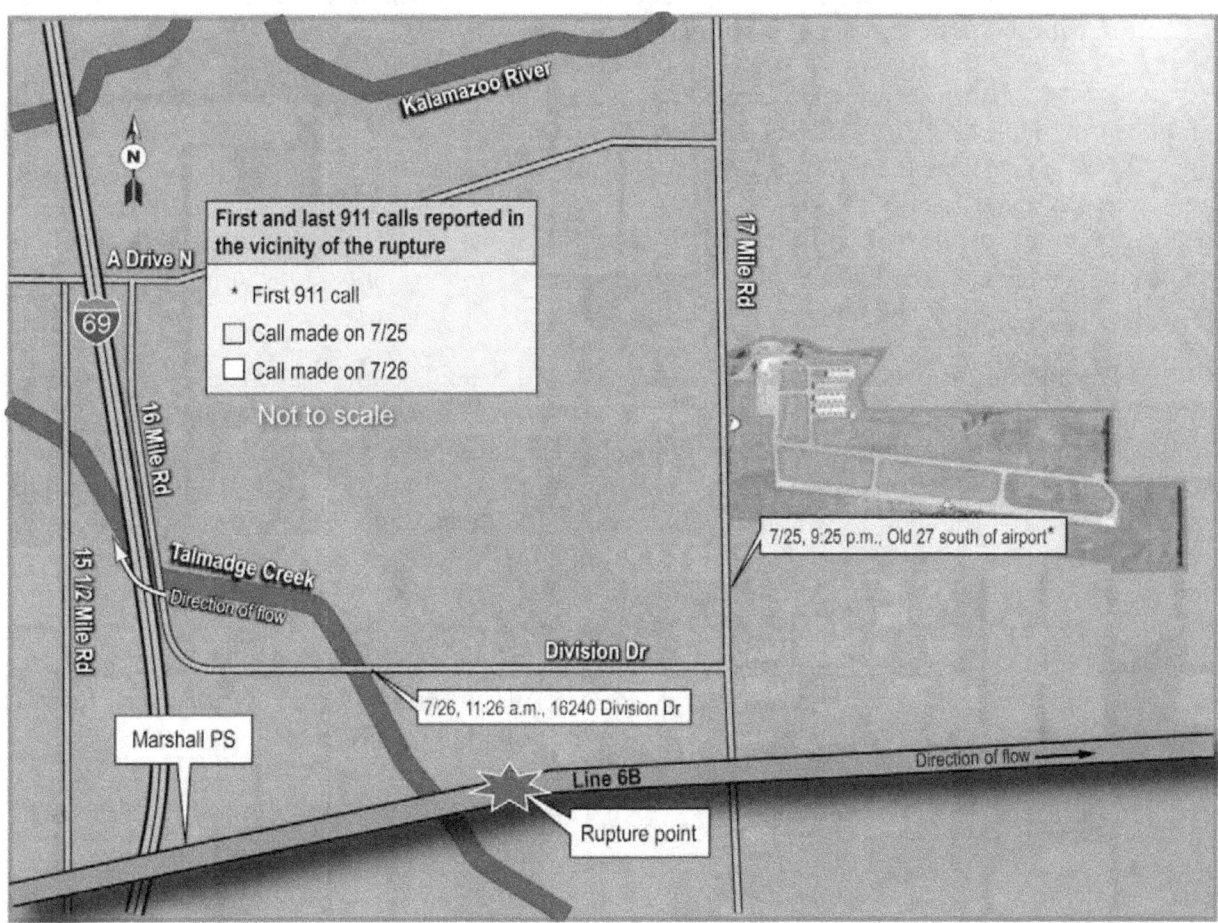

**Figure 8.** Emergency response and 911 calls from nearby residents. First and last calls are noted.

---

[21] Because a combustible gas indicator measures percentage of the lower explosive limit, it likely would not detect the oil unless it was very close to the source.

[22] Over the next 14 hours, the local 911 received seven more calls reporting strong natural gas or petroleum odors in the same vicinity. The 911 dispatcher repeatedly informed the callers that the fire department had been dispatched to investigate the reported odors.

On Monday, July 26, at 4:00 a.m., while preparing to start Line 6B for deliveries into the Marysville and Sarnia Terminals, operator B1 reduced pressure settings at two PSs (Marshall and Mendon) upstream of a valve that had lost communication.[23] Line 6B was going to be started without the Niles PS, which remained out of service for the in-line inspection tool.

About 4:04 a.m., operator B1 started Line 6B from the Griffith PS to the Mendon PS, and by 4:12 a.m., the first 5-minute MBS alarm appeared on his SCADA display. Operator B1 called MBS analyst B about the alarm. MBS analyst B told operator B1 that the alarm was due to column separation. After talking with operator B1, the MBS analyst realized that the MBS software had not been set up correctly[24] because the Niles PS valves were closed. According to MBS analyst B, the valve closure at the Niles PS might have resulted in additional column separation indications that morning.[25]

By 4:24 a.m., operator B1 had received a 20-minute MBS alarm and another 5-minute MBS alarm. He notified shift lead B2 that Line 6B had been operating for 10 minutes but pressure remained less than 1 psig downstream of the Marshall PS. Enbridge's control center procedures required operators to shut down the pipeline when column separation could not be restored within 10 minutes.[26] Shift lead B2 and MBS analyst B told operator B1 to continue pumping oil to restore the column. Operator B1 started a larger pump upstream of the Marshall PS to increase the pipeline pressure.

During this time, operator B2[27] referred shift lead B1 to a draft column separation procedure that she had used earlier in the year. According to the draft procedure, when known column separation existed, an operator would calculate the time needed to fill the pipeline before starting the line. Once started, if column separation were present 10 minutes beyond the calculated time, the pipeline would be shut down. In effect, the draft procedure allowed the pipeline to operate in excess of the 10-minute limit under certain conditions. As operator B1 continued to pump additional oil into the pipeline, shift lead B1 attempted to estimate the time needed to restore the pressure downstream of the Marshall PS.[28] To do this, shift lead B1 tried to determine (1) the volume of oil that had settled throughout Line 6B during the shutdown and (2) the volume of oil that had drained into the Marysville Terminal during startup. Shift lead B1 estimated it would take about 20 minutes to bring the column back together.

---

[23] These were settings that protected the pipeline from overpressure in the event that the valve that had lost communication was closed.

[24] When the station valves at the Niles PS were closed to accommodate an in-line inspection tool, following the shutdown, the SCADA pressure transmitters used by the MBS were no longer using the real-time pipeline pressures, which resulted in errors in the MBS. To correct the MBS software, the MBS analyst had to override the pressures on both sides of the Niles PS. The MBS analyst stated that the lack of live pressures at the Niles PS may have affected the MBS alarms that morning.

[25] According to Enbridge, the software showed more instances of column separation before the software was adjusted.

[26] This duration was commonly referred to as the "10-minute rule" by the control center staff and represented the amount of time a pipeline was allowed to operate in instances of column separation or abnormal operations before being shut down.

[27] This was the shift mate of operator B1, who was operating Lines 4 and 14. Operator B2 had just over 2 years of experience as a pipeline operator. See table 3 for further information about control center staff experience.

[28] By dividing the amount of oil drained out into delivery locations during shutdown by gallons per hour, the shift lead can estimate how long the system must be run to restore pressure.

Operator B1 continued to start pumps on Line 6B and received multiple MBS alarms from 4:24 a.m. until 4:57 a.m. During this time, the Marshall PS discharge pressure never exceeded 3 psig. During this time when the Sarnia Terminal operator called operator B1 and remarked on the slow startup, operator B1 stated that "I'm just wondering either they really drained [Line 6B] out, which I think they did, because I don't have any pressure farther down the line…Or else I'm—or else I'm leaking. One of the two." Operator B1 called shift lead B1 about 5:00 a.m. to report that he had exceeded the estimated time to resolve the column separation issue. Operator B1 stated that the flow into the pipeline, upstream of the Marshall PS, was about 396,000 gallons per hour. After confirming with the Sarnia Terminal operator that only 71,062 gallons had been received since the startup, shift lead B1 instructed operator B1 to shut down Line 6B. About 5:03 a.m., Line 6B was shut down.

## 1.2.4  Second Line 6B Startup—Shift B

At 6:35 a.m., shift lead B2 called the on-call control center supervisor, and he then asked MBS analyst B to participate in the call. Shift lead B2 explained that they had been unable to resolve the column separation at the Marshall PS and that they had exceeded the estimated time needed to fill the pipeline. Shift lead B2 and the control center supervisor questioned MBS analyst B about the difference in pumped versus received volume. MBS analyst B explained that because of what he believed to be the severe column separation, the oil was filling the line rather than flowing through it to the delivery location.

The control center on-call supervisor stated that there were two choices: identify the alarms as a leak or identify the alarms as column separation and try to restart the pipeline again. Shift lead B2 asked MBS analyst B whether the MBS alarm was valid or invalid. MBS analyst B told shift lead B2 that the alarm was "false" because the MBS software was unreliable when column separation was present. The control center supervisor told shift lead B2, "To me it sounds like you need to try again and monitor it. Like [MBS analyst B] said, do it over again."

About 7:09 a.m., operator B1 notified the Sarnia Terminal[29] operator that they were going to start Line 6B for a second time. The Sarnia Terminal operator expressed disbelief at the idea of a second startup. He told investigators that he had voiced his concerns about a Line 6B leak to shift leads B1 and B2 and MBS analyst B that morning. He stated that MBS analyst B had dismissed his concerns and, because he was dealing with other issues that morning, he had not pursued the matter.

Line 6B was started a second time about 7:20 a.m. By 7:36 a.m., as the Marshall PS discharge pressure started to increase, the first 5-minute MBS alarm appeared, followed by a 20-minute MBS alarm. Many additional 5-minute and 20-minute MBS alarms subsequently appeared through 7:42 a.m. During this time, operator B1 unsuccessfully attempted to start additional Line 6B pumps at the La Porte PS; the Marshall PS downstream pressure never increased above 4 psig. After shutting down Line 6B at 7:52 a.m., just before ending his shift, operator B1 made the following comment to the Sarnia Terminal operator.

---

[29] Because Line 6B was delivering oil into the Sarnia Terminal, the Sarnia Terminal operator was involved in the startup, opening valves and moving oil into the terminal tanks. The Sarnia Terminal operator stated that he was able to watch the Line 6B operation on his SCADA display.

I've never seen this...and to me like it looks like a leak...like I've never ever heard of that where you can't get enough—I can pump as hard as I want and I—I'd never over pressure the line. I don't know. Something about this feels wrong.

## 1.2.5 Discovery—Shift C

The shift C rotation occurred between 8:00 a.m. and 8:30 a.m. on Monday morning, July 26. The shift staff included the control center supervisor, who had been contacted during shift B while on call, and MBS analyst A, who had been on duty when the rupture occurred. During the shift exchange, shift leads C1 and C2 were informed about the presumed Line 6B column separation. Shift leads C1 and C2 called the control center supervisor to discuss the column separation issue.

Operator C1 told investigators that he had questioned the volume loss information during the shift exchange. By 8:46 a.m., operator C1 explained to shift leads C1 and C2 that in the past he had started Line 6B using every other PS and without operating the Niles PS. Operator C1 told investigators that he had reviewed SCADA data from the previous shifts that morning, saw the large pressure drop at the Marshall PS during the shift A shutdown, and immediately notified shift lead C1.

At 10:16 a.m., acting on the findings from operator C1 and discussions with shift lead C1, shift lead C2 called and asked the Chicago regional manager whether to send someone to walk along the pipeline, upstream and downstream of the Marshall PS. The Chicago regional manager replied, "I wouldn't think so. If it's right at Marshall—you know, it seems like there's something else going wrong either with the computer or with the instrumentation. ...you lost column and things go haywire, right?" He went on to say, "...I'm not convinced. We haven't had any phone calls. I mean it's perfect weather out here—if it's a rupture someone's going to notice that, you know and smell it." The Chicago regional manager told shift lead C1 that he was okay with the control center starting Line 6B again.

At 11:17 a.m., the control center was notified about the rupture via its emergency line. The caller said, "I work for Consumers Energy[30] and I'm in Marshall. There's oil getting into the creek and I believe it's from your pipeline. I mean there's a lot. We're getting like 20 gas leak calls and everything." Remote valves were closed at 11:18 a.m., sealing off the rupture site within a 2.95-mile section. By 11:20 a.m., the shift lead had called the Chicago regional manager to tell him about the notification. By 11:37 a.m., another Consumers Energy employee notified 911 about the crude oil leak in a creek near Division Drive. The Fredonia Township Fire Department was dispatched by the 911 center shortly after the call. At 11:41 a.m., the Edmonton control center received confirmation from an Enbridge crossing coordinator located at the Marshall pipeline maintenance (PLM) shop confirming the oil on the ground.

---

[30] Consumers Energy is an electric and gas utility provider with services in Calhoun County and Marshall, Michigan.

### 1.2.6 Enbridge Initial Response

At 11:45 a.m. on July 26, the initial Enbridge personnel at the accident location included the Marshall PLM shop crossing coordinator, an electrician, and two senior pipeline employees. After confirming the presence of oil near the ruptured pipeline, the crossing coordinator followed Talmadge Creek downstream to determine the extent of the oil discharge. He found that the oil had not migrated past A Drive North, about 1.5 miles downstream of the rupture, but he observed a large amount of oil at a creek crossing on 15 1/2 Mile Road, about 1 mile downstream of the rupture.

The four-person crew returned to the Marshall PLM shop and retrieved a vacuum truck, a work truck, a semi-truck, and an oil boom trailer. About 12:10 p.m., they returned to A Drive North and installed a double 20-foot length of sorbent boom across Talmadge Creek, where they observed only a little oil flowing. They also installed 20-foot lengths of sorbent boom across Talmadge Creek upstream of A Drive North and at a culvert on the south side of A Drive North. The Enbridge crossing coordinator told NTSB investigators that the Marshall PLM crew was not aware of the severity of the oil spill when it used these initial oil containment measures. The Enbridge first responders did not have an estimate of released volumes when they began their efforts to contain the oil. (See figure 9 for a map of the area around the rupture site where response efforts began.)

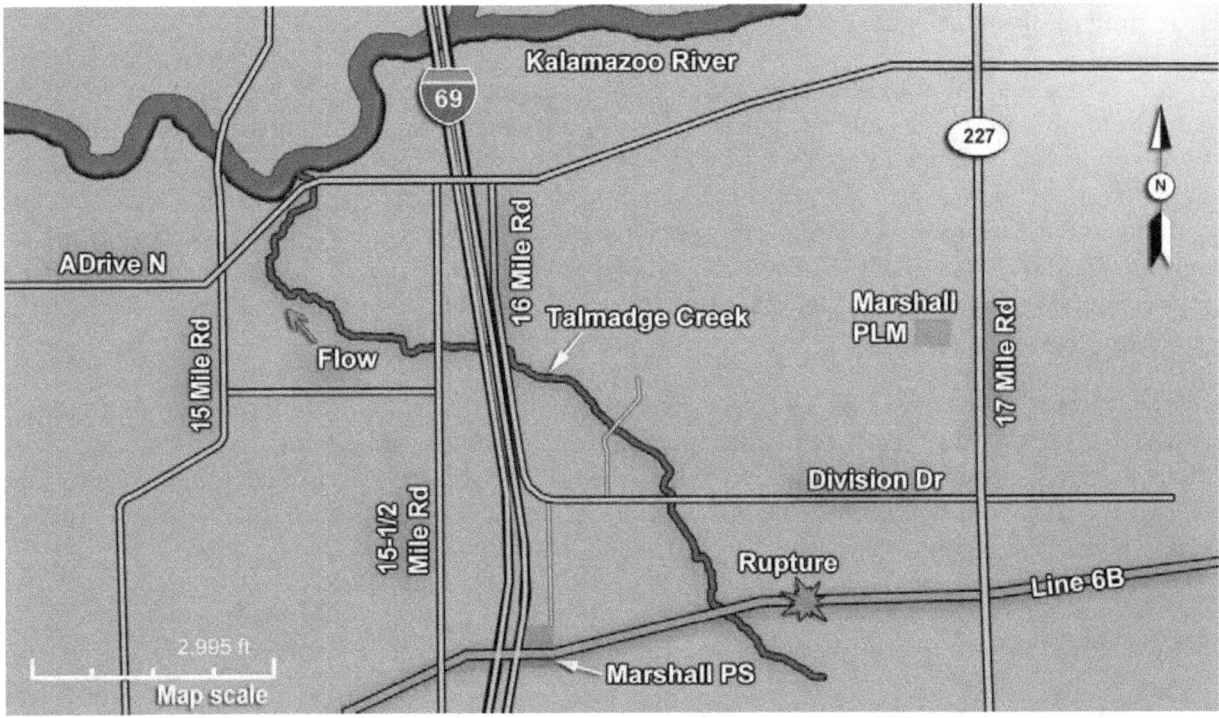

**Figure 9.** Area between rupture site and the Kalamazoo River where first responders concentrated efforts to contain the released oil.

About 12:30 p.m., the Marshall PLM crew moved upstream to the 15 1/2-Mile Road crossing of Talmadge Creek. The crew installed a 40-foot containment boom and sections of sorbent boom on the upstream side of the culvert and spent the remainder of the day, until 11:00 p.m., using the Marshall PLM vacuum truck and skimmer to recover oil.

The Enbridge Bay City PLM supervisor (the interim incident commander until the Chicago regional manager arrived on site) told NTSB investigators that upon his arrival about 12:46 p.m., he observed an oily mixture discharging at a high rate through a 48-inch-diameter steel culvert pipe under Division Drive and continuing downstream in Talmadge Creek. He said the bulk of the released oil was contained upstream (south) of Division Drive. The supervisor stated that he considered having the culvert pipe plugged with earth; however, the water flow was too strong to enable him to do that.

About 1:30 p.m., the Marshall PLM supervisor arrived on scene and conferred with the Bay City PLM supervisor. They decided that the Marshall PLM supervisor would focus on stopping the leak source while the Bay City PLM supervisor would focus on installing oil boom at downstream locations ahead of the advancing oil. The National Response Center (NRC) was notified of the release about this same time on July 26. The NRC notified 16 Federal and state agencies about the spill.

About 2:45 p.m., the Bay City PLM supervisor worked with the Battle Creek Fire Department hazardous materials chief to locate an area for deploying boom for recovering the oil. About 15 minutes later, an Enbridge vacuum truck from the Bay City PLM shop began skimming oil from the water surface near Division Drive.

Between 4:30 and 6:30 p.m., four oil storage tanks were delivered to the Marshall PLM shop to temporarily store the oil that was being collected by the vacuum trucks. The Bay City PLM supervisor estimated that a total of 14 Enbridge personnel and between 6 and 10 personnel from Terra Contracting and Baker Corporation (contractors contacted by the incident commander for oil recovery and storage equipment) were working on scene to contain the oil during this time. The first U.S. Environmental Protection Agency (EPA) on-scene coordinator arrived in Marshall to assess the extent of the spill into Talmadge Creek about 4:32 p.m. The Marshall PLM shop was used as the incident command center.

Working with a six-person crew, the Marshall PLM supervisor constructed an earthen underflow dam, which consists of a mound of soil holding back oil-contaminated water with pipes submerged on the dam side and rising toward the discharge end. The angle of the pipe allows the deeper water in the dam to flow downstream, preventing the contaminated surface waters from flowing into Talmadge Creek. (See figure 10.)

**Figure 10.** Underflow dam on Talmadge Creek on July 30, 2010.

However, the crew found the width of the marsh too great and the ground too soft to construct an earthen dam near the source; instead the crew constructed a gravel-and-earth underflow dam at the confluence of the contaminated marsh and Talmadge Creek, which was accessible by heavy equipment. Enbridge crews used sections of 12-inch-diameter surplus polyvinyl chloride pipe they had found at the Marshall PLM shop to construct the underflow dam. Enbridge crews had learned of this oil containment strategy from participating in drills and exercises; this dam was the first they created during an actual emergency response. The heavy-equipment operators encountered significant difficulty because of the muddy conditions and the high-water flows. The construction of the first underflow dam began early in the afternoon on July 26, but it was not functional until 9:00 p.m. that evening. Crews had to tow the vacuum trucks through the mud to the underflow dam site and to the oily marsh locations until the first gravel roadway was constructed. The Marshall PLM supervisor told NTSB investigators that a considerable volume of oil was present in Talmadge Creek between the first underflow dam that Enbridge constructed and Division Drive. On July 26, Enbridge also deployed at least 12 vacuum trucks to begin recovering oil from the source area underflow dam, the Talmadge Creek stream crossings on Division Drive and 15 1/2 Mile Road, and from the Kalamazoo River at Calhoun County Historic Bridge Park (referred to as Heritage Park).[31]

---

[31] The two initial EPA on-scene coordinators noted that only five vacuum trucks were operating on July 26, while seven additional vacuum trucks that were ordered did not arrive on site until July 27.

Additional contractors would not arrive until the following day to continue a larger scale oil response effort.

## 1.3 Injuries and Evacuations

### 1.3.1 Injuries

No immediate injury reports were made as a result of the Marshall release. The Michigan Department of Community Health conducted a followup study and issued its results in a November 2010 report titled *Acute Effects of the Enbridge Oil Spill*. The study was based on four community surveys along the affected waterways, 147 health care provider reports on 145 patients, and 41 calls placed to the poison center. The study identified 320 people and an additional 11 worksite employees who reported experiencing adverse health effects. Headache, nausea, and respiratory effects were the most common symptoms reported by exposed individuals. The report concluded that these symptoms were consistent with the published literature regarding potential health effects associated with crude oil exposure, which include irritation to the eyes, nose, and throat, as well as dizziness and drowsiness. Contact with the skin and eyes may also cause irritation or burns.

### 1.3.2 Evacuations

On July 26, the residents of six houses self-evacuated because of odors associated with the oil spill. On July 29, an EPA contractor produced a map outlining the recommended evacuation area, which extended from the spill area north and northwest to the Kalamazoo River, beyond the 15 Mile Road bridge crossing, and included 61 houses.[32] The Calhoun County Public Health Department issued a voluntary evacuation notice to about 50 houses. The health department developed residential evacuation recommendations based on the concentration of benzene in the air. Benzene is a toxic constituent of crude oil that can cause drowsiness, dizziness, and unconsciousness. Long-term exposure to benzene causes effects on bone marrow and can cause anemia and leukemia. On August 12, the recommended evacuation of houses near the oil spill site was lifted after the benzene concentrations in the air were below the levels requiring evacuation.

## 1.4 Damages

### 1.4.1 Pipeline

The *Enbridge Inc. 2010 Annual Report* listed revenue losses for the Line 6B accident at $13.2 million. Enbridge has stated that the cost to replace the 50-foot section of Line 6B was $2.7 million.

---

[32] See "Emergency and Environmental Response Attachment 39—Recommended Evacuation Zone Map," in the NTSB public docket for this accident.

## 1.4.2 Environment

Enbridge's estimated costs for emergency response equipment, resources, personnel, and professional and regulatory support in connection with the cleanup of oil discharged from Line 6B were about $767 million as of October 31, 2011.[33] This figure also encompasses the estimated cost of the Federal government's role in the cleanup, including employing contractors, which was an estimated $42 million.

## 1.5 Environmental Conditions

### 1.5.1 Meteorological

The National Weather Service data recorded from Brooks Field Airport, Marshall, Michigan, at 5:55 p.m. near the time of the rupture showed the wind was from 10° at 4 knots, with good visibility and clear skies, the temperature was 79° F, and the dew point was 59° F. A light to moderate rain had occurred on the morning of July 24. On July 25, skies were clearing during the afternoon and evening hours, the high temperature was 79° F, and the low temperature was 69° F.

Weather reports from the W.K. Kellogg Airport, Battle Creek, Michigan, about 13 miles west of Marshall, reported rainfall amounts of about 2.4 inches on July 22 and July 23, 0.6 inch on July 24, and 1.37 inches on July 25.

### 1.5.2 Kalamazoo River Conditions

On July 26 at 12:45 p.m., the U.S. Geological Survey (USGS) reported the Kalamazoo River level in Marshall, Michigan, was 7.19 feet. Within 24 hours, the river level fell below 6 feet. The established flood state for this location is 8 feet. The USGS gauging station on the Kalamazoo River in Marshall, Michigan, reported the average current velocity at 1.44 mph.

## 1.6 Pipeline Information

### 1.6.1 Pipeline History

Enbridge documentation showed that the ruptured pipe segment was part of a purchase of 30-inch pipe from Siderius Inc. of New York on November 14, 1968, which was manufactured by Italsider s.p.a.[34] An inspection report dated March 18, 1969, noted that the chemical analysis and mechanical tests met the requirements of API and Enbridge specifications. Upon fabrication, the pipe was shipped bare from the Italsider s.p.a. facility located in Taranto, Italy, to the Port of Windsor, Ontario, and was delivered by truck to staging sites within Michigan. According to Enbridge, a field-applied spiral wrap of polyethylene tape coating was put on the pipe by machine at the time of Line 6B's construction.

---

[33] This was the most recent figure available at the time of this report.

[34] S.p.a. refers to Societa Per Azioni, a joint stock company with shareholders.

The ruptured segment was tested hydrostatically on November 21, 1969. No leaks or ruptures were documented. The certification letter, from the hydrostatic testing contractor, dated February 3, 1970, indicated that the ruptured segment had been tested to a minimum pressure of 783 psig and a maximum pressure of 820 psig for a 24-hour period. Enbridge used 796 psig as the hydrostatic test pressure of the ruptured segment in the integrity management assessments. The SMYS[35] of the ruptured segment was about 867 psig.

## 1.6.2 Pipeline Operating Pressure

The pipeline segment that ruptured had a maximum operating pressure (MOP) of 624 psig. However, the Marshall PS downstream pressure was limited to 523 psig at the time of the accident based on defects identified during a 2007 in-line inspection for corrosion (these features did not contribute to the rupture) of Line 6B. Historical pressure trends show that the Marshall PS was operating at 624 psig until 2004 when Enbridge imposed a 525 psig pressure restriction. No pressures in excess of 532 psig were noted from 2005 up until the time of rupture. Based on the SCADA pressures readings at the time of the rupture, the highest recorded discharge pressure at the Marshall PS, immediately preceding the rupture, was 486 psig. (See appendix C).

## 1.6.3 Site Description

The ruptured segment was buried about 5 feet below the ground surface and located 0.60 mile downstream from the Marshall PS. The rupture and release occurred in a wetland area near mile point (MP) 608.22 in Marshall, Michigan. The wetlands were located in an undeveloped, mostly rural area about 0.4 mile west of 17 Mile Road and about 0.2 mile south of Division Drive. Industrial complexes were located north and west along 17 Mile Road, less than 1 mile from the rupture site. The ruptured segment of Line 6B was operating in a high consequence area (HCA) identified as an "other populated area," which is defined at Title 49 *Code of Federal Regulations* (CFR) 195.450(3) as a place "that contains a concentrated population, such as an incorporated or unincorporated city, town, village, or other designated residential or commercial area."

## 1.6.4 Other Enbridge Pipeline Incidents

In 49 CFR 195.50, the Pipeline and Hazardous Materials Safety Administration (PHMSA) requires that pipeline operators submit an accident report for hazardous liquid releases, not related to a maintenance activity, that are 5 gallons or more and resulting in $50,000 property damage, explosion, or fire. PHMSA publishes the summaries from these reports on its website.[36] The PHMSA incident and accident statistics for liquid transmission onshore crude oil releases sorted by volume from 1986 through 2011 show that Enbridge releases represent the second and fifth largest crude oil spills and that the company is included in

---

[35] The *SMYS* is the internal pressure that produces a calculated hoop stress equivalent to the minimum yield strength of the material assuming a nominal wall thickness and outside diameter.

[36] Information obtained from PHMSA's website <http://phmsa.dot.gov/pipeline/library/data-stats> (accessed June 5, 2012).

$3^{37}$ of the top 15 releases. The NTSB[38] and the Transportation Safety Board of Canada (TSB) have investigated previous Enbridge leaks and ruptures that resulted from defects not remediated through the Enbridge integrity management program.

### 1.6.4.1 Cohasset, Minnesota

In 2004, the NTSB issued a report on an Enbridge failure that occurred on July 4, 2002, when Enbridge experienced a rupture and 252,000-gallon oil release on its Line 4, near Cohasset, Minnesota.[39] The fractured segment was a United States Steel tape-coated 34-inch-diameter API Standard 5LX grade X52 DSAW pipe with 0.312-inch wall thickness, installed in 1967. Examination of the failed pipe revealed a 13-inch-long transportation-induced metal fatigue[40] crack that had initiated from the internal surface of the pipe at multiple regions where the longitudinal seam weld intersected with the body of the pipe. The ruptured segment had been hydrostatically pressure tested in 1991 to 1,002 psig, and in-line inspections had been conducted twice in 1995 and once in 1996. Neither in-line inspection identified the fatigue crack that eventually grew to failure under repeated pressure cycling. Following the Cohasset accident, a PII (PII Pipeline Solutions) review of the data found that the 1996 inspection data did not meet the reporting criteria used by the PII analysts at the time and there had been problems with the in-line inspection tool. Examination of the 1995 tool runs revealed that the data quality issues prevented any detection of the crack that led to the eventual failure of the pipeline.

At the time of the NTSB investigation into the Cohasset accident, Enbridge stated that it had just introduced the more sophisticated UltraScan Crack Detection (USCD) inspection tool in the United States in 2001. In addition, Enbridge prepared a pipeline inspection procedure that called for "the excavation of all crack-like indications unless an engineering assessment determines that either the indication is acceptable based on a fitness-for-purpose calculation...." Enbridge analyzed crack growth rates using information from the 2002 failure in Cohasset to develop the worst-case scenario crack and its predicted time to failure. Based on these findings, Enbridge proposed to the Research and Special Programs Administration, the predecessor of PHMSA, that a portion of Line 4 be reinspected using the new in-line inspection technology at intervals of 3 years.

---

[37] Onshore, crude oil releases attributed to Enbridge are Grand Rapids, Minnesota, 1.7 million gallons; Pembina, North Dakota, 1.3 million gallons; Marshall, Michigan, 0.8 million gallons.

[38] At the time of this report, the NTSB is also investigating a release from Enbridge's Line 6A that occurred on September 9, 2010, in Romeoville, Illinois. The release is estimated at 316,596 gallons of crude oil. Line 6A is a 34-inch-diameter pipeline with 0.281-inch wall thickness. It was constructed in 1968 and protected with a polyethylene tape coating. The pipe was manufactured by A.O. Smith Corp. with a flash welded longitudinal seam, manufactured to API Standard 5LX grade X52.

[39] *Rupture of Enbridge Pipeline and Release of Crude Oil near Cohasset, Minnesota, July 4, 2002,* Pipeline Accident Report NTSB/PAR-04/01 (Washington, D.C.: National Transportation Safety Board, 2004).

[40] *Transportation-induced metal fatigue* is a failure mechanism for pipe transported primarily by railroad and has also been associated with marine transportation. This type of fatigue is found along the longitudinal seam weld of the pipe and is caused by the cyclic stresses imposed during transportation as the pipe is subjected to frequent motion.

### 1.6.4.2 Glenavon, Saskatchewan

The TSB investigated a rupture involving Enbridge's Line 3 near Glenavon, Saskatchewan,[41] that resulted in a release of nearly 200,000 gallons of crude oil on April 15, 2007. The pipeline was installed in 1968. It was manufactured to the 1967 API 5LX grade X52 specification with 0.28-inch wall thickness and a DSAW longitudinal seam. The pipe was originally protected with a polyethylene tape wrap coating and had an MOP of 652 psi. The TSB noted in its findings that the coating had tented[42] over the longitudinal seam weld, exposing it to a corrosive environment. The rupture was caused by cracking that had initiated at a shallow area of corrosion (a corrosion groove) on the external surface of the pipe with a depth of less than 0.016 inch (5 percent of the wall thickness) where the external longitudinal seam weld intersected with the body of the pipe and had propagated by fatigue up to a depth of 0.112 inch (40 percent of the wall thickness) through the pipe wall. The Enbridge integrity management program did not identify this defect for excavation following an engineering assessment of the defect after the last in-line inspection was conducted in 2006, 1 year before the rupture.

According to the TSB's report findings:

> The verification procedure used by Enbridge was to compare [in-line inspection] estimated crack sizes, and associated calculated failure pressures, with results obtained in the field by non-destructive ultrasonic inspection or crack grinding, or a combination of the two. Enbridge considers field and [in-line inspection] data to be sufficiently accurate if the data falls within an error band of plus or minus 10 percent.

The TSB's report also raised several issues regarding the quality of the inspection results and the analysis:

- In 2005, although Enbridge recalculated the crack growth rate to reflect the more aggressive pressure cycles, the parameters Enbridge used during that analysis did not accurately reflect the actual crack growth rate.

- The analysis of the 2006 in-line inspection data underestimated the depth of the deepest section of the fatigue crack.

The TSB determined that "The accuracy of the predictions of the crack growth model depends on the accuracy of the input parameters, including initial crack size. If any of these parameters have been underestimated, actual crack growth rates will exceed predicted values." The TSB stated the following:

> When input parameters for the modeling of crack growth rates do not reflect probabilities and tolerances associated with the detection and sizing capabilities of [in-line inspection] ultrasonic crack detection tools as well as actual pipe conditions, actual crack growth rates may exceed estimated values.

---

[41] Transportation Safety Board of Canada, *Crude Oil Pipeline Rupture, Enbridge Pipelines Inc. Line 3, Mile Post 506.2217, Near Glenavon, Saskatchewan, 15 April 2007*, Pipeline Investigative Report P07H0014.

[42] See section 1.7.1, "Coating," of this report for further information about tenting.

## 1.7  Examination of the Accident Pipe

The ruptured pipe segment was 39 feet 10.75 inches long. The longitudinal seam was oriented at 99.5° clockwise.[43] A 50-foot length of pipe that included the rupture was removed and cut into two sections for shipping to the NTSB's Materials Laboratory for examination. The upstream section measured 23 feet 4 inches. The downstream section measured 26 feet 10.25 inches. (See figure 11.)

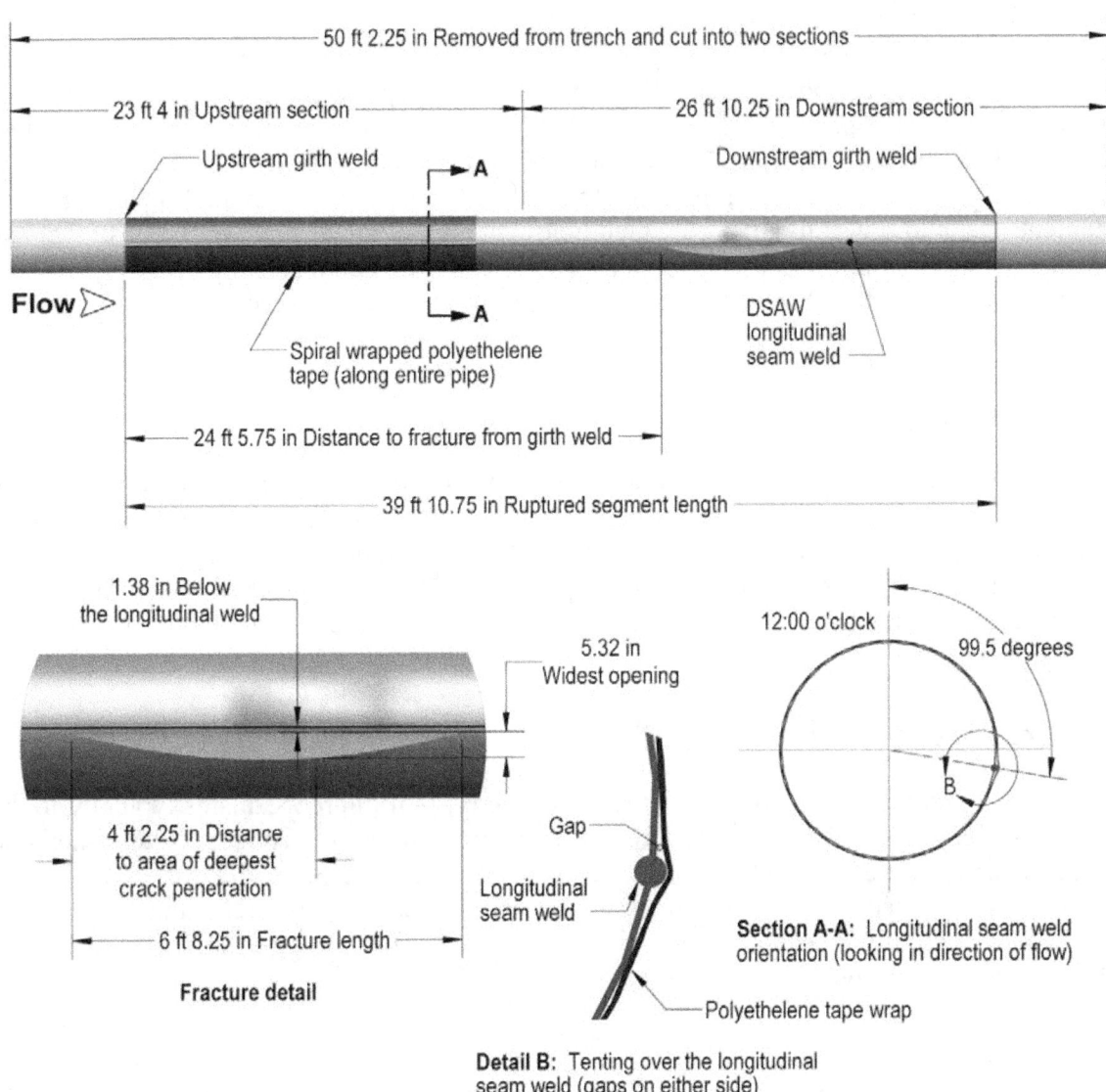

**Figure 11.** Line 6B ruptured segment showing upstream and downstream sections used for Materials Laboratory examination. Detail B shows tented coating over the longitudinal seam weld.

---

[43] Clockwise means as viewed facing the direction of flow. The top of the pipe is 0°, or the 12 o'clock position.

### 1.7.1  Coating

The ruptured segment was coated with a single wrap of Polyken 960-13 polyethylene tape with an adhesive backing. Enbridge reported that the tape coating had been applied in the field by a machine using Polyken 919 primer on the pipe. Examination revealed longitudinally oriented wrinkles in the coating, mostly near the 3 and 9 o'clock positions (viewed in the direction of flow). Wrinkling and tenting were observed along most of the ruptured segment, most pronounced at the 3 o'clock position over the longitudinal seam. Wrinkling and tenting are forms of disbondment of the coating. (The loss of the bond [the adhesion] between a pipeline and its protective coating commonly is called disbondment, which has been known to allow moisture to become trapped between the surface of the pipe and the tape, creating an environment that may be corrosive.) The pattern and location of the wrinkles in the tape coating were consistent with soil loads acting on the pipe.[44] Corrosion was observed beneath the areas where the adhesive bond between the pipe and its protective tape coating had deteriorated. In the areas of disbondment, metal loss was found around and below the longitudinal seam in the upstream and downstream sections of pipe. Because the tape had become disbonded, the pipeline's cathodic protection[45] was prevented from reaching the pipe; it no longer prevented corrosion from occurring.

### 1.7.2  Corrosion

External corrosion was observed along the length of the pipe in areas where the coating had disbonded. The corrosion was generally shallow with interspersed deeper pits and did not show a morphology typically associated with microbial-induced corrosion. The deepest corrosion pit measured in the vicinity of the rupture, near the deepest crack penetration, was 0.078 inch. The internal surface of the pipe was free from any apparent corrosion or other visible surface anomalies.

### 1.7.3  Microbial Corrosion

The EPA and the NTSB conducted testing for activity of microorganisms typically found to cause corrosion in pipes. Microbial test results depend upon many factors, such as, when and where the samples were taken. During its testing, the EPA used liquid samples that were collected from the space between the pipe surface and the coating; whereas, the NTSB used samples that were collected several weeks after the accident from the pipe surface immediately after the coating was removed.

---

[44] Soil loads can act to either open or close tenting gaps, and soil loads can cause wrinkles to form after a pipe's installation. Soil loads on top of a pipe tend to close tenting gaps, whereas soil loads on a side of the pipe tend to open tenting gaps and wrinkles. Tenting gaps and wrinkles are most prevalent near the 3 o'clock and 9 o'clock positions of a pipe.

[45] *Cathodic protection* is a corrosion mitigation method used by the pipeline industry to protect underground steel structures. The system uses direct current power supplies at selected locations along the pipeline to supply protective electrical current. Cathodic protection current is forced to flow in the opposite direction of currents produced by corrosion cells. The protective current is supplied to the pipeline through a ground bed that typically contains a string of suitable anodes, with soil as an electrolyte. A wire connected to the pipeline provides the return path for the current to complete the circuit.

On August 6, 2010, after the ruptured pipe was exposed in the trench, the EPA conducted three microbial tests of the liquid samples extracted from the space between the longitudinal seam and the tape coating. A high concentration (that is, at least 100,000 cells/milliliter) of various microorganisms—including sulfate-reducing bacteria, acid-producing bacteria, and anaerobic bacteria—were found in two of the three samples.

On August 27, 2010, the NTSB conducted additional microbial tests at its materials laboratory. Corrosion products and deposit samples were taken from the external surface at the longitudinal seam and from another area away from the longitudinal seam. Low concentrations (that is, 1 to 10 cells/milliliter) of anaerobic and acid-producing bacteria were detected in the longitudinal seam sample, and a low concentration of anaerobic bacteria was found in a base metal sample. No sulfate-reducing bacteria were detected. In addition, features typically associated with microbial corrosion were not observed on the corroded areas of the pipe.

## 1.7.4  The Fracture

The fracture measured 6 feet 8.25 inches in length with the upstream end of the fracture located 24 feet 5.75 inches away from the upstream girth weld. The widest point along the fracture measured 5.32 inches and was about 4 feet from the upstream end of the rupture. The upper fracture face at the widest opening was measured at 1.38 inches below the longitudinal seam weld away from the heat-affected zone, with this offset ranging from 0.5 to 1.5 inches below the longitudinal weld seam for the length of the fracture face. (See figure 12.)

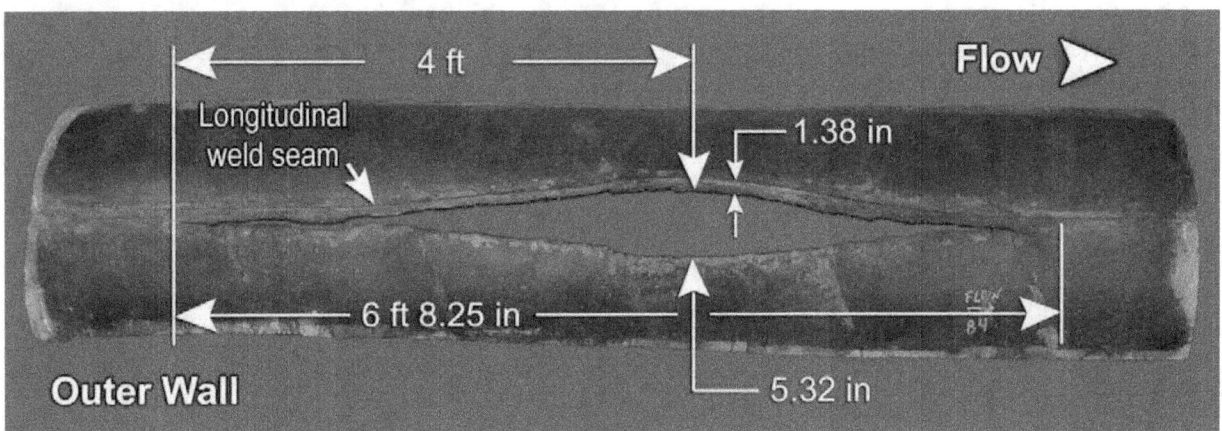

**Figure 12.** The outside surface of the pipe looking at the fracture area cut for lab examination.

Examination of the fracture face revealed features on slightly offset planes consistent with preexisting cracks initiating from multiple origins in corroded areas on the exterior surface. Evidence of preexisting cracks at various penetration depths was observed across nearly the entire length of the fracture surface. The area of deepest preexisting crack penetration, relative to the original local wall thickness, was located 50.25 inches from the upstream end of the rupture.

A continuous series of preexisting cracks was found extending from the outer edge of the fracture surface, linked together on the fracture surface, up to 10.8 inches upstream and 7.9 inches downstream from the area of deepest penetration. (See figure 13.) Black oxide was observed on the preexisting crack portion of the fracture consistent with oxidation in an oxygen-poor environment.

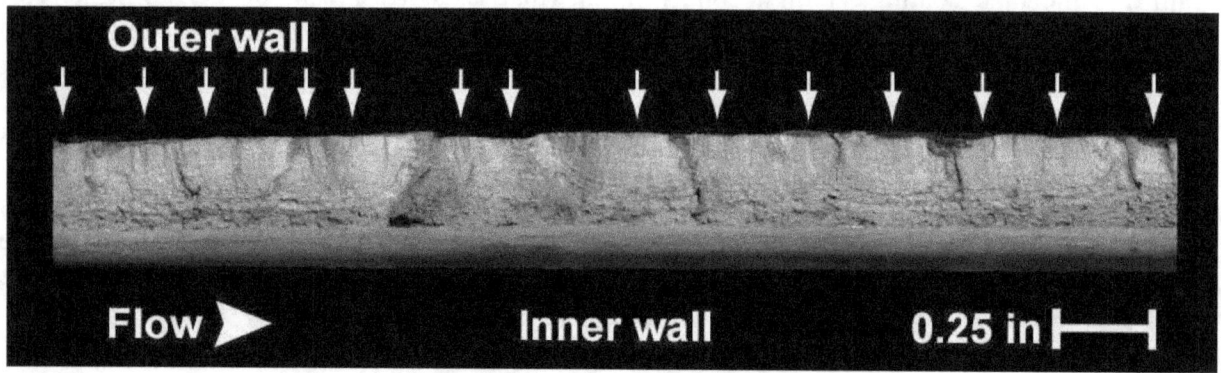

**Figure 13.** Curving arrest lines of preexisting cracks along the upper fracture face shown after cleaning to remove oxides. White arrows indicate multiple origin areas of preexisting cracks.

At the deepest crack penetration (see figure 14), the preexisting cracks extended 0.213 inch deep into the wall of the pipe relative to the original exterior surface, or 83.9 percent of the original wall thickness of 0.254 inch. The curving line in figure 14 indicates the extent of preexisting crack growth near the deepest penetration. The remainder of the fracture face had rough, matte gray features consistent with an overstress fracture. The preexisting cracks had fracture features perpendicular to the outside surface, consistent with corrosion fatigue[46,47] or near-neutral pH stress corrosion cracking (SCC).[48] Fine crack arrest features were present within about 0.015 inch of the crack origins with broader crack arrest features appearing farther away from the origins. These crack arrest features were indications of progressive crack growth and can be associated with corrosion fatigue or near-neutral pH SCC.

---

[46] *Corrosion fatigue* is a mode of cracking in materials under the combined actions of cyclic loading and a corrosive environment. Corrosion fatigue crack growth rates can be substantially higher in the corrosive environment than fatigue crack growth under cyclic loading in a benign environment.

[47] (a) National Energy Board Report of the Inquiry MH-2-95, *Public Inquiry Concerning Stress Corrosion Cracking on Canadian Oil and Gas Pipelines*, National Energy Board Canada (1996). (b) *Fractography*, Metals Handbook, Ninth Edition, Vol. 12, ASM International, 1987. (c) J.I. Dickson and J.P. Bailon, "The Fractography of Environmentally Assisted Cracking," in A.S. Krausz, ed., *Time Dependent Fracture: Proceedings of the Eleventh Canadian Fracture Conference, June 1984, Ottawa, Canada* (Dordrecht: M. Nijhoff Publishers, 1985).

[48] *Near-neutral pH SCC* is a form of cracking produced under the combined action of corrosion and tensile stress typically manifesting as clusters of small cracks in the external body of the pipe that can form long shallow flaws. Near-neutral pH SCC cracks propagate through the metal grain boundaries and with little secondary branching. It was first noted on a polyethylene-tape-coated pipeline in the TransCanada Pipelines system in the 1980s.

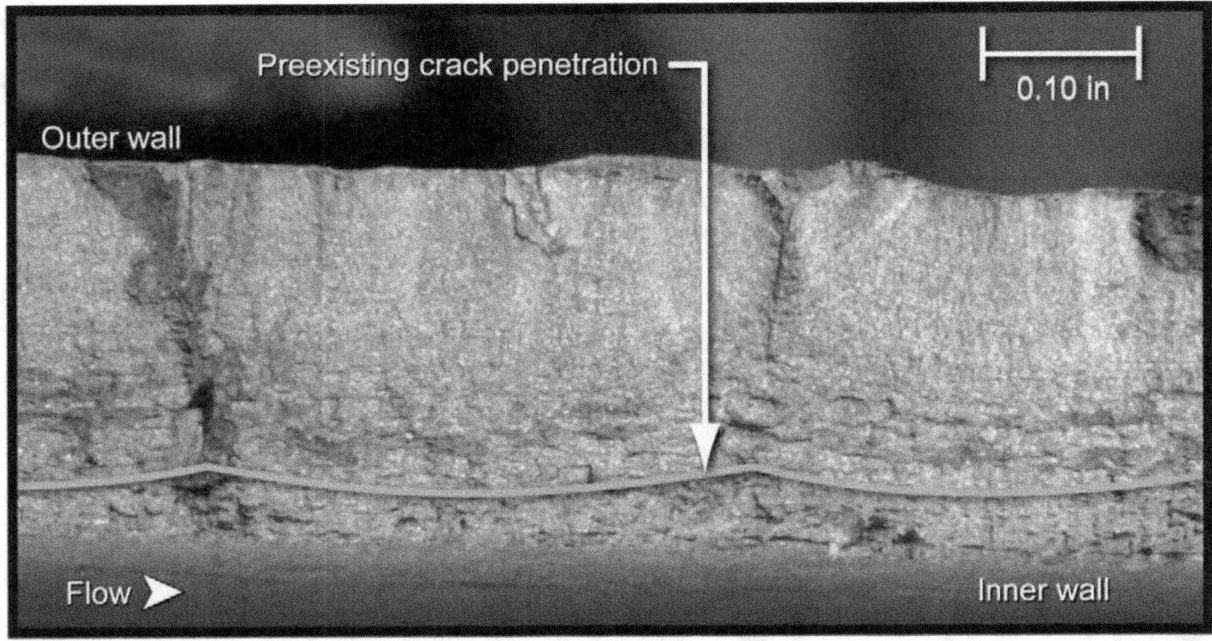

**Figure 14.** Close view of fracture surface area in the area of deepest crack penetration. The solid blue line indicates the extent of the preexisting crack penetration.

A cross-section through the fracture was prepared as shown in figure 15. The preexisting crack portion of the fracture showed a transgranular[49] fracture path with limited crack branching, consistent with near-neutral pH SCC or corrosion fatigue. Multiple closely spaced and parallel secondary cracks (with transgranular propagation paths and limited crack branching) emanated from corrosion pits on the outside wall near the fracture face, also consistent with corrosion fatigue or near-neutral pH SCC. The deepest secondary crack extended through about 43 percent of the wall thickness.

---

[49] A fracture that propagates through the metal grains rather than following the grain boundaries.

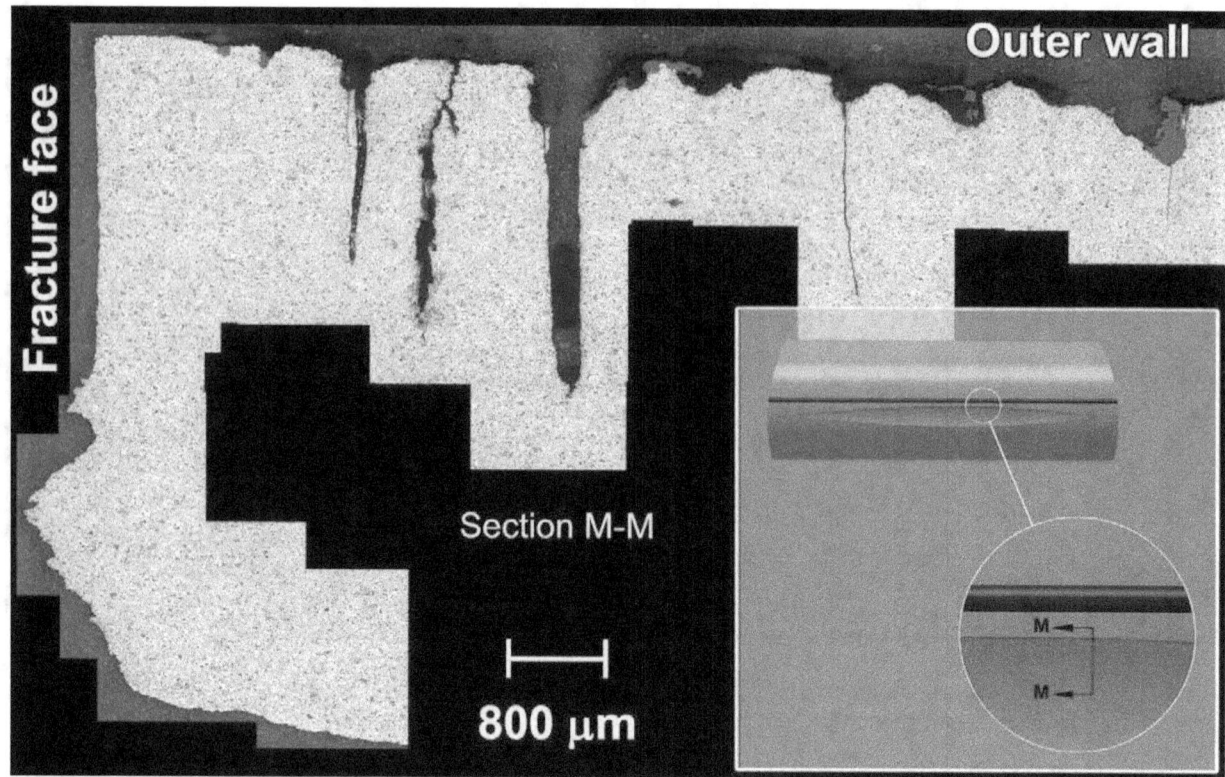

**Figure 15.** Transverse section through the top of the fracture showing multiple parallel cracks emanating from corrosion pits on the outside surface.

### 1.7.5  Crack and Corrosion Depth Profile

The preexisting crack depth and corrosion depth along the length of the rupture was measured relative to the original local wall thickness (as shown in figure 16).[50] The corrosion depths, which were measured on the fracture face under a microscope, did not necessarily reflect the deepest corrosion within the field of view but reflected the corrosion depth at the location where the crack depth was measured for each point. The corrosion depth at the location of deepest penetration measured in the plane of fracture was about 0.030 inch relative to the original wall thickness. The maximum depth of penetration of the preexisting cracks relative to the approximate original exterior wall surface was 0.213 inch at a location corresponding to approximately 28 feet 8 inches (344 inches) downstream of the upstream girth weld.

---

[50] Original wall thickness was measured adjacent to the fracture in areas appearing free of corrosion. The original outer wall location relative to the fracture was determined from the thickness measurement relative to the inner edge of the fracture face.

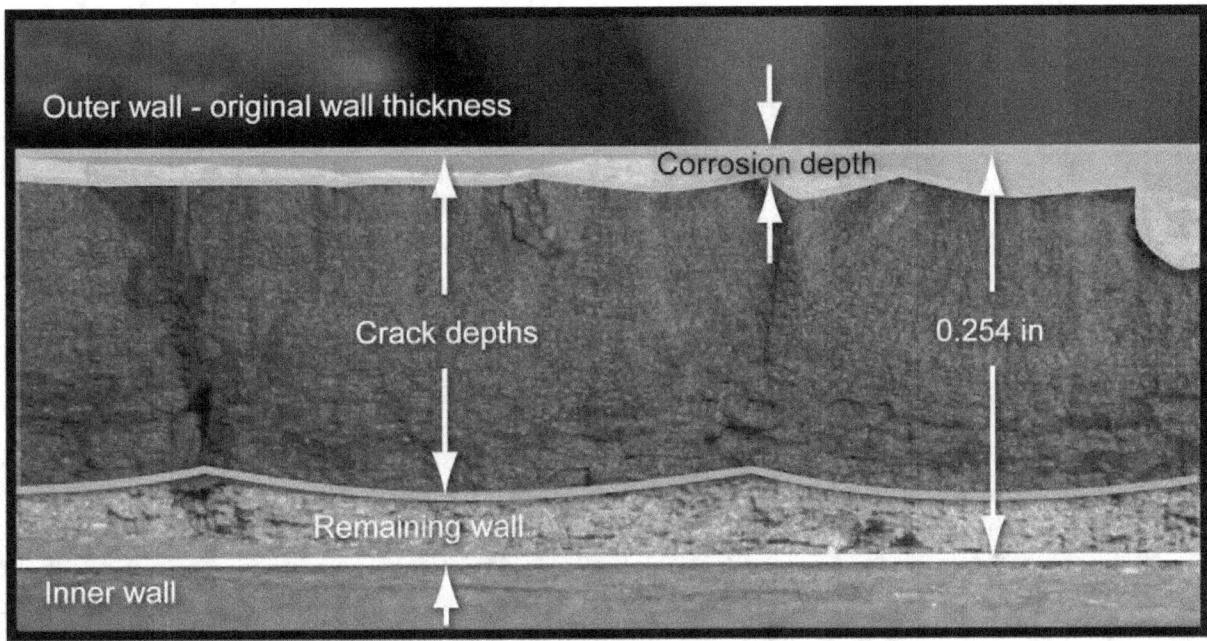

**Figure 16.** Lab measurements of crack and corrosion depths along the fracture face measured from images similar to figure 14 near area of deepest penetration (about 344 inches from upstream girth weld).

### 1.7.6 Mechanical Testing and Chemical Analysis

Tensile properties of all test specimens conformed to the requirements for yield strength, tensile strength, and elongation of grade X52 pipe as specified in the 1968 API Standard 5LX, *Specification for High-Test Line Pipe*. The chemical analysis for each sample tested conformed to the requirements for X52 pipe as specified in the 1968 API Standard 5LX, *Specification for High-Test Line Pipe*.

## 1.8 PHMSA Integrity Management Regulation

### 1.8.1 Pipeline Integrity Management in High Consequence Areas

On December 1, 2000, PHMSA amended 49 CFR Part 195 to require pipeline operating companies with 500 or more miles of hazardous liquid and carbon dioxide pipelines to conduct integrity management in HCAs.[51] On January 16, 2002, PHMSA extended this regulation to include operators who owned or operated less than 500 miles of hazardous liquid and carbon dioxide pipelines.[52]

---

[51] *Federal Register*, vol. 65, no. 232 (December 1, 2000), p. 75378.

[52] *Federal Register*, vol. 67, no. 11 (January 16, 2002), p. 2135.

Based on the comments PHMSA received in 2001, it amended the integrity management regulation, including the repair and mitigation provisions on January 14, 2002,[53] which became effective on May 29, 2001, except for paragraph (h) of 49 CFR 195.452, which became effective on February 13, 2002. According to PHMSA, the API had objected to the use of the word "repair" to describe the action required to address anomalies that could reduce a pipeline's integrity. PHMSA agreed with the API that the word "repair" might be too narrow to cover the range of actions an operator could take to address a safety issue. PHMSA replaced the word "repair" with "remediate." PHMSA also stated that although it firmly believes that repair is necessary to address many anomalies, it may not be necessary in all cases.

## 1.8.2 Elements of Integrity Management and Integration of Threats

As published, 49 CFR 195.452(e) lists risk factors (that is, pipe size, material, leak history, repair history, and coating type) that a pipeline operator must consider for establishing both baseline and continued pipeline assessment schedules. The elements of an integrity management program are listed in 49 CFR 195.452(f). Specifically, an operator must include, "an analysis that integrates all available information about the integrity of the entire pipeline and the consequences of a failure" in its written integrity management program.

The director of PHMSA's engineering and research division told investigators that "integration of all information about the integrity of the pipeline" in 49 CFR 195.452(f)(3) means that all threats are to be evaluated using an overlay or side-by-side analysis that would include cathodic protection, coating surveys, in-line inspection tool findings (for example, geometry, crack, and corrosion), and previous dig reports. He expected PHMSA inspectors to look for issues during an inspection to ensure that operators are implementing this methodology.

## 1.8.3 Discovery of Condition

Title 49 CFR 195.452(h) explains the actions an operator must take to address integrity issues for liquid pipelines in HCAs. Under the general requirements, "an operator must take prompt action to address all anomalous conditions the operator discovers through the integrity assessment or information analysis." The regulation further states the following:

> Discovery of a condition occurs when an operator has adequate information about the condition to determine that the condition presents a potential threat to the integrity of the pipeline. An operator must promptly, but no later than 180 days after an integrity assessment, obtain sufficient information about a condition to make that determination, unless the operator can demonstrate that the 180-day period is impracticable.

---

[53] *Federal Register*, vol. 67, no. 9 (January 14, 2002), p. 1650.

### 1.8.4  Immediate and 180-Day Conditions

Title 49 CFR 195.452(h)(4)(i) requires immediate repair for several conditions, including those exhibiting "metal loss greater than 80 percent of [the] nominal wall regardless of dimensions" and those for which "a calculation of remaining strength of the pipe shows a predicted burst pressure less than the established maximum operating pressure at the location of the anomaly." The regulation identifies two acceptable methods of calculating the remaining strength of corroded pipe. Title 49 CFR 195.452(h)(4)(iii) addresses nine conditions that require remediation within 180 days. Four of these are listed below:

(D) a calculation of the remaining strength of the pipe that shows an operating pressure that is less than the current established maximum operating pressure at the location of the anomaly. Suitable remaining strength calculation methods include, but are not limited to, [American Society of Mechanical Engineers (ASME)]/[American National Standards Institute] B31G ("Manual for Determining the Remaining Strength of Corroded Pipelines" (1991)) or AGA Pipeline Research Committee Project PR-3-805 ("A Modified Criterion for evaluating the Remaining Strength of Corroded Pipe" (December 1989)).

(G) A potential crack indication that when excavated is determined to be a crack.

(H) Corrosion of or along a longitudinal seam weld.

(I) A gouge or a groove greater than 12.5 percent of nominal wall.

On March 15, 2012, NTSB staff met with PHMSA representatives to discuss regulations covering hazardous liquid pipelines. During the meeting, the director of PHMSA's engineering and research division stated that in accordance with 49 CFR 195.452 (h)(4)(iii)(G), PHMSA expects that all cracks will be excavated.

## 1.9  Enbridge Integrity Management Program

The Enbridge pipeline integrity department has been responsible for monitoring and implementing repair or remediation activities that are pertinent to mainline pipelines. The department is divided into three groups responsible for evaluating the risks associated with corrosion, cracks, and geometry-related issues. All of the groups rely on in-line inspection technologies to assess the integrity of the pipeline and identify potential threats. The crack and corrosion groups perform engineering assessments on the data received from the final in-line inspection reports to prioritize and schedule pipeline excavations. Excavations are conducted to evaluate the in-line inspection results, to remediate or repair defects, and to examine the condition of the pipeline segment.

### 1.9.1  Corrosion Management

Enbridge's corrosion management group is responsible for both internal and external pipeline corrosion. SCC is evaluated under the crack management program.

Enbridge evaluated pipeline internal corrosion susceptibility by integrating and evaluating data on pipeline characteristics, in-line inspection data, operating conditions, pipeline cleanliness, crude and sludge sampling, and historical leak data. In 1996, Enbridge began a chemical inhibition program to prevent internal corrosion of Line 6B by using an inhibitor.

The corrosion management group monitors and inspects for external corrosion primarily through in-line inspections. The integrity analysis engineer is responsible for developing a list of features to be excavated (that is, the dig list) based on an analysis of the corrosion in-line inspection data. The corrosion group relies on two different tool inspection technologies (ultrasonic and magnetic flux leakage [MFL]) to locate and detect corrosion defects in the pipeline. The dig list developed from the inspection final report will include all features that meet the excavation criteria that have not been excavated, assessed, and repaired in the past. Enbridge's corrosion excavation criterion is to excavate any feature that either exceeds 50 percent wall thickness loss or has a predicted failure pressure of less than 1.39 times the MOP. Enbridge had no clearly documented procedure that required the integrity analysis engineer to share corrosion in-line inspection data and excavation data with the people responsible to develop a dig list from crack or geometry tool in-line inspection data. According to Enbridge procedures, Enbridge would impose a pressure restriction for any feature requiring immediate repair. For a corrosion feature, the pressure restriction was based on ASME-sponsored code B31G, 2009 edition, *Manual for Determining the Remaining Strength of Corroded Pipelines: Supplement to ASME B31 Code for Pressure Piping.*[54] This is an approved method for calculating the remaining strength of the pipe for corrosion specified at 49 CFR 195.452.

### 1.9.2  Crack Management

To monitor its pipelines for cracks, Enbridge used in-line inspections, direct assessment (excavation and examination), and fitness-for-service[55] engineering assessment techniques.[56] Enbridge performed engineering assessments to manage crack defects identified through in-line inspections of its pipelines. Enbridge relied on a single ultrasonic crack inspection technology (the USCD tool) to perform crack inspections.

---

[54] The ASME-sponsored codes for pressure piping in this report are referred to as ASME codes, even though several other organizations have also been associated with their development over time. The ASME code for pressure piping was originally developed in cooperation with the American Engineering Standards committee, which later changed its name to the American Standards Association, and then to the American National Standards Institute, Inc.

[55] Fitness-for-purpose and fitness-for-service have been used interchangeably, representing engineering assessments used to calculate the adequacy of a structure for continued service under current conditions.

[56] The fitness-for-service techniques were consistent with the British Standard 7910, "Guide to Methods for Assessing the Acceptability of Flaws in Metallic Structures," and API 579-1/ASME FFS-1 2007, *Fitness-for-Service*.

Enbridge's crack management group received a finalized in-line inspection report characterizing defects, which included crack-like or crack-field features. Enbridge interpreted crack-like as single linear cracks and crack-field indications as SCC colonies and applied separate criteria for excavation to each characterization. For crack-like features, the report included a maximum length and depth. For crack-field features, the report included the length of the colony, the longest crack indication (individual crack) in the colony, and a maximum depth. In 2005, Enbridge requested all crack depths be reported as a percentage of the tool-reported wall thickness. The crack depths were reported in ranges of less than 12.5 percent, 12.5 to 25 percent, 25 percent to 40 percent, and greater than 40 percent of wall thickness.

Enbridge excavation criteria for crack-like features was a predicted failure pressure from an engineering assessment less than the hydrostatic test pressure, which is defined as 1.25 times the MOP under 49 CFR 195.304. For crack-field features, Enbridge selected features that had a longest indication greater than 2.5 inches long or had a depth of 25 to 40 percent of the wall thickness. For a crack feature, the pressure restrictions were imposed based on a remaining strength calculation that showed a failure pressure less than the hydrostatic test pressure.[57] (The MOP was 624 psig for the ruptured segment.)

Enbridge provided the crack management excavation program summary worksheet from its 2005 crack tool in-line inspection showing over 15,000 defects on Line 6B. The worksheet listed 929 crack-like features identified by the in-line inspection tool; 29 of these features had a calculated failure pressure that was less than the hydrostatic test pressure (Enbridge crack excavation criteria). More than twice as many features (61 of the 929) had a calculated failure pressure that was less than 1.39 times the MOP (Enbridge's corrosion excavation criteria). All crack-field features 2.5 inches long or greater had been excavated.

## 1.9.3  In-line Inspection Intervals

Fatigue crack growth analysis was conducted by Enbridge on crack-like, crack-field, and notch-like features. Pressure cycle loading based on historical pressure data was used in the crack growth model, and a resulting fatigue life was determined. The time for the next scheduled in-line inspection for cracks was set to be no more than half the calculated fatigue life of any feature remaining in the line. Title 49 CFR 195.452(j)(3) requires that operators set 5-year intervals not to exceed 68 months for continually assessing the pipeline's integrity. Enbridge fatigue life calculations conducted using the 2005 in-line crack inspection data for Line 6B resulted in an estimated reinspection interval greater than the 5-year interval mandated under the regulation. Enbridge was performing the next in-line crack inspection of Line 6B in 2010 at the time of the accident.

---

[57] Under 49 CFR 195.304, this is stated as a minimum of 1.25 times the MOP.

### 1.9.4  Stress Corrosion Cracking

Enbridge's crack management plan focused on fatigue and SCC. The Enbridge SCC plan is part of its overall crack management program. About 39 percent of the Enbridge pipeline system is considered to have susceptibility to SCC based on the Canadian Energy Pipeline Association (CEPA) 1997 standard on SCC. About 35 percent of the total pipeline system has high susceptibility to SCC. The SCC management plan was developed about 1996 following the National Energy Board (NEB) public hearings on SCC in pipelines.

As a policy, Enbridge examined all excavated pipeline segments for SCC.[58] CEPA's recommended SCC mitigation approach included hydrostatic retesting, in-line inspection if appropriate tools were available, extensive pipe replacement, and recoating. CEPA considered hydrostatic retesting and in-line inspection to be temporary mitigation techniques. In contrast, repairs such as recoating the pipe, installing sleeves, grinding away the defects, and replacing the pipe were permanent mitigation techniques. According to CEPA, hydrostatic retesting has been shown to be an effective means for identifying near-critical axial defects, such as SCC.

### 1.9.5  Coating and Cathodic Protection

Line 6B was coated with field-applied Polyken number 960 polyethylene tape coating. Enbridge operates over 1,100 miles of polyethylene-tape-coated pipelines in the United States, which represents about 25 percent of its U.S.-based transmission mileage. Tape-coated portions of Line 6A (410 miles) and Line 6B (283 miles) represent the two longest pipelines making up the 25 percent. Enbridge Lines 6A and 6B were both installed in the late 1960s. The coating on Line 6B was composed of a 9-mil-thick[59] polyethylene backing and a 4-mil-thick synthetic rubber (synthetic resin) adhesive. According to Enbridge, this type of external tape coating and its typical degradation mode are key factors in determining the pipeline's potential susceptibility to SCC. This susceptibility to SCC was due to the higher tendency of this tape coating to lose adhesion (disbondment), exposing the pipe to a potentially corrosive environment while preventing cathodic protection from reaching the pipe.

In addition to the polyethylene tape wrap on Line 6B, Enbridge operated a cathodic protection system to protect the line from corrosion. Pipe-to-soil electrical potential readings taken on July 31, 2010, showed operating levels were above the minimum acceptable criteria established under 49 CFR 195.571. Even with cathodic protection levels operating in excess of the minimum levels specified in the regulations, disbonded tape coating can shield the cathodic protection current from reaching the exposed pipe wall, allowing corrosion to form on the external pipe surface.

---

[58] An SCC colony is assessed to be "significant" if the deepest crack, in a series of interacting cracks, is greater than 10 percent of wall thickness, and the total interacting length of the cracks is equal to or greater than 75 percent of the critical crack length of a 50-percent through wall crack at a stress level of 110 percent of SMYS.

[59] One mil equals 1/1,000 inch.

---

## 1.9.6  In-line Inspection Tools

A variety of in-line inspection tool technologies are used to estimate the size and location of defects that may be on the inside or outside surfaces of the pipe wall. Different tools and technologies are employed by operators depending on the type, orientation, and location of the defects. Since 2004, Enbridge had inspected Line 6B using three types of tools: UltraScan Wall Measurement (USWM), USCD, and MFL.

The USWM tool, which is an Elastic Wave tool, works by sending ultrasound in two directions through the pipe wall and is useful for detecting wall thickness lost to corrosion. The USCD tool detects longitudinal defects (cracks) in a pipe wall using the reflected ultrasonic signals from the defects in the pipe wall to locate and size cracks. The transverse MFL tool relies on magnetic fields to detect defects (cracks and corrosion) in the pipe wall and longitudinal seams.

Despite their sophistication, the detection capabilities of in-line inspection tools have limitations. Each tool technology has a stated minimum defect size that can be detected and the tool can be subjected to interference from nearby anomalies or geometry. The ability of the tool to detect a feature of minimum size is known as the probability of detection. Probability of indication represents the uncertainty involved in the post-processing and interpretation of the raw signals. Once detected, tool data are analyzed through sizing and selection algorithms and, finally, by a data analyst, who characterizes the feature by type.

Enbridge told NTSB investigators that, when the right technology and processes are implemented, in-line inspection has been shown to be more effective than hydrostatic testing at maintaining a reliable pipeline. At the time of the accident, Enbridge had not performed hydrostatic pressure testing on Line 6B since the time of its construction. Enbridge stated it preferred to assess line integrity using in-line inspection tools.

## 1.9.6.1  USCD Tool

The USCD tool was designed to detect, locate, and size axially aligned cracks in liquid pipelines; it requires a liquid coupling between the ultrasonic sensors and the inner pipe wall to allow sound waves to pass between the tool and the pipeline. The amplitude of the sound returning at 45° allows estimation of the depth of a crack or cracks in the pipeline. A crack must be more than 1.18 inches long and 0.0393 inch deep to be detected by the tool and characterized by the in-line inspection analyst. The tool reports single (crack-like) and multiple cracks (crack fields) that are axially aligned, in both the body of the pipe and the seam weld area. To account for uncertainty in the depth sizing, the USCD tool has a tolerance of ±0.02 inch for reported feature depths. However, Enbridge did not account for a tool tolerance in its analysis of the crack depths in the 2005 USCD analysis.

In 2005, Enbridge requested that the crack depth be reported in depth ranges expressed as a percentage of the tool-reported wall thickness. Crack depths are reported in ranges to account for error in the tool's ability to estimate depth. The tool-reported depth ranges were as follows: 0–12.5 percent, 12.5–25 percent, 25–40 percent, and greater than 40 percent.

The USCD tool reported a wall thickness value for each segment of pipe. According to PII, the wall thickness was measured by the tool to facilitate feature sizing; the measurement was not intended to be an accurate representation of the local wall thickness of the segment.

PII stated that for cracks above the detection threshold and located in shallow corroded areas, the detection and identification would be distinctive and based on the reflected echo; however, the reported depth would relate only to the crack indication, not to the depth of the corrosion. (Therefore, it is important to note that the corrosion depth must be added to the crack estimated depth to establish the true extent of the crack depth.) An exception to this occurs when a crack is located at the edge of steep-sided corrosion. In this case, corrosion depth will not affect the depth sizing and the tool will report the actual crack depth. PII further stated that the information regarding the impacts of corrosion on crack sizing was not mentioned in its brochures and had not explicitly been given to Enbridge. The following impacts on performance may occur when an in-line inspection tool is detecting a crack in shallow corrosion:[60]

- [Probability of detection] – Signals reflected by corrosion could be diffused and overlaid on the signals of shallow cracks.

- [Probability of indication] – Weak signals could be identified as rough surface and therefore not sized and reported.

- Depth Estimation – The sizing performance could be affected by diffused and overlaid signals of the corrosion.

Enbridge's director of the integrity management program told NTSB investigators that an operator should consider the corrosion and crack features identified by in-line inspection tools; however, Enbridge prefers to monitor tool accuracy by comparing the in-line inspection tool reported depths with the actual depths measured at the time of excavation. The Enbridge 2005 and 2006 field excavation evaluation procedures stated that defect depth should include crack depth plus wall loss, but in 2005 no similar process was in place under the integrity crack management program to incorporate the findings from field evaluations of the tool-reported crack depth into the engineering assessments.

### 1.9.7  Enbridge Postaccident Threat Assessment Review

Dynamic Risk Assessment Systems, Inc., a contractor, conducted a systemwide threat assessment review for Enbridge in 2011. Based on Enbridge's 1984–2010 leak report database, the review concluded that external corrosion had caused 14 percent of the past failures. Environmentally assisted cracking[61] was responsible for 3 percent of the failures. The review report stated, "External metal loss is one of the morphological traits associated with near-neutral pH SCC and corrosion fatigue." The report further stated, "the environmentally assisted cracking mechanism that is most prevalent along Enbridge's liquid pipeline system is either near-neutral

---

[60] See the item titled "IMP [Integrity Management Program] PII Documents" in the NTSB public docket for this accident.

[61] An environmentally assisted crack is corrosion fatigue or stress corrosion cracking that is accelerated by a corrosive environment.

pH SCC or corrosion fatigue." For Line 6B, the review report categorized manufacturing defects and external corrosion as significant threats and SCC as a moderate threat.

## 1.9.8  Prior In-Line Inspections of Line 6B

In-line corrosion inspections were performed in 2004, 2007, and 2009 using both MFL and ultrasonic in-line inspection tools. The first in-line crack inspection performed on Line 6B, following the introduction of the integrity management rule, was in 2005 using the USCD tool. The following are summary findings from those inspection reports.

### 1.9.8.1  2004 Ultrasonic Wall Measurement In-Line Inspection

In 2004, Enbridge contracted PII to conduct an in-line corrosion inspection on Line 6B using an USWM tool. The PII inspection report for this inspection listed 50,270 corrosion features on Line 6B, with 1,037 of those features having predicted failure pressures of less than 1.39 times the MOP or SMYS. Sixteen external corrosion features identified from the inspection were located on the ruptured segment; 12 of these were on the longitudinal seam weld, and 4 were near the seam weld. Four regions of external corrosion were identified within the immediate rupture location (see figure 17); however, none of these features met the Enbridge criteria for excavation (predicted failure pressure that was less than 1.39 times the MOP). At the location within the fracture corresponding to the deepest preexisting crack penetration[62] identified by the NTSB Materials Laboratory, the 2004 USWM inspection report documented an area of corrosion measuring 18.5 inches long located about 0.80 inch below the longitudinal seam weld with a maximum recorded depth of 0.087 inch (34 percent of the wall thickness). This area of corrosion was located 27.92 feet from the upstream girth weld. In June 2004, Enbridge imposed a pressure restriction at the Marshall PS based on corrosion findings (downstream of the Marshall PS near MP 611) from the 2004 in-line inspection that limited the discharge pressure to 525 psig. The 2004 inspection results included some corrosion indications with estimated depths that might have been undersized due to echo loss.[63] To supplement the readings affected by the echo loss, Enbridge performed a second corrosion inspection in 2007.

---

[62] Located 28 feet 8 inches from the upstream girth weld.

[63] Echo loss occurs when the sound signal is not reflected back to the transducer of the inspection tool, resulting in missing or lost data. PII stated that it used an algorithm to determine the depth of features in cases where echo loss occurred.

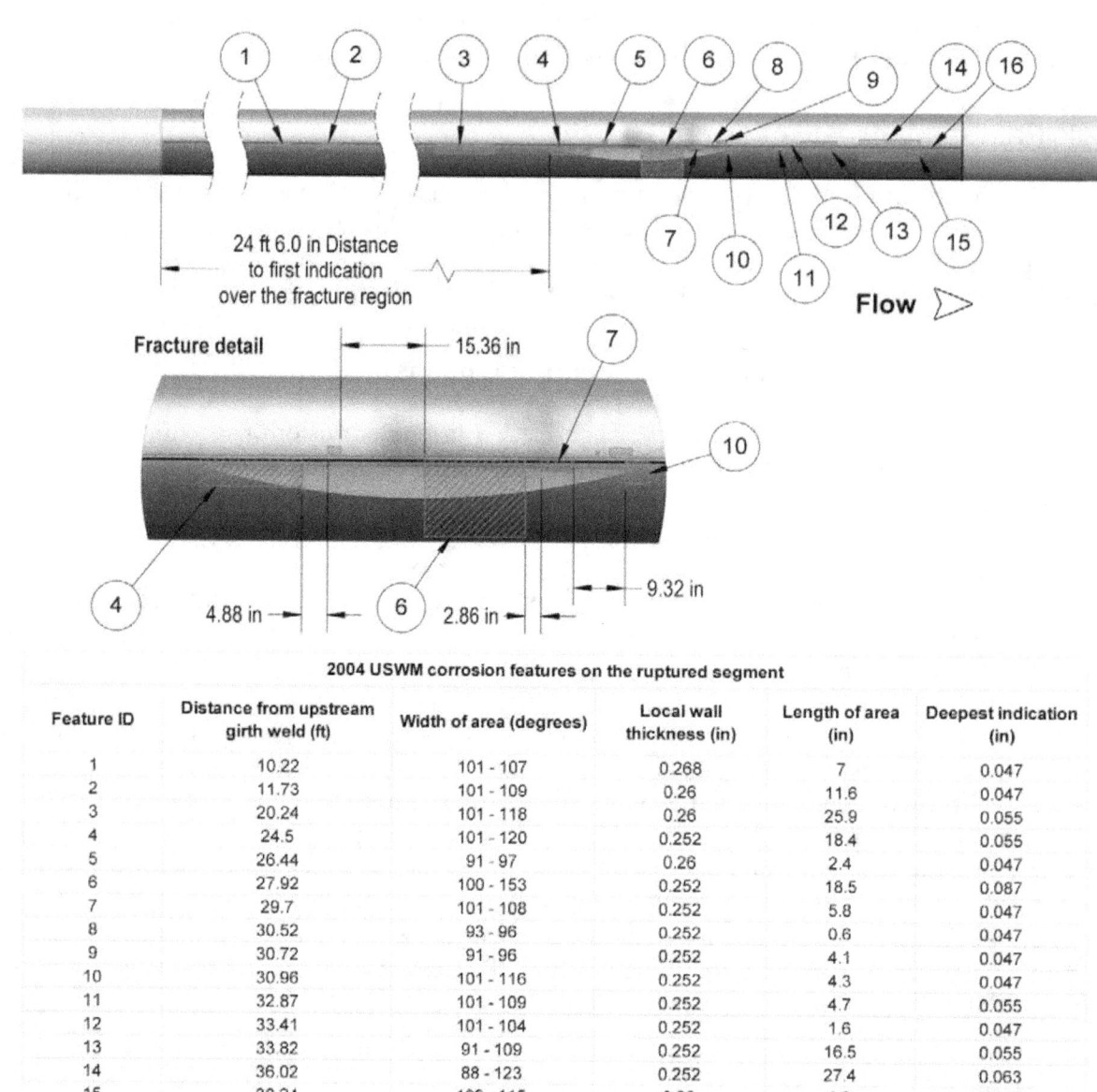

2004 USWM corrosion features on the ruptured segment

| Feature ID | Distance from upstream girth weld (ft) | Width of area (degrees) | Local wall thickness (in) | Length of area (in) | Deepest indication (in) |
|---|---|---|---|---|---|
| 1 | 10.22 | 101 - 107 | 0.268 | 7 | 0.047 |
| 2 | 11.73 | 101 - 109 | 0.26 | 11.6 | 0.047 |
| 3 | 20.24 | 101 - 118 | 0.26 | 25.9 | 0.055 |
| 4 | 24.5 | 101 - 120 | 0.252 | 18.4 | 0.055 |
| 5 | 26.44 | 91 - 97 | 0.26 | 2.4 | 0.047 |
| 6 | 27.92 | 100 - 153 | 0.252 | 18.5 | 0.087 |
| 7 | 29.7 | 101 - 108 | 0.252 | 5.8 | 0.047 |
| 8 | 30.52 | 93 - 96 | 0.252 | 0.6 | 0.047 |
| 9 | 30.72 | 91 - 96 | 0.252 | 4.1 | 0.047 |
| 10 | 30.96 | 101 - 116 | 0.252 | 4.3 | 0.047 |
| 11 | 32.87 | 101 - 109 | 0.252 | 4.7 | 0.055 |
| 12 | 33.41 | 101 - 104 | 0.252 | 1.6 | 0.047 |
| 13 | 33.82 | 91 - 109 | 0.252 | 16.5 | 0.055 |
| 14 | 36.02 | 88 - 123 | 0.252 | 27.4 | 0.063 |
| 15 | 38.24 | 109 - 115 | 0.26 | 1.2 | 0.047 |
| 16 | 38.7 | 100 - 104 | 0.26 | 1 | 0.055 |

The longtiudinal seam weld was reported by the tool as oriented 100 degrees clockwise from the top of the pipe

**Figure 17.** 2004 corrosion inspection of Line 6B and 16 regions of corrosion identified by the tool on the ruptured pipe segment. The detail view shows the areas of corrosion overlapped with the rupture location.

### 1.9.8.2 2005 In-Line Inspection—PII USCD Crack Tool Results

The 2005 USCD tool report identified 7,257 crack-like, crack-field, and notch-like features on Line 6B. The report included six indications of crack-like features located on the external surface that were adjacent to the weld in the ruptured segment. All of the features in the ruptured segment were oriented between 98° to 102° relative to the top of the pipe and were located below the longitudinal weld seam, which the inspection report stated was at 96° relative to the top of the pipe.

Wall thickness of the ruptured segment was measured by the 2005 USCD in-line inspection tool and reported as 0.285 inch for the entire segment length. This tool reported wall thickness was used by PII when reporting the depths of all crack features as a percentage of wall thickness. PII stated that the wall thickness measured by the tool is not intended to be a local indication of wall thickness in the pipe segment. The tool-reported wall thickness value and crack depths[64] (reported as a percentage of tool-reported wall thickness) were used by Enbridge when conducting the engineering assessments of predicted failure pressure and fatigue life of the cracks. The assessments were the basis of selection for pipeline excavation and reinspection intervals.

PII identified six crack-like indications in the 2005 Line 6B in-line inspection report for the ruptured pipe segment. (See figure 18.) Two of the crack defects had depths of 12 to 25 percent of the tool-reported wall thickness. These features were 25.5 inches and 51.6 inches long and were located directly over the area of rupture. The deepest (with a depth of 25 to 40 percent of the tool-reported wall thickness) of the six crack-like features was 9.3 inches long and was located 11.04 feet from the upstream girth weld of the ruptured segment.

---

[64] The Enbridge procedure required that the maximum depth range be used for an initial engineering assessment; however, if the result of the initial calculation was less than the hydrostatic test pressure, a second assessment was performed using a refined crack depth (profile) requested from the in-line inspection vendor. PII stated that it does not stand behind the accuracy of refined depths or profiles. A profiled depth for the 9.3-inch crack-like feature was requested during the analysis of the 2005 in-line inspection data that resulted in the crack not being excavated.

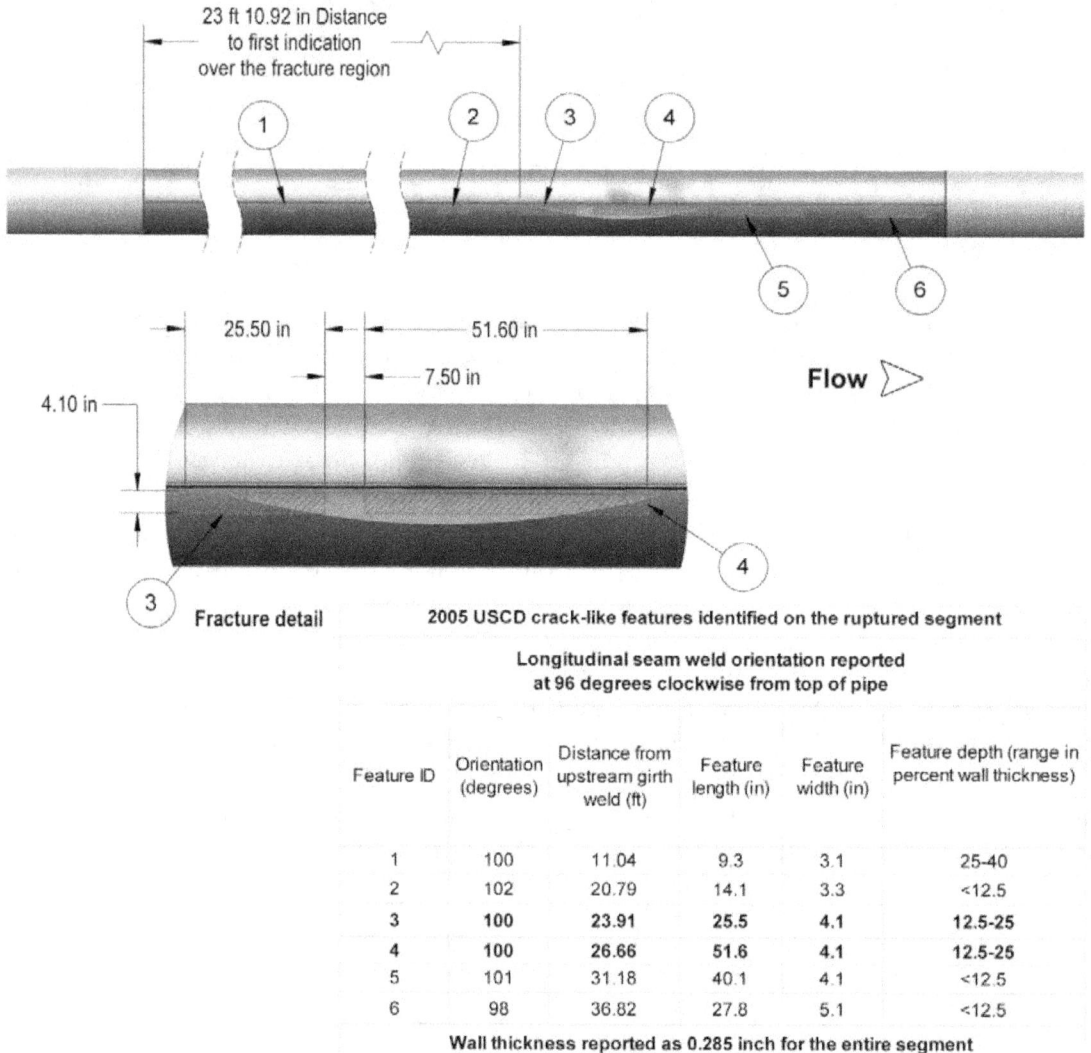

Longitudinal seam weld orientation reported
at 96 degrees clockwise from top of pipe

| Feature ID | Orientation (degrees) | Distance from upstream girth weld (ft) | Feature length (in) | Feature width (in) | Feature depth (range in percent wall thickness) |
|---|---|---|---|---|---|
| 1 | 100 | 11.04 | 9.3 | 3.1 | 25-40 |
| 2 | 102 | 20.79 | 14.1 | 3.3 | <12.5 |
| 3 | 100 | 23.91 | 25.5 | 4.1 | 12.5-25 |
| 4 | 100 | 26.66 | 51.6 | 4.1 | 12.5-25 |
| 5 | 101 | 31.18 | 40.1 | 4.1 | <12.5 |
| 6 | 98 | 36.82 | 27.8 | 5.1 | <12.5 |

Wall thickness reported as 0.285 inch for the entire segment

**Figure 18.** 2005 in-line inspection regions where crack-like characterizations were reported by PII on the ruptured segment of Line 6B.

According to PII, all six features identified on the ruptured segment, including the 51.6-inch-long crack, were originally characterized as crack-field indications by a junior analyst; however, a supervisor changed the analyst's characterizations to crack-like defects during a final quality check.

The Enbridge excavation criteria for crack fields required that features with a longest indication of 2.5 inches or larger or with a depth of 25 to 40 percent of the wall thickness be scheduled for excavation. Features reported as crack-like were selected for excavation if the depth was greater than 40 percent of the wall thickness or an engineering assessment resulted in a predicted failure pressure that was less than the hydrostatic pressure of the pipeline.

Using fitness-for-service software, Enbridge conducted engineering assessments for predicted failure pressures on all six of the reported crack-like defects. Enbridge used the reported wall thickness and crack depths as they appeared on the final 2005 inspection report from PII or as profiled for the 9.3-inch-long feature. Each of these defects had a calculated failure pressure greater than the hydrostatic test pressure of the pipeline (796 psig). Further, none of those indications had a reported depth of greater than 40 percent of the tool-reported wall thickness. Based on the results of the engineering assessment, Enbridge did not identify any of the six crack-like defects on the ruptured pipeline segment for excavation and examination.

After the Marshall accident, PII reanalyzed the raw signal data from all of the six indications and stated that each should have been classified as crack-field features. A PII analysis of the 51.6-inch-long crack-like defect detected during the 2005 USCD in-line inspection showed that this defect should have been reported as a crack-field feature with a longest individual crack length of 3.5 inches. Also, using newer PII depth estimating algorithms, developed in 2008 for crack-field features, the depth of the 51.6-inch-long crack-field feature was characterized as 0.091-inch deep (32 percent of the tool-reported wall thickness). By comparison, the depth algorithm used in 2005 for the same 51.6-inch-long feature (crack-like feature depth analysis) showed a depth of 0.063 inch (22 percent of the reported wall thickness).

Following the accident, in 2011, Enbridge completed a crack inspection of Line 6B. The 2011 ultrasonic crack tool report identified 4,478 crack-like, crack-field, and notch-like features, which was a decrease from the 2005 inspection. (PII had made changes to its feature identification process in 2008.)

### 1.9.8.3 2007 In-Line Inspection—PII High-Resolution MFL Tool Results

Enbridge contracted PII to conduct a 2007 MFL inspection of Line 6B to confirm the depth estimates in areas of echo-loss identified during the 2004 USWM inspection. The 2007 MFL report included 67 corrosion features identified on the ruptured segment starting at about 4 feet and extending to 39.64 feet from the upstream girth weld. The inspection report for the 2007 MFL in-line inspection included a calculation of the predicted failure pressure for each defect on the pipe segment. Neither the deepest feature reported nor the feature with the lowest predicted failure pressure was located at the rupture location.

### 1.9.8.4 2009 In-Line Inspection—PII USWM Tool Results

In June 2009, PII conducted an in-line corrosion inspection of Line 6B using an USWM tool. The report issued to Enbridge in December 2009, which was revised by PII and reissued in June 2010, identified 273,759 metal loss features, and 6,791 of those features had predicted failure pressures that were less than 1.39 times the MOP and met the Enbridge excavation criteria. Nineteen features were found in the ruptured segment; however, none of them met the excavation criteria. All but four of the reported features in the ruptured segment were listed as external corrosion located near the seam weld, oriented between 87° and 99°.[65] The feature with the lowest calculated predicted failure pressure in the ruptured segment was 28.2 feet from the upstream girth weld and measured 68.03 inches long by 17.05 inches wide.

---

[65] These positions are located clockwise from the 12 o'clock position or the top of the pipe (0°).

## 1.10 Pipeline Public Awareness Programs

### 1.10.1 Regulatory Requirements

Pipeline operators are required to develop and implement a written continuing public education program in accordance with 49 CFR 195.440. The regulation states that the program must provide awareness information to the public, appropriate local government officials, and emergency responders. The awareness information must include information about the possible hazards associated with releases, use of a one-call notification system, physical indications that a release has occurred, steps that should be taken in the event of a release, and procedures for reporting such a release.

### 1.10.2 API Recommended Practice 1162

Public awareness programs (PAP) must follow the guidance in API's Recommended Practice (RP) 1162, *Public Awareness Programs for Pipeline Operators* (December 2003). RP 1162 was incorporated by reference into the pipeline regulations (49 CFR 195.3(c)).

RP 1162 establishes guidelines for pipeline operators to develop, manage, and evaluate PAPs. RP 1162 identifies audiences that should receive awareness messages, the content of baseline awareness messages, and the frequency of the messages for each audience. Audiences defined in the standard include the affected public, emergency officials (including fire departments and police departments), and local public officials. RP 1162 states that the evaluation should include both the process and the program effectiveness. RP 1162 states that operators should evaluate the process annually and evaluate program effectiveness at intervals not greater than every 4 years. This evaluation should determine if the awareness messages are reaching the audiences and if the audiences understand the messages.

### 1.10.3 Enbridge's PAP

Enbridge's PAP was completed in June 2006 and revised in 2010. According to Enbridge, direct mail brochures were mailed to all audiences annually. Prior to the Marshall accident, the most recent direct mailings were in May 2010. For Calhoun County, 2,304 mailing addresses were listed. For Marshall, 509 mailing addresses were listed.

On February 28, 2010, Enbridge, along with six other pipeline companies, hosted safety awareness training in Jackson, Michigan, for emergency officials. Topics included product hazards and characteristics and leak recognition and response. One attendee was from the Marshall City Fire Department, and two attendees were from the Marshall Township Fire Department. Enbridge mailed its *2010 Michigan Pipeline Emergency Response Planning Information* manual to emergency response organizations that were not present for the safety awareness training.

Enbridge's program plan was reviewed informally by Enbridge's program awareness manager and formally through the Public Awareness Program Effectiveness Research Survey

(PAPERS) program.[66] The program was conducted every 2 years, and the most recent program was conducted in 2009 (prior to the accident). According to the PAPERS report, the objective of the survey was to determine if the public awareness information is reaching the intended stakeholder audiences and if the audiences understand the messages delivered. Twenty-six operators participated in the survey. For Enbridge's survey, the report notes that there were 314 respondents from the affected public audience and 267 additional attendees from other audiences.[67] Tables 1 and 2 show the responses (in percentages) to two key questions about pipeline awareness and pipeline information.

**Table 1.** Awareness of pipelines in the community.

| Question: How well informed would you say you are regarding pipelines in your community? | | | |
|---|---|---|---|
| Response | Affected Public | Public Officials | Emergency Officials |
| Very well informed | 23% | 39% | 47% |
| Somewhat informed | 36% | 32% | 38% |
| Not too informed | 27% | 21% | 16% |
| Not at all informed | 15% | 8% | 0% |
| Don't know/refused | 0% | 0% | 0% |

**Table 2.** Pipeline information received.

| Question: Within the past two years (Affected Public)/12 months (Excavators, Emergency Officials)/three years (Public Officials), do you recall receiving any information from a pipeline company, or companies, relating to pipelines? | | | |
|---|---|---|---|
| Response | Affected Public | Public Officials | Emergency Officials |
| Yes | 55% | 64% | 77% |
| No | 45% | 34% | 21% |
| Don't know/refused | 0% | 2% | 2% |

---

[66] The PAPERS review is sponsored by the API, the Association of Oil Pipelines, and the Interstate Natural Gas Association of America. The PAPERS program is an industrywide survey conducted to assess the effectiveness of PAPs.

[67] This includes excavators, emergency officials, and public officials.

## 1.11 Enbridge Operations

### 1.11.1 Edmonton Control Center

The Enbridge pipeline system is controlled from a single SCADA control center located in Edmonton, Alberta, Canada. According to Enbridge's HCA management plan, dated March 2010, the Edmonton control center is the hub of emergency response and shuts down a pipeline within 8 minutes[68] of an abnormal condition when the condition cannot be identified or corrected. During a shutdown, control center staff contact operational personnel in the area to respond.

At the time of the accident, the control center was staffed by 22 control center operators, 2 shift leads, and an MBS analyst, all of whom worked in 12-hour shifts. Control center operators were grouped in pairs in what Enbridge referred to as "pods." Each console within a pod controlled two or more pipelines. A control center supervisor and the MBS analyst were either available at the control center or were on call on nights and weekends.

At the time of the accident, the MBS analyst reported to the information technology department. The MBS analyst position had been added to the control center in July 2008. Before the position existed, MBS alarms were handled by an on-call engineer; alarms were not analyzed in the control center. Operator A2 stated that over the last few years, the MBS analyst's role had evolved from determining whether the MBS program was working and an MBS alarm was valid to determining whether the operator should shut down the pipeline.

The control center was staffed by four groups of individuals involved in pipeline operational decisions. The control center operator was responsible for direct control of the movement of products through the pipeline. The control center operator was to start or stop pipeline flow according to a schedule determined by another Enbridge department, and in accordance with pipeline operating restrictions. The control center procedures gave authority to the control center operator to shut down the pipeline under specific circumstances or for any other reason that the control center operator determined to be in the best interests of safety.

Shift leads served as liaisons between operators and others involved in pipeline operations to facilitate pipeline operations. Their role was tailored toward managing the control center operators and assisting them in troubleshooting rather than solving pipeline operational issues. In this capacity, the shift leads were required to have had some technical experience in operations (typically that of an operator); however, a shift lead was not required to demonstrate a technical proficiency in pipeline operations on a regular basis. Operator B1 told investigators, "We don't have anybody that's designated as a technical person. They (shift leads) are people-people—people persons...they both have more experience than I do. So I would—I'm going to assume that they would know as much or more than I do." Shift lead B2 described his role as follows: "... I'm there to first and foremost be a people leader to the operators in the room and then also provide support where needed, whether that's technical support, whether

---

[68] Enbridge used an 8-minute timeframe for recognition and for shutting valves when calculating worst-case discharges on the pipeline. This time was different from the control center's 10-minute restriction, which required the control center operator to stop a pipeline under specific circumstances.

that's, I guess support as a leader with personal issues or anything that is involved in the control center."

The on-call supervisor was above the shift lead in authority. His or her direct position within the Enbridge organizational structure varied according to the title of the person serving as on-call supervisor at that time. In general, the on-call supervisor, a position that varied according to a predetermined rotation schedule, was at the first or second level above the shift lead. His or her role was to confer with the shift lead and others in the control center when a pipeline operating issue could not be settled at the shift lead/operator level and approve or disapprove of a decision regarding pipeline operations. The MBS analyst, while not in the chain of command of the control center operator, shift lead, or on-call supervisor, provided expertise in response to MBS alarms. The role of the MBS analyst was to determine, according to his or her analysis of the data provided by the MBS software, whether the MBS software was operating correctly; however, the control center procedures set the expectation that the MBS analyst would tell the shift leads and control center operators whether a leak alarm was "valid" or "false".

According to Enbridge's vice president of customer service, who oversaw the control center and the pipeline scheduling department at the time of the accident, the company's emphasis on shift leads' leadership skills was based on an increase in the number of control center staff. On January 1, 2007, Enbridge employed 89 control center operators and 15 control center support staff. On July 15, 2010, these staff numbers rose to 117 and 37, respectively. The addition of new pipelines to the Enbridge system had necessitated increasing the control center staff. Some operators told NTSB investigators that the experience level in the control center had decreased as staff numbers increased.

### 1.11.2 Control Center Personnel Experience

NTSB investigators examined Enbridge control center documents to assess the experience levels of the control center staff who were on duty at the time of the accident. The shift leads had held their positions from 3 to 6 years and had obtained varying levels of experience before becoming shift leads. The control center operators working on shifts A, B, and C had from 3 to 30 years experience. Because the MBS analyst position was new to the control center as of 2008, the two MBS analysts had been in their positions 1.5 to 2 years. MBS analyst A had no prior pipeline operations experience. MBS analyst B had more than 20 years of experience as a control center operator before becoming an analyst. Table 3 lists the people involved in the Line 6B shutdown and startups on July 25 and 26, as well as their experience and position in the control center.

**Table 3.** Key control center staff involved in the accident and their years of experience.

| Shift A: Sunday 8:00 a.m.–Sunday 8:00 p.m. | | |
|---|---|---|
| Shift lead A1 | Pipeline/Terminal Consoles | 6 years as operator<br>3 years as shift lead |
| Shift lead A2 | Pipeline/Terminal Consoles | 25 years with Enbridge<br>6 years as shift lead |
| Operator A1 | Lines 3, 17, 6A, and 6B operator | 29 years as operator<br>Requalifying on Line 6B after 6-month absence |
| Operator A2 | Mentor to operator A1 | 30 years experience |
| MBS analyst A | Responsible for MBS (leak detection) | Level II MBS analyst<br>1.5 years experience |
| **Shift B: Sunday 8:00 p.m.–Monday 8:00 a.m.** | | |
| Shift lead B1 | Pipeline/Terminal Consoles | 11 years with Enbridge<br>3 years as shift lead |
| Shift lead B2 | Pipeline/Terminal Consoles | 8 years with Enbridge<br>2.5 years as shift lead |
| Operator B1 | Lines 3, 17, 6A, and 6B operator | 3.5 years as operator |
| Operator B2 | Lines 4 and 14 operator and shiftmate to operator B1 | Just over 2 years as operator |
| MBS analyst B | Responsible for MBS (leak detection) | 20 years as operator<br>2 years as Level III MBS analyst |
| Control center supervisor (on-call) | On-call designated supervisor | 20 years operations experience<br>1.5 years as supervisor |
| **Shift C: Monday 8:00 a.m.–Monday 8:00 p.m.** | | |
| Shift lead C1 | Pipeline/Terminal Consoles | 15 years with Enbridge<br>5 years as shift lead |
| Shift lead C2 | Pipeline/Terminal Consoles | 8 years with Enbridge<br>2 years as shift lead |
| Operator C1 | Lines 3, 17, 6A, and 6B operator | 6 years as operator |
| MBS analyst A | See Shift A information | |

### 1.11.3 Toxicology

After the accident, as required by 49 CFR 199.105(b)[69] and 199.221,[70] Enbridge conducted drug[71] and alcohol tests for each shift lead and Line 6B operator on duty during shifts A, B, and C. Specimens were collected from all the shift leads and operators A2 and C1 between 8:50 and 10:50 p.m. on July 27. Specimens were collected from operators A1 and B1 between 12:00 and 12:40 p.m. on July 28. The results of the drug tests were negative. However, these results were not valid because the alcohol testing was not conducted within the maximum time allotted after the rupture as specified in the regulations.

Enbridge did not explain to PHMSA why alcohol testing was not carried out within 8 hours of discovery of the rupture, as required by 49 CFR 199.221 and 199.225(a). Still, Enbridge tested these individuals even though more than 8 hours had passed since they had been on duty. The control center supervisor told investigators that the delay in testing was due to the delay in confirming the rupture and the fact that many of the personnel who had been on duty during the accident sequence had gone home by the time the rupture was identified.

### 1.11.4 Training and Qualifications

### 1.11.4.1    Control Center Operations

Enbridge's supervisor of training and compliance for control center operations was responsible for control center training. He also oversaw the operator qualification process required in 49 CFR 195.505. During postaccident interviews, he stated the following regarding operator training: "...the goal is for the operator to operate independently, but also with the support of the team members."

Operator training was conducted in five phases and typically lasted about 6 months. The initial phase of instruction consisted of classroom and web-based instruction covering material such as hydraulics, vapor pressure, viscosity, and specific gravity. The remaining phases incorporated on-the-job training with a mentor, problem solving, and abnormal operation recognition presented through a simulator. By the completion of the fifth phase, students were expected to recognize and respond appropriately to abnormal operating conditions, including column separation and leak scenarios. Upon successfully completing additional classroom

---

[69] The regulation states, "(b) Post-accident testing. As soon as possible but no later than 32 hours after an accident, an operator shall drug test each employee whose performance either contributed to the accident or cannot be completely discounted as a contributing factor to the accident. An operator may decide not to test under this paragraph but such a decision must be based on the best information available immediately after the accident that the employee's performance could not have contributed to the accident or that, because of the time between that performance and the accident, it is not likely that a drug test would reveal whether the performance was affected by drug use."

[70] "Each operator shall prohibit a covered employee who has actual knowledge of an accident in which his or her performance of covered functions has not been discounted by the operator as a contributing factor to the accident from using alcohol for eight hours following the accident, unless he or she has been given a post-accident test under §199.225(a), or the operator has determined that the employee's performance could not have contributed to the accident."

[71] The drug test included five classes of illegal drugs: marijuana, cocaine, opiates, amphetamines, and phencyclidine.

training, passing a written and oral examination administered by a trained evaluator, and demonstrating proficiency by operating a pipeline for 10 shifts without intervention from a mentor, students were considered qualified operators.

Operator training emphasized individual knowledge, skills, and performance. Enbridge did not conduct team training involving shift leads, operators, and MBS analysts, nor did PHMSA or the NEB require such training. According to Enbridge, although it did not conduct formal team training programs, control center operators were introduced to team aspects of the control center during initial training and were expected to rely on available control center staff to accomplish training objectives. When operators were introduced to simulator scenarios, instructors and other course participants used role playing to assist or distract the operator trainees, portraying, for example, on-site or on-call field personnel. According to Enbridge, part of the evaluation of student performance was based on the quality of the student's teamwork.

After qualifying, operators and shift leads participated annually in simulator training where they were presented with leak and column separation scenarios, as well as other abnormal operating conditions. PHMSA required operators to demonstrate their technical knowledge and pipeline operating proficiency on a regular basis through an evaluation process known as operator qualification. Enbridge conducted operator qualifications at 3-year intervals, in accordance with PHMSA regulations. PHMSA did not require, nor did Enbridge regularly evaluate, the technical proficiency of shift leads, MBS analysts, or other control center supervisors or managers.

Many of the operators told NTSB investigators that the emergency scenarios were the only occasion they had to observe a leak scenario after completing their initial training. One operator described the emergency scenarios they practiced in the following manner, "They have some preconfigured programs that we run and some of them have station lockouts and some of them have leaks and some of them have just com [communications devices] fails and different scenarios that we go through to help us to understand what we're seeing." The operator added that they practice leak scenarios on the simulator, but, because the simulators do not have MBS alarms, they recognize leaks by line pressure variations.

According to Enbridge's control center supervisor, applicants for control center operator positions came from two groups: (1) graduates with degrees in engineering technology from 2-year technical schools in Alberta and (2) people with experience as control center operators. Enbridge gave applicants written tests and simulator exercises, and those who performed satisfactorily were interviewed by control center supervisors and managers. Interviews sought to determine the ability of applicants to perform satisfactorily with others in Enbridge's control center.

### 1.11.4.2    MBS Analyst

MBS analyst training typically takes 3 months to complete. According to Enbridge's director of the pipeline modeling group, the curriculum contained two instructional segments: (1) learning basic hydraulic information and the Enbridge MBS and (2) participating in on-the-job training and observing qualified MBS analysts perform their duties. In addition, students practiced scenarios on a simulator and determined the validity of MBS alarms.

Upon successfully completing a written examination and a performance assessment on a simulator-presented scenario, students were considered qualified as MBS analysts.

## 1.11.5 MBS Leak Detection

### 1.11.5.1    Federal Regulations

PHMSA requires pipeline operating companies to have effective leak detection methods under 49 CFR 195.452(i)(3), "An operator must have a means to detect leaks on its pipeline system. An operator must evaluate the capability of its leak detection means and modify, as necessary, to protect the HCA. An operator's evaluation must, at least, consider, the following factors—length and size of the pipeline, type of product carried, the pipeline's proximity to the HCA, the swiftness of leak detection, location of nearest response personnel, leak history, and risk assessment results." In addition, 49 CFR 195.134 requires that each hazardous liquid pipeline transporting liquid in single phase, with an existing CPM system, comply with section 4.2 of API RP 1130 in its design. Title 49 CFR 195.444 requires that the CPM system be compliant with API RP 1130 with respect to operating, maintaining, testing, record-keeping, and dispatcher training.

### 1.11.5.2    API 1130 Computational Pipeline Monitoring for Liquids

API's RP 1130[72] for CPM of liquid lines offers guidance to pipeline operating companies on how to establish and to operate CPM leak detection systems. This RP addresses technology, infrastructure, SCADA, data presentation, system integration with SCADA, CPM operations, and system testing. The RP addresses the use of a support person to help a control center operator distinguish between types of CPM alarms. The RP states,

> The causes of the Pipeline Company CPM Alarms are not usually determined by a separate piece of software, (i.e. an expert system) that provides the cause or probability of cause, but by the Pipeline Controller or CPM support person. Simply understanding the cause of the alarm condition on a monitored pipeline may not be the end of the alarm evaluation.

According to the RP, the CPM system should use three alarms to help "justify the CPM system credibility and sensitivity of the CPM system." The RP further states,

> Many CPM systems provide just one type of alarm and so in this case the determination of the cause and categorization of alarm should be made by the person who evaluates the alarm (the Pipeline Controller or perhaps jointly with a CPM support person) or by a separate piece of software (i.e. an expert system) that provides the cause or probability of cause. Automatic alarm cause evaluation would be a desirable CPM system feature.

---

[72] API RP 1130, *Computational Pipeline Monitoring for Liquids*, third edition, September 2007.

The Edmonton control center staff relied on the MBS analyst as their support person for MBS alarm evaluation.

The RP states that past instances of alarm causes can be a useful guide in alarm evaluation but every alarm should be evaluated individually and assumptions of previous causes should not be readily made. API's RP 1130 further emphasizes the need for review of past CPM alarms when they become excessive so as to maintain CPM credibility, "an excessive number of alarms will detract from the system credibility and may create complacency."

API's RP 1130 states that a CPM alarm is probably the most complex alarm that a control center operator will experience. To correctly recognize and respond to this type of alarm, the RP states that an operator needs specific training and appropriate reference material.

### 1.11.5.3    Enbridge's MBS

Enbridge's MBS software was one of several leak detection methods Enbridge used. Additional leak detection methods included aerial patrols, emergency hotline calls, a batch tracking system, and SCADA data.

At the time of the accident, the Enbridge MBS used a real-time pressure transient pipeline model, which operated in parallel with the SCADA system and consisted of a hydraulic model with the actual pipeline's attributes.[73] The MBS software incorporated real-time pressure, flow, temperatures, and density from the SCADA and the batch-tracking system to calculate an expected flow and pressure between the pipeline sections and then compare those values to the actual flow meter readings. The system monitors volume imbalances between the estimated and actual flows in the pipeline. One flow meter installed along the mainline at the Marshall PS, divided Line 6B into two separate volume balance sections: (1) the Griffith Terminal to the Marshall PS, and (2) the Marshall PS to the Sarnia Terminal. Additional flow meters were installed at the delivery and injection terminals. During times of stable operation, the MBS relied upon both flow measurement and pressure data to calculate imbalances. Losing one or the other would affect the level of accuracy.

When the volume imbalance of the MBS software exceeded the alarm or threshold value, an audible alarm and visual alert were displayed to the control center operator[74] that required interpretation by an MBS analyst. The shift lead and control center operators had a limited set of MBS displays, including pipeline elevation and hydraulic gradient profiles; however, operator A1 and shift lead B2 told investigators they were not familiar with the MBS console displays and were not trained to use the MBS software. Enbridge used a single MBS alarm indication that displayed as a 5-minute, 20-minute, or 2-hour alarm (the shorter the time, the larger the leak indication). A second alarm sounded when the condition continued for more than 10 minutes.

---

[73] This included diameter, length of line, valves, fittings, PSs, and elevations.

[74] Enbridge's SCADA system used only one sound for all alarms, regardless of pipeline condition or urgency of operator action needed in response.

Because the MBS software relied on SCADA pressures and flow meter readings, transient operations such as shutdowns and startups could impact the MBS software's leak detection capabilities. MBS analyst B also stated that the shift leads were aware that when column separation was present, the MBS software was "not reliable." The supervisor of the MBS group told investigators that it was commonly known that MBS alarms clear upon shutting down a pipeline.

The Enbridge MBS procedure (that is, flowchart) indicates that when column separation is present, the MBS software is unreliable. As explained by an Enbridge MBS specialist and MBS analyst B, the MBS software is no longer able to predict the pipeline performance accurately so the MBS analyst does not believe the MBS software when there is column separation present in a pipeline segment. Just because an MBS event clears in the SCADA system, it does not mean the underlying condition has been resolved. Column separation is a known limitation to pressure transient leak detection systems because the systems are built to estimate the flows and pressures of a homogenous liquid line.

MBS analyst B told investigators that over a typical 12-hour shift, three of five calls were due to column separation. According to Enbridge, calls to the MBS analyst to research MBS alarms averaged from 1.6 to 4.2 calls per shift in 2010. More than one operator interviewed stated that a majority of the MBS alarms were related to either column separation or instrumentation. Historical alarm records showed that no MBS alarms attributed to column separation occurred on Line 6B before the pressure restrictions were implemented at the Marshall PS in July 2009. Following the 2009 pressure restrictions, the control center reported three MBS alarms[75] associated with column separation. None of the reported column separation indications were near the Marshall PS or ruptured pipe segment.

During the initial startup on July 26, 2010, the MBS analyst B had to override the pressures in the MBS software[76] to reflect actual conditions at the Niles PS because the MBS system did not reflect the closed valves. A second pressure transmitter at the Stockbridge Terminal (downstream of Marshall) had been disabled in the MBS software on July 22 and re-enabled at 10:00 p.m. on July 25, 2010.

## 1.11.5.4    Column Separation

Column separation, sometimes called slack line, commonly occurs in areas of higher elevation where the line pressure is lowest on a pipeline; however, column separation can occur at any point in a pipeline where the pressure in the line is below the pressure at which the oil becomes a vapor[77] resulting in liquid-and-vapor mix. The vapor within the pipeline forms a void that restricts the flow of liquid. Any void in the internal volume of the pipeline, including a large

---

[75] These alarms occurred on October 18, 2009; April 28, 2010; and June 27, 2010. All of the MBS alarms were in the Marshall PS to the Stockbridge PS section with column separation indications at the Marysville Terminal, downstream of the Stockbridge PS.

[76] The Niles PS pressure transmitters used by the MBS were located behind the isolation valves that were shut when the station was taken out of service for the in-line inspection tool; therefore, the pressure readings were disabled in the MBS software following the shutdown on July 25, 2010.

[77] The point at which a liquid turns to vapor is a function of both temperature and pressure and is referred to as the vapor pressure of the liquid.

loss of oil either from a rupture or drain off into lower elevations, would result in column separation indications over the leak detection software. The terrain between the Marshall PS and the next PS was relatively flat with a net elevation rise between the two of about 30 feet and a maximum rise of 100 feet. To eliminate column separation, pressure must be increased above the vapor pressure of the liquid.[78] This may require generating back pressure in the line by closing a downstream valve or increasing the delivery rate or pressure from an upstream PS.

### 1.11.6 Procedures

#### 1.11.6.1      10-Minute Restriction

Multiple control center operational procedures reference a restriction to operation of the pipeline in excess of 10 minutes when operating under unknown circumstances. The 10-minute limit appears in the control center *Suspected Column Separation*, *MBS Leak Alarm-Analysis by MBS Support*, and *Suspected Leak* procedures, among others and was commonly referred to in the control center as the "10-minute rule."

The 10-minute limitation was adopted as a result of the March 1991 Enbridge rupture and release that occurred on Line 3, spilling 1.7 million gallons of crude oil in Grand Rapids, Minnesota.[79] The oil release polluted a tributary of the Mississippi River with a reported cleanup cost of $7.5 million. The failure occurred in fatigue cracks at the base of the DSAW longitudinal seam weld (where the weld meets the body of the pipe). During the 1991 accident, personnel in Enbridge's Edmonton Control Center interpreted the SCADA alarms and indications to a condition of column separation and instrument error and continued to pump oil into the ruptured 34-inch-diameter line for more than an hour until the leak was recognized.

In 1991, Enbridge stated in its response to PHMSA that a revision to the operation maintenance procedures manual was adopted stating, "If an operator experiences pressure or flow abnormalities or unexplainable changes in line conditions for which a reason cannot be established within a 10-minute period, the line shall be shut down, isolated, and evaluated until the situation is verified and or [sic] corrected."

#### 1.11.6.2      Suspected Column Separation

The control center's suspected column separation procedure (see appendix B) required that the control center operator notify the shift lead in the event of a suspected column separation. According to the procedure, if the column separation had not been restored within 10 minutes, the control center operator was to notify the shift lead, shut down the pipeline, close the mainline valves and record the event electronically as an abnormal operation. The shift lead had the responsibility of making emergency notifications to the field and having field personnel confirm a leak. If no leak were found then the line could only be restarted with permission from the pipeline control on-call designated supervisor.

---

[78] According to Enbridge, on the evening of the rupture, Cold Lake crude was being pumped through Line 6B, which has a stated vapor pressure below atmospheric pressure.

[79] PHMSA investigated this accident.

A draft version of the suspected column separation procedure was sent out to control center staff for review in May 2010. The draft version of the procedure included a new section to the existing procedure addressing "starting up into a known column separation." Under the draft procedure, the control center operator was to notify the shift lead of the column separation and calculate an estimated time to restore the column prior to starting the pipeline. Under known column separation procedure, the 10-minute restriction became effective only after the estimated time to restore the column had expired.

According to operator B2, the draft procedure was used once prior to the accident, when starting a pipeline that had been intentionally drained into storage tanks. According to shift lead B1 who used this procedure during the first startup, he believed that there had been an excessive volume lost due to drainage to lower elevations and delivery locations after the shutdown. He had also attributed volume lost to a valve that had been opened at the Marysville Terminal delivery location during startup that morning. Shift lead B1 stated that he was aware that this was a draft procedure.

### 1.11.6.3    MBS Alarm

According to the control center procedures on leak alarms, the control center operator notified the shift lead and recorded the event as an abnormal operation in the facility and maintenance database. The shift lead had the responsibility of assessing the alarm and calling it a temporary alarm or notifying the MBS analyst to review the alarm. Shift leads nearly always gave the MBS alarms to the MBS analyst for review. The procedure required that the control center operator shut the line down if an analysis of the MBS alarm was not complete within 10 minutes. The control center staff expected that either the MBS analyst would report the alarm as "valid" or "false"; however, these terms do not appear in the MBS flowchart for examining MBS alarms. Temporary or false alarms resulted in the pipeline being allowed to start again or resume normal operations without approval. Valid alarms required approval of the on-call supervisor or regional management to start the pipeline.

MBS analyst B told investigators that "valid" and "false" were control center terms and were not used by MBS analysts. According to the Enbridge flowchart[80] used by the MBS analyst, if the MBS software showed that vapor was present in the pipeline, the MBS analyst was to contact the shift lead and tell the shift lead that the software was showing column separation but that the software was not reliable. The Enbridge flowchart directed the MBS analyst to tell the shift lead that it was the control center operator's decision to start the line. After the accident, MBS analyst B told investigators that it was the operator's job to examine the pressures on the pipeline to determine if there was a leak or not.

### 1.11.6.4    SCADA Leak Triggers

The Enbridge control center procedures included a leak triggers list, that is, indications in the SCADA system of possible leaks. The procedure defined leak triggers as unexplained, abnormal operating conditions or events that indicate a leak. Enbridge included suspected

---

[80] See Enbridge's MBS and control center operations procedures provided in appendix B of this report.

column separation, MBS alarms, MBS malfunction, leak triggers from SCADA data, a suspected leak from SCADA data, and sectional valve alarms as some of the conditions constituting abnormal events that required reporting to management.

The control center operator was to use the suspected leak procedures to determine whether a leak was present on the pipeline through SCADA indications. Leak triggers included active MBS alarms, sudden drops in discharge or suction pressure, sudden increases or decreases in flow rate, and the local shutdown of PSs in combination with pressure drops. One or two leak triggers required that the suspected leak procedure be followed, which monitored the line conditions for further leak triggers. If a leak could not be ruled out in 10 minutes then the line was to be shut down. Three or more leak triggers required the immediate shutdown of the pipeline and emergency notifications to the field under the confirmed leak triggers procedure.

### 1.11.6.5      Suspected Leak—Volume Difference

A suspected leak procedure for volume differences associated with pipeline estimates performed by the control center operator from the commodity movement and tracking system (CMT)[81] stated that if the difference between the volume injected into the pipeline and the volume received at the terminals is more than 10 percent, or if the volume imbalance was not accompanied by a corresponding increase in pipeline pressures, the confirmed leak procedure was to be executed.

### 1.11.6.6      Leak and Obstruction Trigger—On Startup from SCADA Data

The leak and obstruction trigger procedure required that the control center operator review the holding pressures on a pipeline segment if the pressure changes did not propagate throughout a pipeline segment within a specified time (about 1 minute). If sufficient holding pressure was maintained on the pipeline segment during shutdown, the control center operator was to execute the procedure for a confirmed leak. If insufficient holding pressure was maintained on a pipeline during shutdown, the control center operator was to execute the procedure for suspected column separation.

### 1.11.7 Fatigue Management

Title 49 CFR 195.446(d), regarding methods to reduce the risk of control center operator fatigue, was effective on November 30, 2009, and required procedures to be in place by August 1, 2011, and implemented by February 1, 2012. Enbridge developed and distributed a fatigue risk management plan that took effect on July 30, 2011. PHMSA's regulations governing hours of service required pipeline control center operators to receive at least 8 hours of rest between shifts. Enbridge followed PHMSA requirements to provide operators with "off-duty time sufficient to achieve eight hours of continuous sleep" and limited emergency coverage to seven 12-hour shifts in succession. According to Enbridge's control center supervisor, control

---

[81] At Enbridge, CMT is a system that performs real-time monitoring of the oil in the pipeline. Control center operators manually perform an accounting of the volumes of oil in the pipeline every 2 hours to check delivery volumes and potential leaks.

center shifts were 12 hours long, although operators worked overtime beyond those 12 hours on occasion. Thus, a typical control center operator's schedule began at 8:00 a.m.[82] on Friday, Saturday, and Sunday, ending at 8:00 p.m. each day, followed by Monday and Tuesday nights in which the schedule was reversed. After 4 to 5 days off duty, the operator would then work 2 nights followed by 3 days, or 3 days followed by 2 nights, scheduled in such a way as to preclude anyone from working without at least 24 hours of rest when alternating between night and day shifts.

### 1.11.8 Enbridge Health and Safety Management System

Prior to this accident, Enbridge implemented a health and safety management system, which primarily pertained to on-site safety. In May 2010, Enbridge created the position of director of safety culture after three pipeline employees had been killed in two on-site accidents in the 5 months between November 2007 and March 2008. This position, which reported to the senior vice president of operations, was given to Enbridge's director of construction, safety, and services within its major project group. The focus of the program was in the areas of workplace safety, process safety management, and contractor safety. Within these areas, the company concentrated on five general safety areas: driving safety, confined space entry, ground disturbance, isolation of energized systems, and reporting of safety-related incidents.

In November 2008, the company retained the services of a consultant to produce a safety benchmarking assessment.[83] The director of safety culture stated that after the Marshall accident, Enbridge realized that safety encompassed more than workplace safety and individual safety, and the company began to develop a better understanding of the need for process safety management and also the need to make sure that control center operations were included within the scope of the safety culture. There is no PHMSA requirement for pipeline operating companies to implement safety management systems (SMS).

## 1.12 Environmental Response

### 1.12.1 Volume Released

At the time of the rupture, two batches of crude oil were located in the pipeline on either side of the rupture location. These were 2.6 million gallons of Cold Lake Blend and 2.7 million gallons of Western Canadian Select crude oil. When Enbridge first notified the NRC about the rupture and release, it reported that an estimated 819,000 gallons of oil had been spilled. NTSB investigators learned that this was an inaccurate estimate based on the wrong diameter pipe. Enbridge performed a second analysis, which included oil lost from higher elevations as well as pumped volumes during the two startups. Based on this analysis, on November 2, 2010, Enbridge revised its estimated release volume to 843,444 gallons. The NTSB examined flow meter trends from the SCADA system for injected volumes of oil at Griffith Terminal during the two Line 6B startups on July 26, 2010. Based on this examination, the NTSB determined about

---

[82] This is expressed in eastern daylight time for the report; 8:00 a.m. eastern daylight time is 6:00 a.m. local Edmonton time.

[83] This was the second such assessment after an initial one in May 2005.

683,436 gallons (81 percent of the total release) of crude oil were pumped into Line 6B during the two startups. (See appendix C).

## 1.12.2 Hazardous Materials Information

Cold Lake Blend and Western Canadian Select crude oil condensate mixtures[84] are regulated by the U.S. Department of Transportation (DOT) as class 3 flammable hazardous materials. Heavy crude typically is a mixture of crude oil (from 50 to 70 percent) and hydrocarbon diluent[85] (from 30 to 50 percent). The material contains 20 to 30 percent volatiles by volume. The mixture is used as raw material in the production of fuels and lubricants. It is a brown or black liquid with a hydrocarbon odor; it is lighter than water with a specific gravity of 0.65 to 0.75. It exhibits a flashpoint of -31° F. The vapor is heavier than air, with a lower explosive limit of 0.8 percent and an upper explosive limit of 8 percent vapor concentration in air.

## 1.12.3 Overview of the Oil Spill Response

During the first day of the response, the Marshall PLM responders were assisted by contractors and regional personnel. Late on the first day of the response, the first responders constructed an underflow dam in the wetland near the source area and installed additional oil sorbent and containment boom in the Kalamazoo River at Heritage Park and at Linear Park in Battle Creek, about 8.9 and 14.8 miles downstream of the rupture, respectively. On July 26, Enbridge also deployed vacuum trucks to recover oil from the source area underflow dam, from the Talmadge Creek stream crossings on Division Drive and 15 1/2 Mile Road, and from the Kalamazoo River at Heritage Park. (See table 4.)

**Table 4.** Enbridge resources deployed as reported at midnight on July 26, 2010.

| Location | Resources Deployed | Personnel |
|---|---|---|
| Leak site | One underflow dam, vacuum trucks[a] | 7 Enbridge |
| 15 1/2 Mile Road | One skimmer, 30-ft oil boom, three vacuum trucks | 4 Enbridge |
| Division Drive | Two, 50-ft oil boom, two vacuum trucks | 14 Enbridge 10 Contractors (est.) |
| A Drive North | 50-ft oil boom, one vacuum truck | |
| Heritage Park | 600-ft oil boom, two vacuum trucks | |
| Linear Park | 400-ft oil boom, one vacuum truck | |

[a] The number of vacuum trucks servicing the underflow dam was not tracked on the first day of the response, although Enbridge reports as many as three trucks were pumping at the same time.

---

[84] Without the addition of condensate, heavy bituminous crude oil does not flow easily.

[85] Hydrocarbon diluent is a substance used to dilute a viscous or dense substance so that it will flow more easily.

During the first week of the response, Enbridge assigned between 29 and 36 workers (day) and 22 to 26 workers (night) to river oil containment operations. These workers were supplemented with as many as 356 day personnel and 160 night personnel that were employed by private oil spill response organizations.

In the days following the accident, Enbridge and its contractors established about 33 oil spill containment-and-control points (from the release site to the west end of Morrow Lake in Kalamazoo County, covering about 38 miles of the river). (See figure 19.) The control points consisted of a variety of oil containment strategies, including underflow dams, oil booming, and sorbent booming. Vacuum trucks and oil skimmers were used to remove oil at these locations.

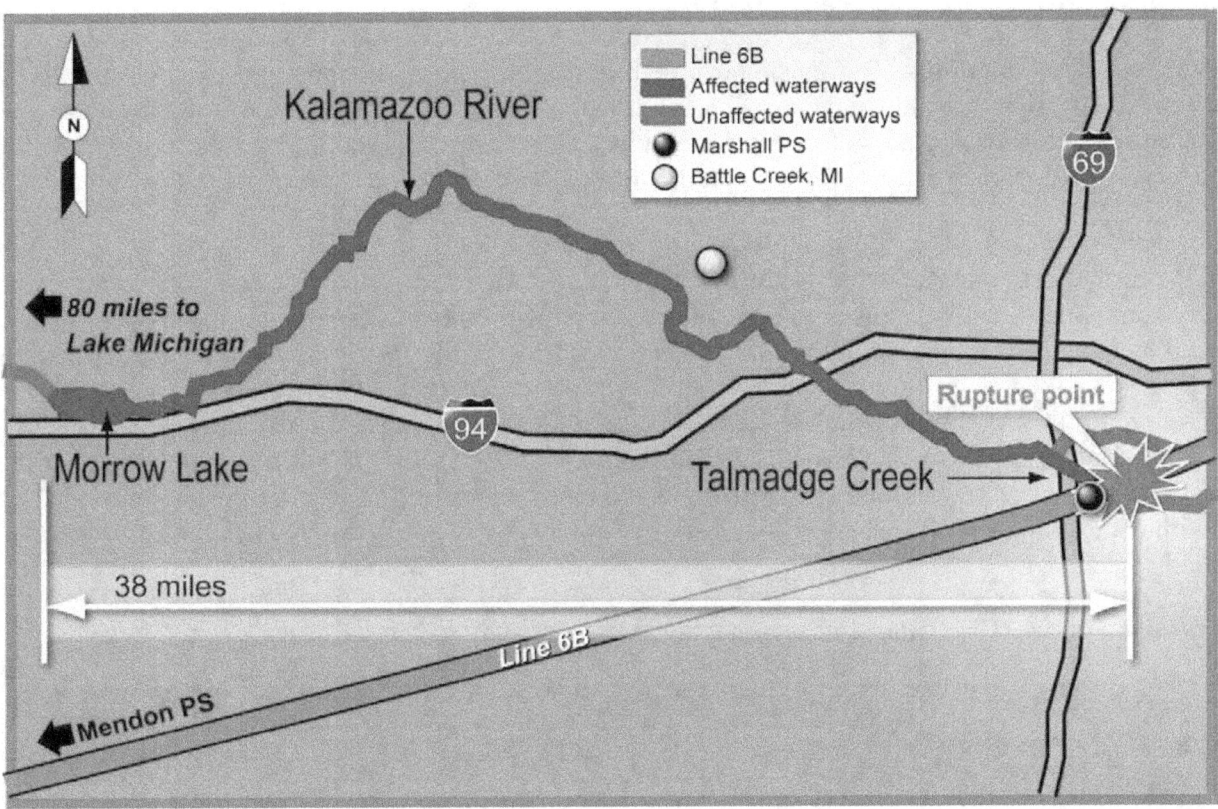

**Figure 19.** Map showing rupture location and affected waterways from Talmadge Creek to Morrow Lake.

By July 29, the third day of operations, 51,090 feet of oil boom had been deployed and 647 field personnel were on site. On August 17, the peak deployment of 2,011 personnel occurred. The greatest amount of oil boom deployed in the affected waterways was 176,124 feet, which was deployed on August 20.

As of April 30, 2012, the EPA reported that over 17 million gallons of oil and water liquid waste had been collected, from which an estimated 1.2 million gallons of oil had been recovered by the spill response contractors. In addition, about 186,398 cubic yards of hazardous and nonhazardous soil and debris were disposed of, including river dredge spoils.

### 1.12.3.1      Notifications

The Enbridge supervisor of regional engineering initially contacted the NRC about 1:09 p.m. on July 25, 2010; however, his call was placed on hold for about 6 minutes. He called the NRC again about 1:23 p.m. and was placed on hold before he was able to report the release about 1:33 p.m. Between 1:47 and 1:49 p.m., the NRC notified 16 Federal and Michigan state agencies, including the EPA, the U.S. Coast Guard (Coast Guard), PHMSA, the Michigan Department of Environmental Quality, the Michigan Intelligence Operations Center, and the Michigan Department of Community Health.

### 1.12.4 Enbridge Facility Response Plan

Each operator of an onshore pipeline, for which a response plan is required by 49 CFR 194.101, may not handle, store, or transport oil in a pipeline unless the operator has submitted a response plan that meets the requirements of this regulation. Every 5 years, pipeline operating companies must review, update, and resubmit facility response plans to PHMSA for approval.

The response plan must address a worst-case discharge, identify environmentally and economically sensitive areas, and describe the responsibilities of the operator and Federal, state, and local agencies in removing such a discharge. Title 49 CFR 194.115(a) states, "Each operator shall identify and ensure, by contract or other approved means, the resources necessary to remove, to the maximum extent practicable, a worst case discharge and to mitigate or prevent a substantial threat of a worst case discharge." Title 49 CFR 194.115(b) directs pipeline operating companies to identify in their response plans the response resources that are available to respond within the time-specific response tiers after discovery of a worst-case discharge, as shown in table 5.

**Table 5.** Title 49 CFR 194.115 response tiers.

|                   | Tier 1   | Tier 2   | Tier 3   |
|-------------------|----------|----------|----------|
| High volume area  | 6 hours  | 30 hours | 54 hours |
| All other areas   | 12 hours | 36 hours | 60 hours |

The regulation does not provide guidance for determining the amount of response resources that should be on site within the Tier 1, 2, and 3 timeframes. In the absence of guidance, Enbridge developed its own interpretation of the three-tier requirement.

The Enbridge senior compliance specialist told NTSB investigators that Tier 1 refers to resources that provide initial containment and recovery efforts, such as Enbridge equipment and personnel that are available from the nearest PLM facilities. Tier 2 includes Enbridge's internal emergency response resources from anywhere within the Chicago region in addition to those local contractors listed in the Enbridge emergency response directory. Tier 3 consists of oil spill response organizations that are identified in the facility response plan. Even with Enbridge's definitions of the tiered resources, an Enbridge North Dakota Region supervisor of measurement, audit, and compliance stated that the regulation was vague and lacking in guidance for the level of response required for each tier.

On February 23, 2005, PHMSA published a final rule establishing oil spill response planning requirements for onshore oil pipelines in accordance with 49 CFR Part 194.[86] The final rule purported to harmonize certain PHMSA requirements with related oil spill response regulations developed by the Coast Guard. PHMSA received several comments on its interim final rule published in 1993 expressing concern that 49 CFR 194.115 does not identify the level of capability that PHMSA would consider sufficient within the three tiers. In the final rule, PHMSA did not amend the response resources requirement to include specific tiered response planning criteria.

Enbridge determined that pipeline facilities within its Chicago response zone met the significant and substantial harm criteria outlined in 49 CFR 194.103 and developed a *Chicago Region Specific Emergency Response Plan (#867)*, most recently revised on April 10, 2010. The Chicago response zone covers 11 pipelines and 3 terminal lines that transport crude oil, diluents, and natural gas liquids within 2,108 miles of pipeline. The accident involved the approximate worst-case discharge of 1,111,152 gallons specified in Enbridge's facility response plan[87] for Line 6B. The worst-case discharge is based, in part, on the maximum flow rate of the pipeline and an assumed response time of 8 minutes, the time allotted for the control center to recognize a leak and close the necessary valves.

Enbridge's plan states that the company owns and maintains emergency response equipment throughout its Chicago region at 13 office locations and strategic locations, including the Marshall, Michigan, PLM shop. The plan lists the amounts and types of spill response equipment maintained at each PLM station for responding to a worse-case discharge, including the Marshall PLM. According to the plan, the single Marshall PLM inventory response trailer (see figure 20) was packed with 1,100 feet of river containment boom; 200 feet of small containment boom; 200 feet of sorbent boom; and 1,000 sorbent pads to respond to the stated worst-case discharge of 1,111,152 gallons. In addition to the trailer, the PLM shop equipment included 3 skimmers, 18 pumps, 1 storage tank, 3 boats, and a single 1,680- to 2,520-gallon-capacity vacuum truck. According to Enbridge's interpretation of response planning regulations, this equipment constitutes its Tier 1 response resources.

---

[86] *Federal Register*, vol. 70, no. 35 (February 23, 2005), p. 8734.

[87] The worst-case discharge takes into account the design flow rate and the time to shut down the pipeline plus the amount released due to the elevation profile. The Enbridge response plan identified Line 6B as having a design capacity of 12.6 million gallons per day with an estimated time to recognize a leak and shut down valves of 8 minutes.

**Figure 20.** Enbridge PLM emergency response trailer containing the company's Tier 1 oil containment equipment, October 17, 2010.

According to its facility response plan, Enbridge employed 112 hazardous waste operations and emergency response-trained pipeline personnel and technicians who are available for emergency response to oil releases in the company's Chicago region. The plan stated that Enbridge has working agreements with Bay West and Garner Environmental Services, Inc. to supplement Enbridge's resources to respond to a worst-case discharge. Bay West, based in Minneapolis, Minnesota, is an established Coast Guard oil spill response organization that provides 24-hour emergency spill response. Garner Environmental Services, Inc., based near Houston, Texas, advertises that it has numerous locations and many away teams, which are capable of providing timely response upon notification. Enbridge maintained lists of other local contractors that may be used for emergencies in each Enbridge response zone.

When notified of the Marshall accident, Bay West assembled its available resources, including 20 response personnel equipped with one boat and one trailer containing spill response equipment. After a 10- to 11-hour drive, Bay West's crews arrived on July 27. Garner Environmental Services, Inc.'s crews arrived by Thursday, July 29.

Enbridge's facility response plan referred to control point maps that Enbridge had developed for use during spill response activities. The maps provided emergency responders with a reference to accessible locations for deploying containment boom. The two mapped locations closest to Talmadge Creek on the Kalamazoo River were not accessible to the responders because of the heavy rains that had increased the water levels, and a containment boom was not deployed.

## 1.12.5 EPA Oversight of Spill Response Efforts

On July 26, 2010, about 1:40 p.m., an EPA official in the EPA's Region 5 Chicago office verified the information contained in Enbridge's report to the NRC. About 1:51 p.m., the EPA official contacted two other on-scene coordinators and advised them to respond to the accident to verify the content of the NRC report and to initiate response activities as necessary. About 4:32 p.m., the first EPA on-scene coordinator arrived and saw the oil in Talmadge Creek from the Division Drive crossing and concluded that the oil spill was significant. He observed one vacuum truck but no oil boom on the discharge side of the culvert under Division Drive.

EPA on-scene coordinators attempted to collect information about the Enbridge response effort but noted that the Chicago regional manager was not able to provide sufficient information about either the company's response actions or the amount of resources it had deployed. The EPA response effort on July 26 consisted primarily of monitoring Enbridge's emergency response activities.

At the end of the first day of the response, the EPA on-scene coordinators stressed that Enbridge should make all efforts necessary to protect a Superfund[88] site, which extended about 80 miles from the Morrow Lake Dam to Lake Michigan to prevent comingling of the contaminants. The EPA on-scene coordinators directed that oil boom be installed 30 miles downstream of the rupture at Morrow Lake as a collection point. About 8:40 p.m., the senior on-scene coordinator contacted the EPA Region 5 emergency response branch chief and requested mobilization of an incident management team, the Superfund Technical Assessment and Response Team,[89] and Emergency and Rapid Response Services[90] contractors.

The EPA on-scene coordinators told NTSB investigators that they determined during the initial hours of the response that Enbridge did not have the resources on site to contain or control the flow of oil into Talmadge Creek and the Kalamazoo River. The EPA directed Enbridge to secure more resources for the response. Upon learning that some crews were responding from Minnesota, an on-scene coordinator provided Enbridge the names of local contractors to facilitate a quicker response time.

---

[88] Superfund is the name given to the environmental program established to address abandoned hazardous waste sites under the Comprehensive Environmental Response, Compensation, and Liability Act of 1980. Superfund allows the EPA to clean up sites and to compel responsible parties to perform cleanups or reimburse the government for EPA-led cleanups.

[89] The Superfund Technical Assessment and Response Team contractors provide technical support to EPA's site assessment and response activities, including gathering and analyzing technical information, preparing technical reports on oil and hazardous substance investigations, and technical support for cleanup efforts.

[90] The Emergency and Rapid Response Services contractors provide the EPA with time-critical cleanup services, including personnel, equipment, and materials to contain, recover, and dispose of hazardous substances. The contract also provides for sample analyses and site restoration activities.

About 8:15 p.m. on July 27, the Federal on-scene coordinator (FOSC)[91] issued an administrative removal order to Enbridge's chief executive officer under Section 311(c) of the Clean Water Act (33 U.S.C. 1321(c)), requiring the company to stop the flow of oil into the Talmadge Creek and the Kalamazoo River, to remediate all oil and contaminated soils in and around the vicinity of the release, and to deploy appropriate oil recovery and containment devices and equipment. The administrative order also required Enbridge to conduct other activities such as air, water, and sediment sampling, and waste disposal at approved facilities.

### 1.12.6 Environmental Monitoring

### 1.12.6.1    Air Quality

On July 26, EPA monitored the air along the Kalamazoo River, in residential areas bordering Talmadge Creek, and at Morrow Lake. The highest concentrations of volatile organic compounds—organic compounds that have a high vapor pressure at normal temperatures causing them to evaporate readily, many of which are dangerous to human health—occurred at crossings of 15 1/2 Mile Road and A Drive North over Talmadge Creek and at the 15 Mile Road bridge crossing over the Kalamazoo River.

Between July 27 and 29, the levels of benzene and petroleum hydrocarbons were sufficient to require respiratory protection for the cleanup workers.

### 1.12.6.2    Potable Water

On July 29, the Calhoun County Health Department and the Kalamazoo County Health and Community Services Department issued an advisory to residents with private wells within 200 feet of the Kalamazoo River and Talmadge Creek to stop using the water for drinking and cooking.

On September 23, 2010, the EPA issued a supplemental order that required (in part) that Enbridge sample all private and public drinking water wells located within 200 feet of all impacted waterways and that Enbridge evaluate potential impacts to groundwater. On October 31, 2010, Enbridge submitted its evaluation report to local health departments. After review of the report and drinking water sampling results collected to date, the local health departments lifted the drinking water advisory.

### 1.12.6.3    Surface Water and Sediment

The EPA ordered Enbridge to sample the surface water and the sediment of the impacted areas by July 27, 2010, and continuously thereafter until notified by EPA. The waters from Talmadge Creek and the Kalamazoo River, from the confluence point of Talmadge Creek to Morrow Lake, were contaminated to varying degrees with petroleum-related hydrocarbons. Once the crude oil mixture entered the water, weathering, volatility, and physical agitation caused the

---

[91] The FOSC is the Federal official responsible for coordinating and directing responses to discharges of oil into waters of the United States.

denser oil fraction to sink and incorporate into river sediments and collect on the river bottom. As of January 2012, the Michigan Department of Environmental Quality continued to evaluate water quality in the affected river system.

On August 1 and 3, 2010, respectively, the Kalamazoo and the Calhoun County health departments prohibited the use of these surface waters for irrigation and the watering of livestock. Calhoun County's ban also applied to recreation activities, including boating, swimming, fishing, and the agricultural use of surface waters.

The Michigan Department of Community Health advised members of the public not to consume fish from either Talmadge Creek or the Kalamazoo River to the west end of Morrow Lake. The Kalamazoo County Health and Community Services partially lifted the water use ban on September 3 in response to improved water sampling test results for the portion of the Kalamazoo River between Morrow Dam and Merrill Park.

Enbridge began collecting sediment samples on July 27 to determine the impact of the spill on the river system. By August 2010, field personnel noticed the presence of submerged oil. Starting in September 2010 and continuing throughout the winter, Enbridge removed the submerged oil by dredging, excavating, and aeration. In spring 2011, an EPA-directed reassessment found a moderate-to-heavy contamination covering over 200 acres of the river bottom. In August 2011, the EPA directed Enbridge to remove the remaining submerged oil. On June 21, 2012, the responding local, state, and Federal agencies announced that impacted areas of Talmadge Creek and the Kalamazoo River, except for Morrow Lake Delta, are open for recreational use.

### 1.12.7 Natural Resources and Wildlife

With the cooperation of U.S. Fish and Wildlife Service and the Michigan Department of Natural Resources and Environment, Enbridge established a wildlife response center in Marshall to accept and treat affected wildlife. The wildlife response center cared for and released about 3,970 animals, including about 3,650 reptiles and 196 birds. Of the 196 birds treated, 144 were released.

The National Oceanic and Atmospheric Administration coordinated with Federal and state agencies and Enbridge to collect data on the oil-impacted natural resources for a natural resources damage assessment, as required by the Oil Pollution Act of 1990. The study has not yet been completed.

## 1.13 Previous NTSB Investigations and Studies

### 1.13.1 NTSB SCADA 2005 Study

In 2005, the NTSB conducted a safety study of SCADA systems for hazardous liquid pipeline operators,[92] examining the design and staffing of SCADA centers and operational issues

---

[92] *Supervisory Control and Data Acquisition (SCADA) in Liquid Pipelines,* Safety Study NTSB/SS-05/02 (Washington, D.C.: National Transportation Safety Board, 2005).

such as SCADA screen graphics, alarm design, fatigue management, controller training and selection, and CPM (leak detection). The study examined the role of SCADA systems in 13 hazardous liquid line accidents investigated between 1992 and 2004. In 10 of the accidents cited by the study, there was a delay in leak recognition by the control center operators. The NTSB issued a report on November 29, 2005, with five recommendations to PHMSA, which included that PHMSA require use of API's RP 1165 for SCADA graphics, pipeline operators review/audit SCADA alarms, that control center operators receive simulator or noncomputerized abnormal operating condition training, that liquid pipeline operators report fatigue information on the PHMSA accident report form and that all pipeline operators install computer based leak detection systems. The 2005 NTSB report concluded that the use of a leak detection technology would enhance the control center operator's "ability to detect large spills, increase the likelihood of spill detection, and reduce the response time to large spills." Partially in response to the study, Public Law 109-468, the Pipeline Inspection, Protection, Enforcement and Safety (PIPES) Act of 2006, was enacted on December 29, 2006. To conform to these recommendations and the requirements of the PIPES Act, PHMSA created the control center management rule contained in 49 CFR Parts 192 and 195. As a result, the NTSB closed the recommendations and classified them, "Closed—Acceptable Action."

### 1.13.2 NTSB 2010 Pipeline Investigation of Pacific Gas and Electric Company

On September 9, 2010, a gas pipeline in San Bruno, California,[93] operated by the Pacific Gas and Electric Company (PG&E), ruptured. Eight people were killed, 10 were injured seriously, 48 people sustained minor injuries, and 38 houses were destroyed. In its investigation of this accident, the NTSB identified a lack of team performance within PG&E's SCADA operations center after the rupture. The report noted,

> …that the lack of assigned roles and responsibilities resulted in SCADA staff not allocating their time and attention in the most effective manner. …The lack of a centralized command structure was also evident in that key information was not disseminated in a reliable manner. …The lack of a centralized command structure was also reflected in the conflicting instructions regarding whether to remotely close valves at the Martin Station. …Finally, the supervising engineer for the SCADA controls group seemed slow to get involved, despite the fact that he is responsible for all SCADA and control systems throughout the PG&E gas transmission pipeline system. …In summary, PG&E's response to the Line 132 break lacked a command structure with defined leadership and support responsibilities within the SCADA center. Execution of the PG&E emergency plan resulted in delays that could have been avoided by better utilizing the SCADA center's capability.

---

[93] *Pacific Gas and Electric Company Natural Gas Transmission Pipeline Rupture and Fire, San Bruno, California, September 9, 2010*, Pipeline Accident Report NTSB/PAR-11/01 (Washington, D.C.: National Transportation Safety Board, 2011).

### 1.13.3 Carmichael, Mississippi

In its report of a pipeline rupture, liquid propane release, and fire near Carmichael, Mississippi, on November 1, 2007,[94] the NTSB noted that although an operator's PAP plan may meet API RP 1162 requirements and Federal pipeline standards, compliance is not a guarantee that implementation is effective or that the operator is exercising adequate oversight. The NTSB made the following recommendation to PHMSA:

> Initiate a program to evaluate pipeline operators' public education programs, including pipeline operators' self-evaluations of the effectiveness of their public education programs. Provide the National Transportation Safety Board with a timeline for implementation and completion of this evaluation. (P-09-3)

In response to this recommendation, PHMSA expanded its state and Federal inspection programs to include a review of operators' effectiveness evaluations, and developed detailed inspection guidance for pipeline safety inspectors. These inspections are currently ongoing and focus on how operators evaluate their PAPs for effectiveness, the results of the evaluations, how the results were documented, and what improvements were identified and implemented. The NTSB classified this safety recommendation "Closed—Acceptable Action."

## 1.14 Postaccident Actions

### 1.14.1 PHMSA Corrective Action Order

On July 28, 2010, PHMSA issued a corrective action order (CAO) requiring Enbridge to ensure the safety of Line 6B before authorizing its return to service. The CAO required Enbridge to submit a return to service plan, including procedures for repairs and monitoring the pipeline if service were resumed. It also required Enbridge to submit an integrity verification plan that includes a comprehensive review of the operating history of Line 6B, further inspections, testing, and repairs within and beyond the immediate rupture area.

On August 9, 2010, Enbridge submitted its response to the CAO and its proposed restart plan. On August 10, 2010, after reviewing the response and the restart plan, PHMSA stated that "(the plan) does not contain sufficient technical details or adequate steps to permit a conclusion that no immediate threats are present elsewhere on the line that require repair prior to any restart of a pipeline, even at a further reduced pressure." PHMSA refused to approve any Enbridge restart plan that did not include a minimum of four investigative excavations and a hydrostatic pressure test. Enbridge completed the investigative excavations and successfully pressure tested a portion of Line 6B that included the rupture site on August 30, 2010. After reviewing the Enbridge integrity verification results and the proposed restart plan, PHMSA issued an amendment to the CAO on September 17, 2010, establishing expectations for repair of known defects and the collection of additional integrity data. Enbridge revised its restart plan again and resubmitted it on September 21. PHMSA approved the revised restart plan 2 days later on

---

[94] *Rupture of Hazardous Liquid Pipeline With Release and Ignition of Propane, Carmichael, Mississippi, November 1, 2007*, Pipeline Accident Report NTSB/PAR-09/01 (Washington, D.C.: National Transportation Safety Board, 2009).

September 22 and authorized a staged restart of Line 6B at a reduced MOP, beginning September 27, 2010.

### 1.14.2 PHMSA's Notice of Probable Violation

On July 2, 2012, PHMSA issued a Notice of Probable Violation (NOPV) to Enbridge citing 24 violations and a total preliminary civil penalty of nearly $3.7 million. Enbridge is required to respond to the NOPV within 30 days of receipt. The violations contained in the NOPV include the following:

- Four violations of 49 CFR 195.452 (integrity management rule) including discovery of condition, risk analysis related to pipeline segments in an HCA, and the integration of all threats during integrity assessments of the pipeline.

- Three violations of 49 CFR 195.401 related to the failure to stop the pipeline when the Edmonton control center received the alarms during the shutdown and the two startups that were indicative of a condition affecting safe operation.

- Eleven violations of 49 CFR 195.402 related to the failure of the Edmonton control center to follow established procedures during the shutdown and startup of Line 6B.

- One violation of 49 CFR 195.440 related to the Enbridge public awareness program effectiveness.

- Two violations of 49 CFR 195.52 related to the timeliness and accuracy of information in the early notifications made by Enbridge to the NRC.

- Two violations of 49 CFR 195.54 related to the timeliness and accuracy of information submitted to the DOT.

- One violation of 49 CFR 195.505 related to the operation of Line 6B by operator A1, an unqualified individual. (Operator A1 was a trainee who had just returned after being on sick leave for 6 months).

### 1.14.3 Enbridge Actions

### 1.14.3.1    Line 6B Replacement Projects

Since the Marshall accident, Enbridge has announced two replacement projects, identified as phase 1[95] and phase 2,[96] that combined will replace the entire 285 miles of Line 6B in the United States. The phase 1 replacement project, announced in May 2011, replaces 75 miles of noncontiguous segments of Line 6B located in Michigan and Indiana. Enbridge expects to complete phase 1 by 2013.

---

[95] Enbridge Phase 1 Line 6B Replacement Project, State of Michigan, The Michigan Public Service Commission Case No. U-16856 (August 26, 2011) and U-16838 (August 12, 2011).

[96] Enbridge Phase 2 Line 6B Replacement Project, State of Michigan, The Michigan Public Service Commission; Case No. U17020.

The application for phase 2 of the Line 6B replacement was filed on Monday, April 16, 2012, with the Michigan Public Service Commission to replace another 160 miles of Line 6B in Michigan and 60 miles of Line 6B in Indiana. The phase 2 request included increasing the diameter of 110 miles of existing 30-inch-diameter pipeline to 36-inch-diameter pipeline between Griffith and Stockbridge to boost the capacity of the line. The remaining 50 miles of pipe would be replaced with 30-inch-diameter pipe between Ortonville and the St. Clair River in Marysville, Michigan.

In the 2012 filing to the Michigan Public Service Commission, Enbridge stated the following:

> Enbridge's decision to replace these segments minimizes the amount and frequency of future maintenance activities. While ongoing integrity inspections, testing and maintenance achieve required safety standards, replacement for the remaining Line 6B segments is the more cost-effective option to meet the current and future capacity requirements of its shippers.

### 1.14.3.2    Enbridge Operator Training

Following the Marshall accident, Enbridge increased the number of emergency response simulator sessions that operators took from one per year to two per year. Students also participated in two additional training sessions annually: one on human factors, which included fatigue, and one on hydraulics. The additional human factors training was administered in response to PHMSA's new rules addressing control center management.

### 1.14.3.3    Integrity Management

Enbridge issued new procedures following the accident in the areas of integrity management and control center operations. Enbridge now requires engineering assessments of cracks to use the smaller of either the nominal wall thickness or the prior measured wall thickness from in-line inspections. Enbridge also adopted a method of analyzing SCC features independently of fatigue by examining the strain rate of the crack. Pipeline excavation and inspection criteria have also been changed so that inspection features identified as crack-field are excavated if the longest indication measures 2.5 inches. Enbridge now includes the tool error, derived from excavation data, in the calculations of failure pressure and fatigue life and inspects overlays to examine overlap between corrosion and cracking. Enbridge also has implemented an excavation program that ensures a statistically significant number of excavations will occur, which establishes a confidence interval based on the tool's results and verifies that the tool bias numbers are reliable.

### 1.14.3.4    Enbridge Control Center

Enbridge added two technical specialists, who have previous control center experience, to the control center to assist operators when required. Before the Marshall accident, Enbridge had planned to move its control center to a new location. The new center was completed in December 2011, and its control center operations moved to the center at that time.

Oversight of the control center was transferred from the vice president, customer service to senior vice president, operations. A new vice president, pipeline control and a new director, control center were selected. The control center operations were divided into a terminal side and a pipeline side with technical specialists added to each. The specialists support the shift lead and the operator in technical issues. The three operators and the two shift leads involved in the accident were temporarily reassigned to positions outside of the control center. The two shift A operators retired from the company: one in September 2011 and the other in November 2011.

All operators, shift leads, and MBS analysts were provided additional technical training on hydraulics, control center roles and responsibilities, procedure compliance, column separation analysis, and the 10-minute operational limit. MBS analysts were required to note to shift leads, operators, and on-call supervisors, in response to an MBS alarm, only whether the alarm was valid or not. Operators were annually given an additional simulated emergency scenario and human factors training on fatigue (a PHMSA requirement that was independent of this accident) and on lessons learned from previous accidents. Procedures governing the documentation of information to be communicated during shift changes were developed and implemented.

Enbridge reemphasized the rule that requires an operator to shut down a line after 10 minutes if a problem remains unresolved. Operators and supervisors were prohibited from overriding approved control-room procedures. On-call procedures were revised to make available additional personnel—including the control center director and the senior vice president—when control center staff needed assistance. These on-call individuals were given (1) specific procedures to follow and (2) questions to be asked in particular circumstances.

Enbridge has also stated that additional flow meters have been installed on Line 6B increasing the number of segments that are calculated within the MBS system and increasing its accuracy.

## 1.15 Federal Oversight

### 1.15.1 Canadian and U.S. Regulation

Enbridge operates pipelines in both Canada and the United States from its Edmonton, Alberta, Canada, operations center. Hazardous liquid pipelines in the United States are subject to U.S. oversight by PHMSA, and those in Canada are subject to Canadian oversight by the NEB. Pipelines that originated in Canada and terminated in the United States were subject to the requirements of both PHMSA and the NEB. PHMSA and NEB currently operate under a memorandum of understanding signed in 2005 that outlines when notifications are to be made between agencies with respect to enforcement and inspections.

According to Enbridge's manager, United States/Canadian compliance, Enbridge did not find conflicts in meeting the requirements of the two regulators. Rather, where reporting requirements of the two regulators were different, the company either met the requirements of the applicable regulator or those of the regulator with more rigorous standards.

## 1.15.2 Enbridge 2010 Long-Term Pressure Reduction Notification

On July 15, 2010, Enbridge filed a notification with PHMSA regarding pressure restrictions on Line 6B that would exceed the 365 days allowed under 49 CFR 195.452(h)(1)(ii).[97] Beginning in February 2004, Enbridge had PII conduct an in-line corrosion inspection of Line 6B, from the Griffith PS to the Sarnia Terminal. The inspection was performed using an ultrasonic USWM tool and the results showed some areas with echo-loss readings near pitting corrosion.[98] To ascertain the depth in these areas of echo loss, a second inspection was conducted on October 13, 2007, using an MFL in-line inspection technology that was not subject to echo-loss. Enbridge originally requested that the 2007 data be overlaid with the 2004 inspection data.

In July 2008, because of difficulties in trying to overlay the two sets of data from the 2004 and 2007 inspections, Enbridge instructed PII to treat the more recent in-line inspection (2007 MFL) as a standalone report. PII issued its initial standalone report in November 2008. This initial report contained an equipment error[99] that affected the sizing and the location of some features in the pipeline. PII issued a revised report in May 2009 that corrected the errors in feature sizing. However, the errors had occurred more than halfway along Line 6B; therefore, the data collected in the first half of the inspection was unaffected.

By July 17, 2009, Enbridge identified 114 corrosion features (downstream of the ruptured segment) from the 2007 inspection that required self-imposed pressure restrictions to maintain the pipeline integrity. Under the regulations, a pipeline operator may impose pressure restrictions on its pipeline as a temporary remediation measure to integrity defects for up to 365 days.

In its filing to PHMSA in 2010, Enbridge referred to the July 17, 2009, date as the "discovery of condition" date. Under 49 CFR 195.452 (h)(2)[100] a "discovery of condition" must be made within 180 days following an integrity assessment; Enbridge noted that the 180 days expired on April 10, 2008. Enbridge's July 17, 2009, "discovery of condition" date was 463 days past the 180 days allowed under the regulations and 643 days past the date that the in-line inspection was originally conducted.

## 1.15.3 PHMSA Inspections

PHMSA regulates the transportation of hazardous liquids and gases by pipeline in the United States. PHMSA conducted an Integrity Management Segment Identification and Completeness Check of Enbridge's integrity management program from February 26 to 27, 2002. The

---

[97] Title 49 CFR 195.452(h)(1)(ii), Long term pressure reduction, states that "When a pressure reduction exceeds 365 days, the operator must notify PHMSA in accordance with paragraph (m) of this section and explain the reasons for the delay. An operator must also take further remedial action to ensure the safety of the pipeline."

[98] Pitting corrosion is a form of localized corrosion that generates small holes in the external surface of the pipe.

[99] This was reported as an error due to slippage of the odometer wheel installed on the tool, which is responsible for recording the start and end of the defect when detected by the sensors.

[100] Discovery of a condition occurs when an operator has adequate information about the condition to determine that the condition presents a potential threat to the integrity of the pipeline. An operator must promptly, but no later than 180 days after an integrity assessment, obtain sufficient information about a condition to make that determination, unless the operator can demonstrate that the 180-day period is impracticable.

audit found deficiencies in the process Enbridge was using to identify segments that could affect HCAs. PHMSA issued a notice of amendment to Enbridge on May 15, 2002. In its final response, dated September 3, 2002, Enbridge agreed to modify its segment identification plan.

From May 12 to June 2, 2003, PHMSA inspected Enbridge's integrity management plan. After the inspection on December 21, PHMSA issued a NOPV, Warning Letter, Notice of Amendment, and Letter of Concern, identifying 14 separate issues that included 3 probable violations, 5 procedural issues, and 6 areas of concerns. The 3 probable violations were changed to "Warning Letter" by PHMSA because no civil penalty or compliance order was proposed. One violation involved the Plummer to the Clearbrook pipeline section of Line 4. The discovery of several anomalies was made within 180 days of completion of in-line inspection of the pipeline, but these anomalies were erroneously classified as "previously repaired" and were excluded from the remediation plan. In another violation, PHMSA stated,

> Enbridge's information analysis procedures did not adequately consider data from other inspections and tests. Also, the process of evaluation of each pipeline segment by analyzing all available data was insufficient to gain a complete understanding of pipeline integrity (195.452(f)(3)(g)(3)).

Enbridge responded on January 28, 2005. Enbridge's response stated that for all hazards (external corrosion, internal corrosion, SCC, weld cracking, mechanical damage), specific defect analysis is conducted. Based on Enbridge's response, PHMSA ultimately closed the file on March 20, 2007. PHMSA conducted a second comprehensive integrity management program review of Enbridge during the weeks of June 12 and June 26, 2006. The detailed protocol inspection format was utilized to review Enbridge's processes for the following:

- Integrating information from all relevant sources to understand location-specific risks for these segments…

- Identifying and implementing remedial actions for anomalies and defects identified during integrity assessments…

- Performing periodic evaluations and on-going assessments of pipeline integrity; and

- Evaluating Integrity Management performance.

A summary report was prepared by PHMSA at the conclusion of the inspection identifying 13 recommendations concerning Enbridge's integrity management plan. Concerning a continual process of evaluation and assessment, PHMSA noted during the inspection that

> The lack of a periodic evaluation process was indicative of the Enbridge approach to integrity management, where the pigging/[pipeline integrity management] activities are largely done separate from risk assessment activities. Utilization of available information/risk analysis information appears to be limited to the evaluation of certain additional [preventive and maintenance] measures and is not well integrated with key integrity/assessment decisions. In effect, Enbridge

[integrity management]-related groups operate semi-independently, and it is not clear that overall integration of knowledge and data is occurring on a consistent basis.

## 1.15.4 Pipeline Safety, Regulatory Certainty, and Job Creation Act of 2011

On January 3, 2012, pipeline safety legislation was signed into law by the President, Public Law 112-90. The new law contains provisions related to public awareness, response plans, leak detection, and the transportation of diluted bitumen.

Under section 6(a) of the law, PHMSA has 1 year to do the following:

...develop and implement a program promoting greater awareness of the existence of the National Pipeline Mapping System to State and local emergency responders and other interested parties. The program shall include guidance on how to use the National Pipeline Mapping System to locate pipelines in communities and local jurisdictions.

Section 8(a) of the statute also requires that PHMSA make the response plans filed by pipeline operators available to the public upon written request.

This law also addresses leak detection systems of pipeline operators and requires that PHMSA study the "technical limitations" of current systems and how to foster the development of better technologies and incorporate the requirements of these systems into the Federal code if feasible. PHMSA is also required to perform a study of the transportation of diluted bitumen to determine whether the existing regulations are sufficient to protect pipelines that transport these products. Line 6B transports diluted bitumen crude oil extracted from the Alberta oil sands.

## 1.15.5 National Energy Board

The NEB is an independent regulatory agency of the Government of Canada charged with overseeing international and interprovincial aspects of the oil, gas, and electric utility industries. Based in Calgary, Alberta, Canada, the NEB regulates the construction and operation of oil and natural gas pipelines crossing provincial or international borders. Because segments of the pipeline infrastructure in Canada and the United States are interconnected, PHMSA and the NEB entered into an agreement on November 22, 2005, to improve pipeline safety and enhance cooperation.[101] The NEB completed an inspection of Enbridge on July 18, 2008; it identified the following issues.

The NEB stated that because Enbridge's integrity management program encompassed multiple departments (for example, integrity management, engineering, and risk management) with interconnected areas of responsibility, Enbridge should create a structured management program and implement a formal documentation process across the organization.

---

[101] Because Enbridge's pipelines extend into the United States, they are subject to PHMSA's regulations.

The NEB further stated that Enbridge's integrity management program needed a hazard and threat identification assessment process that considers fatigue-dependent cracking, among other threats. The NEB noted the following:

> The assessment process and data for determining the crack and corrosion in-line inspection frequency required improvement to prevent failures from reoccurring. Ongoing evaluation of the effectiveness of the crack management plan is required such that [in-line inspection] frequency can be reliable. a) [In-line inspection] Accuracy of crack detection and sizing; b) Validity of Crack Growth Modeling in regards to input data (i.e. material properties and growth coefficients) and ongoing field verification of assumptions; and c) Determination of the crack—susceptible pipelines accounting for the level of identified data uncertainty (i.e. unknown and non-reliable input data) and continuous validation by field investigation.

Similar to PHMSA's findings, the NEB also noted that Enbridge's departments were not well integrated, particularly when performing risk assessments. The NEB found that:

> Validation of the corrosion assessment interval results and the evaluation of their influence in the external corrosion mitigation and monitoring programs are required. Similarly, validation of crack detection [in-line inspection] performance, crack growth modeling, re-inspection frequency, susceptibility to cracking of Enbridge's pipeline segments, and the evaluation of their influence in the crack mitigation and monitoring programs are also required.

During its inspection, the NEB discovered that each of Enbridge's departments was independently assessing coincidental features. The NEB stated that for Enbridge's integrity management program to be effective—that is, to identify, monitor, assess, and mitigate threats—all departments should be participating in an integrated integrity management process. Enbridge submitted its corrective action plan to the NEB on February 2, 2009.

### 1.15.6 PHMSA Inspection of Enbridge's PAP

In May 2011, Enbridge revised its PAP and created a public awareness committee that includes a performance metrics subcommittee. According to the committee charter, the committee will meet four times a year and will be responsible for the annual review of the PAP and the program performance measures.

In July 2011, PHMSA conducted an inspection of Enbridge's May 2011 PAP. PHMSA's inspection report noted the following two findings:

> Enbridge's PAP does not have a written implementation review process that clearly identifies both supplemental and overall PAP implementation.

> Enbridge does not have a process in the PAP that outlines a consistent format and methodology for evaluating program outreach, understandability of message content, desired stakeholder behavior, and bottom-line results.

## 1.15.7 PHMSA Facility Response Plan Review and Approval

PHMSA had reviewed and approved Enbridge's facility response plan before the accident. The EPA consulted the plan during the initial phase of the response to the Marshall accident to gain an understanding of Enbridge's response resources and planning. The EPA noted that the plan did not have information specific to spill response at any particular location. As of the date of this report, PHMSA has not performed a postaccident review of the facility response plan. PHMSA told NTSB investigators that it will review the lessons learned from the Marshall accident either when Enbridge renews its facility response plan in 2015 or when Enbridge amends its facility response plan, whichever Enbridge completes first.

PHMSA's plan review process was supposed to emphasize the adequacy of the pipeline operator's response resources, incident command system, and ability to protect environmentally sensitive areas. PHMSA's environmental planning officer told NTSB investigators that these plans are assessed based on the reviewer's professional experience and judgment.

PHMSA also required plan holders to respond to a 16-element self-assessment questionnaire. On April 1, 2010, Enbridge submitted its responses and affirmed the adequacy of the following elements:

- Whether the facility response plan identifies enough spill containment equipment and recovery capacity to respond to a worst-case discharge to the maximum extent practicable;

- If the facility response plan identifies spill recovery strategies appropriate for the response zones;

- If planned spill recovery activities can be accomplished within the appropriate tier times;

- Whether the plan identifies enough trained personnel to respond to a worst-case discharge.

PHMSA's environmental planning officer reviewed the facility response plan and questionnaire without requesting supplemental information. On April 15, 2010, the environmental planning officer notified Enbridge that its facility response plan had been approved. PHMSA's correspondence to Enbridge did not cite any deficiencies in the plan.

Following the Marshall accident, PHMSA asked the DOT Volpe National Transportation Systems Center (Volpe) to identify the processes used by four Federal agencies responsible for reviewing facility plans that are required under the Oil Pollution Act of 1990. According to Volpe's draft report, at the time of the accident, PHMSA had 1.5 employees to oversee about 450 facility response plans. Until June 2010, one PHMSA environmental planning officer reviewed and approved facility response plans.

Currently, authority to review and approve facility response plans is assigned to a division director. PHMSA reported that another full-time employee has been assigned to oversee spill response plans since the data were collected for Volpe's draft report. In contrast, Volpe's draft report stated that EPA Region 6 had 2 employees, 3 contractors, and 22 on-scene coordinators[102] to review 1,700 facility response plans. The Coast Guard Sector Boston oversees 45 facility response plans with a staff of 4 inspectors and 3 to 4 trainees.

Volpe's draft report stated that PHMSA does not perform on-site audits or unannounced drills for operators who submit facility response plans for approval. Both the Coast Guard and the EPA conduct on-site audits and plan reviews after initial review and approval of the submitted plan. In addition, both the Coast Guard and the EPA conduct announced and unannounced exercises to test the effectiveness of plans. Although the Coast Guard and the EPA report to their headquarters offices on the number of plans, noncompliances, and inspections conducted, PHMSA has not currently implemented performance metrics for its facility response plan program. Table 6 provides key findings of the Volpe draft report, contrasting PHMSA's plan review process with those of the other Federal agencies that are responsible for response plan review.

**Table 6.** Volpe's comparative study of response plan review.

|  | PHMSA | EPA | Coast Guard |
|---|---|---|---|
| Centralized collection of plans | Yes | No | Yes vessel response plan |
| Regional collection of plans | No | Yes | Yes |
| Information system support | No | Yes | Yes |
| Number of plans | 450 | 500 for Region 5 1,500 for Region 6 | 3,000 vessel response plans and hundreds of facility response plans (fixed and mobile) |
| Number of staff involved in plan review | 1.5 | 35 in Region 5 5 in Region 6 | 21 in headquarters (18 for vessel response plan; 3 for facility response plan) and hundreds in the field |
| Completeness review conducted[a] | Yes | Yes | Yes |
| Second level review conducted[b] | No | Yes | Yes |
| Unannounced or announced drills or exercises to verify plans | No | Yes | Yes |

[a] Completeness review involves the staff member using a checklist to ensure all required elements of the plan are present.
[b] A second level review is conducted by a more senior level staff member prior to submitting a recommendation for approval to the approving authority.

---

[102] The on-scene coordinator can be delegated to authorize plans as needed based upon workload.

PHMSA's director of emergency support and security reported that in its 2012 budget request, PHMSA requested eight additional personnel and over $1 million to enhance its field oil-related activities. However, those resources were not approved in the final budget. He reported that PHMSA is developing plans to increase oil-related activities in its field program.

## 1.15.8 PHMSA Facility Response Plan Advisory Bulletin

On June 23, 2010, PHMSA issued Advisory Bulletin PHMSA-2010-0175, in light of the Deepwater Horizon oil spill in the Gulf of Mexico,[103] advising pipeline facility response plan holders to review and update their plans within 30 days to ensure that adequate resources were available to comply with emergency response requirements to address a worst-case discharge. The bulletin noted that the response to the Deepwater Horizon spill had resulted in the relocation of oil spill response resources. The Enbridge senior emergency response engineer responded to the advisory bulletin on July 21, 2010, by stating that Enbridge had assessed its emergency preparedness in relation to a worst-case discharge for each of its response zones. He reported that two oil spill response organizations—Bay West and Garner Environmental Services, Inc.—have confirmed their ability to deploy appropriate spill response resources in the response zones. He further responded:

> In relation to the Advisory Bulletin, we have reassessed our facility response plan and concluded that our plan is complete, complies with 49 CFR Part 194, and is appropriate for responding to a worst case discharge in our Chicago Region Response Zone.

## 1.15.9 Response Preparedness

The National Preparedness for Response Exercise Program (PREP), a unified Federal effort to satisfy the exercise requirements of the Coast Guard, the EPA, PHMSA, and the U.S. Department of the Interior's Minerals Management Service,[104] was developed to establish a spill response exercise program in accordance with the Oil Pollution Act of 1990. PREP became effective on January 1, 1994. PHMSA requires an operator to satisfy the requirement for a drill program by following the *PREP Guidelines*. PREP requirements for onshore transportation-related pipelines require facility response plan holders to participate in both internal (facility-specific) and external (area-specific) exercises.

Section 5 of the *PREP Guidelines* provides for unannounced government-initiated exercises to test plan holder's ability to respond to a worst-case discharge event. These full-scale exercises, which are used to evaluate a plan holder's operational capability, involve all levels of the organization and all aspects of a response operation. Plan holders are not required to

---

[103] Deepwater Horizon was an ultra-deepwater semi-submersible offshore oil drilling rig located in the Gulf of Mexico about 250 miles southeast of Houston, Texas. On April 20, 2010, while drilling, an explosion on the rig killed 11 crewmembers and ignited a fire. By April 22, the rig sank, leaving the well gushing oil at the seabed, resulting in the largest offshore oil spill in U.S. history, with an estimated release of 172.2 to 205.8 million gallons of crude oil.

[104] On October 1, 2011, the Minerals Management Service was succeeded by the Bureau of Safety and Environmental Enforcement.

participate in unannounced exercises if they have already participated in one during the previous 36 months. Although PHMSA recently has not been conducting unannounced government-initiated exercises, it has committed to conducting not more than 20 per year on the regulated pipeline industry. Records indicate that since 2005, PHMSA has participated in only one exercise per year and has not hosted any exercises specific to pipeline facilities.

The *PREP Guidelines* identify 16 facility response plan core components that should be exercised at least once during each triennial cycle. These core components relate to areas such as notifications, mobilization of resources, response management, and the ability to contain and recover a discharge. According to the *PREP Guidelines*, PHMSA is responsible for verifying internal exercises and for conducting and certifying external exercises conducted by the operator and other Federal agencies.

During the 10-year period from 2002 to 2011, PHMSA participated in 26 drills and exercises. Enbridge participated in the September 24, 2003, exercise in Sault Ste. Marie, Michigan, which was led by the Coast Guard and PHMSA, and in the March 10-11, 2004, exercise in Cushing, Oklahoma, led by the Federal Bureau of Investigation, PHMSA, and more than 20 Federal, state, and local government agencies. PHMSA's environmental planning officer told NTSB investigators that Enbridge successfully completed both exercises. Key Enbridge personnel who participated as initial responders to the Marshall accident reported that they have continued to receive annual boat-handling and oil-boom deployment training for creeks and rivers. Several responders had previous experience with much smaller oil spills. None of the Enbridge first responders reported having had experience responding to an oil spill of this magnitude or having had previous training for oil spills in high water and swift moving creeks. The Enbridge response personnel also told NTSB investigators that they had no experience constructing underflow dam oil-containment structures, although some were aware of the technique.

## 1.15.10    PHMSA Control Center Management

PHMSA promulgated the control center management rule in 2009 in response to recommendations generated as part of the NTSB 2005 SCADA study and to fulfill the requirements of the PIPES Act of 2006, Public Law 109-468, which was enacted on December 29, 2006. Section 12(a) of the statute, concerning pipeline control center management, required the U.S. Secretary of Transportation to do the following:

> (a) Issue regulations requiring each operator of a gas or hazardous liquid pipeline to develop, implement, and submit to the Secretary...a human factors management plan designed to reduce risks associated with human factors, including fatigue, in each control center for the pipeline. Each plan must include, among the measures to reduce such risks, a maximum limit on the hours of service established by the operator for individuals employed as controllers in a control center for the pipeline.

Further, section 19 of the act, "Standards," called on the Secretary of Transportation, no later than June 1, 2008, to implement actions corresponding to those called for in Safety Recommendations P-05-1, -2, and -5.

Require operators of hazardous liquid pipelines to follow the American Petroleum Institute's Recommended Practice 1165 for the use of graphics on the Supervisory Control and Data Acquisition screens. (P-05-1)

Require pipeline companies to have a policy for the review/audit of alarms. (P-05-2)

Require operators to install computer-based leak detection systems on all lines unless engineering analysis determines that such a system is not necessary. (P-05-5)

PHMSA modified existing gas and liquid pipeline regulations contained in 49 CFR 192 and 195 to address the requirements of P-05-1 and -2 and both recommendations were classified "Closed—Acceptable Action" on April 28, 2010. PHMSA's rule modifications, which took effect on February 1, 2011, were similar for liquid and gas pipelines and required pipeline operators to comply with the requirements by August 1, 2011. The modified regulations pertaining to liquid pipelines were incorporated into 49 CFR 195.446, "Control Room Management."

Safety Recommendation P-05-5 was classified "Closed—Acceptable Alternate Action" on May 6, 2010, based on PHMSA's integrity management requirements to detect and repair leaks through defect repair prioritization, risk based assessment, repair prioritization of defects by environmental consequence, corrosion management, right-of-way surveillance, public awareness leading to citizen identifications of leaks, emergency preparedness and lessons learned from accident analysis. In addition, PHMSA issued Advisory Bulletin ADB-10-01 informing pipeline operating companies of PHMSA's expectations regarding pipeline leak detection systems. Operators must justify the reasons for not having a leak detection system, and if leak detection systems are not in place, operators must perform hourly balances by hand.

According to PHMSA's Central Region supervisor of accident investigations, its representatives met with DOT personnel involved in overseeing aviation and rail operations, the Coast Guard, and the Nuclear Regulatory Commission between 2004 and 2007, which was before PHMSA developed control room management rules. These meetings were conducted to learn about the best practices in the oversight by Federal regulators from the perspective of the regulators. The meetings also included the Federal Aviation Administration's (FAA) Civil Aerospace Medical Institute to review human factors oversight issues. This was done to assist PHMSA in the development of its new control room regulations.

In addition to its regulations, PHMSA issued several advisory bulletins governing control rooms and SCADA systems. Advisory Bulletin 04-05, issued on November 26, 2006, explained the parts of 49 CFR 192 and 195 that required gas and liquid pipeline operating companies to establish and maintain operator qualification programs. The advisory bulletin advised pipeline operating companies to include periodic requalification for operators at intervals that "reflect the relevant factors including the complexity, criticality, and frequency of the performance of the task."

Advisory Bulletin 05-06 responded to NTSB Safety Recommendation P-98-30, which called upon PHMSA's predecessor agency to "assess the potential safety risks associated with rotating pipeline controller shifts and establish industry guidelines for the development and implementation of pipeline controller work schedules that reduce the likelihood of accidents attributable to controller fatigue."

## 1.16 Other Information

### 1.16.1 Oil Spill Response Methods

Effective oil spill removal strategies largely depend on the crude oil mixture's density and its tendency to float or sink in fresh water. Once the crude oil mixture (oil and diluents) enters the environment, weather factors, volatility, and physical agitation affect the composition, thus allowing some of the oil to sink into river sediments and collect on the river bottom.

The most effective response methods to control the environmental consequences of an oil spill vary according to the specific spill conditions (that is, the type and amount of oil, weather and site conditions, and the effectiveness of the response strategies). The time required to bring needed resources and personnel to the scene is also critical to an effective response. Response actions are most viable and effective very early during a response. When the oil is concentrated near the discharge source, focusing on source control, containment, and removal near the source provides the best opportunity to reduce adverse environmental impact.[105]

Although Talmadge Creek flow data were not available for the day of the accident, Enbridge first responders told NTSB investigators that the water flow was faster than they had previously seen. Coast Guard research indicates that controlling and recovering oil spills in fast moving water (above 1 knot) is difficult because oil flows under booms and skimmers in swift current, thus necessitating quicker and more efficient responses.[106] In a stream with a flow rate greater than 10 cubic feet per second, the Coast Guard recommends the use of underflow dams, overflow dams, sorbent barriers, or a combination of these techniques instead of deploying oil containment boom.

Underflow dams can be erected in shallow rivers and culverts using hand tools or heavy machinery. Pipes are used to form an underflow dam, which allows water to pass, while retaining oil. On the day the release was discovered, Enbridge first responders used surplus pipe and an excavator at the Marshall PLM shop to construct an earthen underflow dam. Underflow dams also can be installed quickly at culverts by using sheets of plywood or another suitable barrier to prevent floating oil from escaping downstream.

On July 26, Enbridge responders installed skirted oil boom and sorbent boom across the corrugated pipe culvert under Division Drive. (See figure 21.) When asked to identify lessons

---

[105] *Characteristics of Response Strategies: A Guide for Spill Response Planning in Marine Environments* (American Petroleum Institute, National Oceanic and Atmospheric Administration, U.S. Coast Guard, and U.S. Environmental Protection Agency joint publication, June 2010).

[106] *Oil Spill Response in Fast Moving Currents, a Field Guide* (Groton, Connecticut: U.S. Coast Guard Research and Development Center, October 2001).

learned from the response, the Bay City PLM supervisor told NTSB investigators that, in the future, he would ensure that sheets of plywood are included in Enbridge's boom trailers so that adjustable underflow dams can be constructed over culvert pipes.

**Figure 21.** (Left) Enbridge employees install sorbent boom in front of a culvert at Division Drive. (Right) Oil residue marks the level of the oil carried through this culvert following the Enbridge release from Line 6B.

The EPA's Region 5 Integrated Contingency Plan discusses response methods for small river and stream environments, in which the primary use of booming should be to divert slicks toward collection points in low-current areas. The plan states that booming is ineffective in fast shallow water and in steep bank environments. The plan also states that sorbent boom should be used to recover sheen in low current areas and along the shore. Although sorbent boom effectively absorbs oil sheen in stagnant water, it is an ineffective barrier to flowing oil.[107]

The Coast Guard's Research and Development Center further describes the proper use of sorbent boom, stating that it is used to recover trace amounts of oil and sheen in stagnant or slow moving water, or as a polishing technique to control escaping sheen from containment boom. The Coast Guard recommends that when containment boom is used in a fast moving current, the maximum deflection angle must be maintained to channel the oil toward calm water along the bank.

The Enbridge operating and maintenance procedure for emergency response identifies methods for containing oil in wetlands, rivers, and sensitive areas. The procedure states that when containing releases in rivers, an attempt must be made to confine the product as close to the source as possible to prevent the product from entering a major river. The procedure states that releases could be contained using one or a number of the following techniques: containment booms, diversion booms, sorbent booms, earth dikes, and containment weirs. The procedure for containing releases in rivers stated that sorbent booms may be used in calm waters when current speeds are less than 1.64 feet per second and the degree of contamination is minor.

---

[107] *Mechanical Protection Guidelines* (Research Planning, Inc., National Oceanic and Atmospheric Administration, and U.S. Coast Guard National Strike Force joint publication, June 1994).

### 1.16.2 API Standard 1160—Managing System Integrity for Hazardous Liquid Pipelines

The API Standard 1160, *Managing System Integrity for Hazardous Liquid Pipelines*, stresses that regulation should be used as the foundation of a high-quality integrity management program, rather than relying solely on a compliance approach. Some of the standard's "Guiding Principles" include the following:

- An integrity management program must be flexible. The program should be customized, continually evaluated, and modified as appropriate to accommodate changes in the pipeline system.

- The integration of information is a key component for managing system integrity. It is important to integrate all available information from various sources in the decision-making process.

- Identifying risks to pipeline integrity is a continuous process. Analyzing for risks in a pipeline system is a continuous reassessment process. The operator will periodically gather additional information and system operating experience. This information should be factored into understanding system risks.

The standard states that all "coincident occurrence" of suspected high-risk conditions or events should be compared using existing data. The standard further stresses that data should be timely, complete, and of high quality.

# 2 Analysis

## 2.1 Introduction

This analysis explains the probable cause of the accident and includes a discussion of the following safety issues identified in this report:

- Multiple aspects of Enbridge's organization, including pipeline integrity management, operations control room management, leak detection and recognition, public awareness, and environmental response.

- PHMSA's oversight of pipeline operating companies' SCADA systems, integrity management programs, and facility response plans.

- Federal pipeline safety regulations governing the assessment and repair of crack defects under operators' integrity management programs.

The remainder of this introductory section discusses those elements of the investigation the NTSB determined were not factors in the accident.

The ruptured segment of Line 6B had a polyethylene tape coating and a cathodic protection system, which was operating in excess of the minimum levels specified in the regulations, to mitigate external corrosion. The coating had disbonded, and the NTSB Materials Laboratory's examination revealed large areas of general corrosion and pitting at and near the pipe's longitudinal seam weld in the disbonded areas. Because Line 6B's polyethylene tape coating had disbonded, the surface of the pipe was exposed to the surrounding environment and susceptible to corrosion. However, the pattern and location of the disbondment were not consistent with degradation associated with cathodic protection systems. Therefore, the operation of the cathodic protection system was not considered a factor in this accident.

To investigate any potential microbial contribution to the corrosion, the EPA and the NTSB conducted microbial testing. The EPA's results from liquid samples showed higher microbial concentrations than the NTSB's results from surface samples. Knowing the microbial concentrations on the metal surface is critical to estimating microbial contributions to corrosion damage; therefore, the NTSB conducted microbial tests using corrosion product and deposit samples obtained from the pipe's surface beneath the coating. The results showed the presence of low concentrations of microorganisms in the samples; however, features typically associated with microbial corrosion were not observed on the corroded areas of the pipe. Therefore, microbial corrosion was not considered a factor in the rupture.

Enbridge had an internal corrosion management program since 1996 that used cleaning tools, biocide, and inhibitors to mitigate internal corrosion of its pipelines. The NTSB's examination of the ruptured pipe segment showed that the internal pipe surfaces were free from any apparent corrosion or other visible surface anomalies. Therefore, internal corrosion was not a factor in the rupture of Line 6B.

The NTSB's examination showed that the location of the fracture was inconsistent with transportation-induced metal fatigue or third-party damage. The fracture originated from corrosion pits on the external surface in the pipe's base metal and away from the longitudinal seam weld heat-affected zone. In addition, the NTSB's examination of the pipe showed no sign of third-party damage. Therefore, transportation-induced metal fatigue and third-party damage were not factors in the rupture.

The NTSB's testing of the chemical and mechanical properties of the steel taken from the ruptured segment showed the pipe met or exceeded the API specifications in place at the time the pipe was manufactured. Further, the rupture did not occur at the longitudinal seam weld or in the weld heat-affected zone, which are locations typically associated with manufacturing defects. In addition, no manufacturing anomalies were noted at the fracture origins. Therefore, pipe manufacturing defects did not contribute to the failure of the pipeline.

Based on the above information, the NTSB concludes that the following were not factors in this accident: cathodic protection, microbial corrosion, internal corrosion, transportation-induced metal fatigue, third-party damage, and pipe manufacturing defects.

## 2.2 Pipeline Failure

### 2.2.1 The Rupture

About 5:57 p.m. during the planned shutdown, the Line 6B operator increased the pressure at a pressure control valve near the Stockbridge Terminal to slow the flow rate in the pipeline and to increase the upstream pressure (toward the Marshall PS) by 150 psig. The pressure increase occurred in 16 seconds. About 45 seconds after the pressure had increased upstream of Stockbridge Terminal and just before the Marshall PS pump was stopped, Line 6B ruptured at a highest recorded pressure of 486 psig,[108] which was lower than the MOP of 624 psig and the pressure restriction of 523 psig. The pipeline segment ruptured due to corrosion fatigue cracks that had grown in size until the pipe failed during the planned shutdown. The corrosion fatigue cracks most likely grew from smaller cracks that were likely initiated by longitudinally oriented, near-neutral pH SCC from a corrosion pit. These cracks initiated from multiple origins along the 6-foot-8.25-inch rupture and in areas of external surface corrosion. The small cracks eventually grew in size and linked together to form one large crack. This segment of pipe was not excavated or repaired and the crack was allowed to grow to a depth of 0.213 inch relative to the original wall thickness of 0.254 inch (83.9 percent), and it resulted in a rupture coinciding with the pipeline shutdown operations on July 25, 2010.

### 2.2.2 Fracture Mechanism

The ruptured pipe segment was wrapped with polyethylene tape at the time of its installation in 1969. Since the late 1960s, coating technology has advanced significantly. The coatings available today follow the pipe's contour better and are more resistant to disbonding. Some of the newer coatings also allow cathodic protection to reach the pipe. Tape coating that is

---

[108] This discharge pressure was recorded locally at the Marshall PS.

well-adhered will remain tightly bonded to the external surface of a pipe; however, the tape coating on the ruptured segment had areas where the tape was loose and wrinkled with areas of localized bulging. Where the tape crossed the longitudinal seam weld, it was "tented" and the failure of the adhesive (that is, disbondment) was evident along multiple areas of the pipe, including areas away from the rupture location. Polyethylene tape-wrap coatings installed on pipelines with DSAW longitudinal seams are susceptible to disbondment due to tenting, particularly when the longitudinal seam weld is located at the 3 o'clock position on the pipe as it was in the ruptured segment.

The pipe had been installed through a wetland; the rupture occurred near the edge of the wetland, which potentially had subjected the ruptured segment to wet-and-dry environmental patterns. Moisture had penetrated areas where the coating was not adhered to the pipe. This disbondment exposed the pipe's surface to conditions that are conducive to corrosion, near-neutral pH SCC, and corrosion fatigue. This observation was evident by the presence of corrosion and clusters of cracks along the length of the ruptured segment. The NTSB's examination showed that fracture features emanated from the bottom of the individual corrosion pits at the external pipe surface. This observation indicated that the corrosion was in place prior to the crack formation and provided locations of concentrated stress for crack initiation.

The fracture features found on the ruptured segment were consistent with near-neutral pH SCC and corrosion fatigue as the fracture mechanism. When cross sections of the cracks were examined at a microscopic level, the cracks were observed extending through the metal grains with limited crack branching.[109] On the fracture surfaces, many fine crack-arrest lines were found near the origin areas of the cracks; farther away, larger broad-band crack-arrest features were found. These crack-arrest lines indicated areas of progressive advancement likely generated from either pressure cycles or changes in environmental conditions.

Near-neutral pH SCC and corrosion fatigue are forms of environmentally assisted cracking and share similar fracture features.[110] However, the NTSB observed distinct differences in the crack arrest lines near the crack origins and those found farther away. These differences suggest a change in the fracture mechanism as the cracks propagated deeper into the pipe wall. Published experimental findings[111] show near-neutral pH SCC cracks that are about 0.020 inch

---

[109] Crack branching refers to crack growth where the crack path diverges into separate crack paths as it grows, appearing in cross section similar to the branches of a tree.

[110] (a) J.I. Dickson and J.P. Bailon, "The Fractography of Environmentally Assisted Cracking," in A.S. Krausz, ed., *Time Dependent Fracture: Proceedings of the Eleventh Canadian Fracture Conference, June 1984, Ottawa, Canada* (Dordrecht: M. Nijhoff Publishers, 1985). (b) G. Gabetta, "Transgranular Stress Corrosion Cracking of Low-Alloy Steels in Diluted Solutions," *Corrosion*, vol. 53, no. 7 (1997), pp. 516–524.

[111] (a) W. Zheng and others, "Stress Corrosion Cracking of Oil and Gas Pipelines: New Insights on Crack Growth Behaviour Gained From Full-Scale and Small-Scale Tests," 12th International Conference on Fracture 2009, July 12–17, 2009, Ottawa, Ontario, Canada. (b) B. Fang and others, "Transition from Pits to Cracks in Pipeline Steel in Near-Neutral pH Solution," 12th International Conference on Fracture 2009, July 12–17, 2009, Ottawa, Ontario, Canada. (c) W. Chen and R.L. Sutherby, "Crack Growth Behavior of Pipeline Steel in Near-Neutral pH Soil Environments," *Metallurgical and Materials Transactions A*, vol. 38, no. 6 (2007) pp. 1260–1268. (d) M.H. Marvasti, "Crack Growth Behavior of Pipeline Steels in Near Neutral pH Soil Environment," master's thesis, University of Alberta, 2010. (e) F. Song and others, *Development of a Commercial Model to Predict Stress Corrosion Cracking Growth Rates in Operating Pipelines*, SwRI Project 20.14080 (Washington, D.C.: U.S. Department of Transportation, Pipeline Hazardous Materials Safety Administration, 2011).

long will likely stop growing under a static load but will grow at a rate consistent with corrosion fatigue under a cyclic load.

Therefore, the NTSB concludes that the Line 6B segment ruptured under normal operating pressure due to corrosion fatigue cracks that grew and coalesced from multiple stress corrosion cracks, which had initiated in areas of external corrosion beneath the disbonded polyethylene tape coating.

## 2.3  Federal Regulations Governing Hazardous Liquid Pipelines

The actions an operator must take to address integrity issues for liquid pipelines are described in 49 CFR 195.452(h). In accordance with these requirements:

> an operator must take prompt action to address all anomalous conditions the operator discovers through the integrity assessment or information analysis. In addressing all conditions, an operator must evaluate all anomalous conditions and remediate those that could reduce a pipeline's integrity. An operator must be able to demonstrate that the remediation of the condition will ensure the condition is unlikely to pose a threat to the long term integrity of the pipeline.

In response to API's comments during PHMSA's rulemaking process, PHMSA amended its integrity management rule by replacing the word "repair" with "remediate." In the preamble[112] to its rulemaking, PHMSA stated that "although actions may consist of repair, other actions such as further testing and evaluation, environmental changes, operational changes or administrative changes could be appropriate."

PHMSA also stated that "remediate can encompass a broad range of actions, which include mitigative measures as well as repair" but that it "firmly believes that a repair is necessary to address many anomalies." However, PHMSA did not identify which anomalies should be repaired.

Title 49 CFR 195.452(h)(4)(i) requires immediate repair for certain conditions, including "metal loss greater than 80 percent of the nominal wall regardless of dimensions" and when "a calculation of remaining strength of the pipe shows a predicted burst pressure less than the established [MOP] at the location of the anomaly." The regulation also identifies two acceptable methods for calculating the remaining strength of corroded pipe. The regulation does not provide an acceptable method for recalculating the remaining strength of cracked pipe.

Title 49 CFR 195.452(h)(4)(iii) addresses nine conditions that require remediation within 180 days. Four of these are the following:

> (D) A calculation of the remaining strength of the pipe that shows an operating pressure that is less than the current established [MOP] at the location of the anomaly. Suitable remaining strength calculation methods include, but are not limited to, ASME/[American National Standards Institute] B31G ("Manual for

---

[112] *Federal Register*, vol. 65, no. 232 (December 1, 2000), p. 75377.

Determining the Remaining Strength of Corroded Pipelines" (1991)) or [American Gas Association] Pipeline Research Committee Project PR-3-805 ("A Modified Criterion for evaluating the Remaining Strength of Corroded Pipe" (December 1989)).

(G) Corrosion of or along a longitudinal seam weld.

(H) A gouge or a groove greater than 12.5 percent of nominal wall.

(I) A potential crack indication that when excavated is determined to be a crack.

During a meeting with NTSB investigators, PHMSA's director of engineering and research stated that PHMSA expects that all cracks will be excavated. However, Enbridge was not excavating all features that had a high probability of being a crack.

Title 49 CFR 195.452(h)(4)(iii) does not address the size, depth, location, or suitable engineering assessment methods associated with the predicted failure pressure or prioritization of crack defects as it does with corrosion defects. The regulation addresses cracks as potential cracks that when excavated are determined to be cracks but does not address what constitutes potential cracks or whether excavation is required of all cracks—an expectation expressed by PHMSA's director of engineering and research. Because the regulation is less explicit regarding the assessment of crack features, it does not clearly state the safety margin that should be applied to a predicted failure pressure, as it does with corrosion, when performing engineering assessments of crack defects. Because the regulation is less prescriptive with respect to the remediation of crack features, the Enbridge crack management program used different and inconsistent excavation criteria for cracks versus corrosion. Enbridge assessed cracking by using fitness-for-service methods that applied a lower margin of safety to the predicted failure pressure than would have been applied to corrosion features assessed under the same section of the regulations.

Therefore, the NTSB concludes that 49 CFR 195.452(h) does not provide clear requirements regarding when to repair and when to remediate pipeline defects and inadequately defines the requirements for assessing the effect on pipeline integrity when either crack defects or cracks and corrosion are simultaneously present in the pipeline.

PHMSA had inspected Enbridge's integrity management program twice prior to the Marshall accident. During PHMSA's first integrity management inspection of Enbridge in 2003 and during its second comprehensive integrity management inspection of Enbridge in 2006, PHMSA identified deficiencies involving Enbridge's inadequate incorporation of data from all in-line inspections and tests. For example, after the 2003 inspection, PHMSA stated, "Enbridge's information analysis procedures did not adequately consider data from other inspections and tests. Also, the process of evaluation of each pipeline segment by analyzing all available data was insufficient to gain a complete understanding of pipeline integrity." After the 2006 inspection, PHMSA stated, "In effect, Enbridge [integrity management]-related groups operate semi-independently, and it is not clear that overall integration of knowledge and data is occurring on a consistent basis." However, no further followup or verification of any corrective actions by Enbridge was conducted by PHMSA. In addition, Enbridge had notified PHMSA of the introduction of changes to the engineering assessment of crack defects, following the Cohasset accident in 2002; however, no evidence was found that PHMSA asked Enbridge for justification in choosing a lower safety margin for the crack excavation criteria versus that of the corrosion excavation criteria.

Therefore, the NTSB concludes that PHMSA failed to pursue findings from previous inspections and did not require Enbridge to excavate pipe segments with injurious crack defects.

Based on its findings, the NTSB recommends that PHMSA revise 49 CFR 195.452 to clearly state (1) when an engineering assessment of crack defects, including environmentally assisted cracks, must be performed; (2) the acceptable methods for performing these engineering assessments, including the assessment of cracks coinciding with corrosion with a safety factor that considers the uncertainties associated with sizing of crack defects; (3) criteria for determining when a probable crack defect in a pipeline segment must be excavated and time limits for completing those excavations; (4) pressure restriction limits for crack defects that are not excavated by the required date; and (5) acceptable methods for determining crack growth for any cracks allowed to remain in the pipe, including growth caused by fatigue, corrosion fatigue, or SCC as applicable.

PHMSA states the following in 49 CFR 195.452(h)(2):

Discovery of a condition occurs when an operator has adequate information about the condition to determine that the condition presents a potential threat to the integrity of the pipeline. An operator must promptly, but no later than 180 days after an integrity assessment, obtain sufficient information about a condition to make that determination, unless the operator can demonstrate that the 180-day period is impracticable.

The regulation does not provide an upper limit to the number of days that an operator can take to complete the determination of threats on the pipeline, only that it must have information within 180 days. In addition, the regulation does not state whether the operator must act when a partial assessment has determined threats to the integrity of the pipeline. As written, the regulation allows a pipeline operating company to define what constitutes an "assessment" of its pipeline system and to delay corrective integrity actions.

If pressure restrictions are imposed to maintain the integrity of a pipeline, 49 CFR 195.452(h)(1)(ii) requires that pressure restrictions extending beyond 365 days be communicated to PHMSA. Enbridge filed a notice of long-term pressure reduction with PHMSA on July 15, 2010, 1 year following what it defined as the "discovery of condition" and the date when pressure restrictions were first imposed on Line 6B to safeguard the pipeline from corrosion defects. These pressure restrictions were imposed on July 17, 2009, more than 600 days after the original October 13, 2007,[113] in-line inspection that identified the defects requiring pressure restrictions and 463 days beyond the 180-day "discovery of condition" deadline. Only through this long-term pressure restriction notification process did PHMSA learn

[113] The 2007 MFL corrosion inspection was a followup in-line inspection to a 2004 inspection of Line 6B, which included some readings with echo-loss problems that impacted the reported depth. The 2007 in-line inspection was originally intended as a "fill-in" to supplement the 2004 inspection.

of the numerous delays to its original date-of-discovery deadline (April 10, 2008), which Enbridge stated were due to revisions and reissues of the 2007 in-line corrosion inspection report.

Enbridge was not required to notify PHMSA that it had exceeded the 180-day "discovery of condition" deadline because Enbridge stated that the revisions constituted inadequate information. However, a portion of the 2007 in-line inspection was unaffected by the errors that required the revisions and could have been used to impose pressure restrictions. The NTSB recognizes that the tool vendor has a role in the operator meeting the deadlines that are established by the "discovery of condition" rule; however, when defects are time-dependent, the regulator should be informed when delays exceed 180 days.

Therefore, the NTSB concludes that Enbridge's delayed reporting of the "discovery of condition" by more than 460 days indicates that Enbridge's interpretation of the current regulation delayed the repair of the pipeline.

The NTSB is concerned that other pipeline operators also may interpret the current regulation in a manner that delays defect repairs on a pipeline. Therefore, the NTSB recommends that PHMSA revise 49 CFR 195.452(h)(2), the "discovery of condition," to require, in cases where a determination about pipeline threats has not been obtained within 180 days following the date of inspection, that pipeline operators notify PHMSA and provide an expected date when adequate information will become available.

## 2.4  Deficiencies in the Integrity Management Program

The Enbridge crack management plan operated under the premise that defects in an aging pipeline with disbonded coating could be managed using a single in-line inspection technology and that prioritization of crack defects for excavation and remediation could be effectively managed through engineering assessments based strictly on the crack tool inspection data.

The program did not account for errors associated with in-line inspections and the interaction of multiple defects on a pipeline. The 51.6-inch-long crack-like feature that eventually led to the Line 6B rupture was one of six features that had been detected on the ruptured segment during an in-line inspection conducted by Enbridge's integrity management program in 2005. Non-detection and improper classification of the defect are inherent risks when relying solely on in-line inspection data to ensure the integrity of the pipeline, yet for nearly 5 years following the inspection, the integrity management program failed to identify the 51.6-inch crack feature located adjacent to the weld as a threat to the pipeline. The Enbridge integrity management program relied entirely on the 2005 USCD tool inspection data and the engineering assessment methods, which applied a lower margin of safety than was applied under the corrosion management program, and analyzed the pipeline integrity without accounting for tool inaccuracies, validating the reported wall thickness, or considering interacting threats. Had the Enbridge integrity management program included any of these aspects, the crack-like defect that eventually resulted in the ruptured pipeline segment in Marshall might have been identified and addressed.

## 2.4.1   Engineering Assessment of Cracks and Margin of Safety

Enbridge applied a lower margin of safety when assessing crack defects versus when assessing corrosion defects. The Enbridge integrity crack management group calculated the predicted failure pressure for each reported defect from data supplied following in-line inspections. From these calculations, Enbridge would select and prioritize pipeline segments for excavation.[114] To Enbridge, the excavation of a pipeline segment would expose the segment and would include a visual inspection and a nondestructive examination[115] for cracks (including SCC) and corrosion. The results from these field assessments were sent to the integrity crack management group and used to assess tool accuracy and to make decisions for repairing the defect.

All crack-like features that had a predicted failure pressure that was calculated to be less than the hydrostatic test pressure of the pipeline segment were scheduled to be excavated.[116] Hydrostatic test pressure is defined by 49 CFR 195.304 as a minimum pressure of 1.25 times the MOP of the pipeline. The Line 6B rupture segment had a MOP of 624 psig with a stated hydrostatic test pressure of 796 psig (or 1.28 times the MOP). By comparison, the corrosion defects on Line 6B were required to be excavated and remediated in accordance with 49 CFR 195.452(h)(4)(i)(B) when calculated predicted failure pressures were less than 1.39 times the MOP of the pipeline or SMYS (867 psig, the pressure that equates to a circumferential stress equivalent to the SMYS of the pipe). Therefore, the calculated margin of safety for a corrosion feature was 11 percent higher than that of a crack feature.

The use of a lower safety factor for crack defects is inconsistent with the growth rate assumptions used by the Enbridge crack management and corrosion management groups. The crack growth rate used in the engineering assessments of cracks is greater than the maximum corrosion growth rate assumption. Furthermore, Enbridge has stated that a greater range of possible errors is associated with crack tools and that a higher reliability exists with corrosion tools. However, neither of these factors was reflected in the lower safety margin used by Enbridge when assessing cracks than when assessing corrosion. A larger margin of safety would have resulted in a larger number of crack defects being eligible for excavation and examination.

## 2.4.2   In-line Inspection Tool Tolerances

To account for uncertainty in the depth sizing of crack features, the USCD tool has a stated tolerance of ±0.02 inch. However, Enbridge did not include this tolerance in its engineering assessment of the crack defects from the 2005 USCD in-line inspection report. Enbridge applied an engineering assessment method that used the maximum depth reported by the tool, without incorporating tool tolerance to predict a failure pressure on the pipeline. If this

---

[114] A reported depth greater than 40 percent of the wall thickness was another trigger that was used to select crack features for excavation. None of the crack-like defects identified on the rupture segment had a reported depth greater than 40 percent.

[115] Magnetic particle testing was performed for SCC, and a USWM tool was used to record remaining wall thickness.

[116] Five features were excluded with the comment "surface breaking lamination." Enbridge stated that experience had shown these features are mid-wall laminations with no surface-breaking component.

predicted failure pressure was lower than the hydrostatic test pressure, rather than excavate the crack, Enbridge requested that PII analyze the in-line inspection data again and refine the estimated crack depth or crack profile. This was the case for the 9.3-inch-long crack and deepest of the six features identified in 2005. The Enbridge method of engineering assessment used the tool-reported crack depths as actual without accounting for tool error. However, PII has stated that the tool tolerance should be incorporated in the reported crack depth. If tool tolerance is not accounted for during an engineering assessment, the size of some defects may be underestimated, resulting in a predicted failure pressure greater than the actual failure pressure. If the predicted failure pressure is greater than the hydrostatic test pressure, these defects may not get excavated and evaluated.

### 2.4.3 Improper Wall Thickness

Enbridge used the wall thickness reported by the 2005 USCD tool (0.285 inch) in its fitness-for-purpose failure pressure assessment and crack-growth calculations used to prepare the excavation list. The reported wall thickness from the USCD tool appeared in the in-line inspection report as a constant for the entire length of the ruptured segment. But, wall thickness can vary significantly along the length of a pipe, and while this value was within the specification tolerance for this pipe, Enbridge did not compare the value to the values reported by the 2004 USWM wall measurement tool. The 2005 USCD tool-reported wall thickness of 0.285 inch was 0.035 inch thicker than the nominal wall thickness of 0.25 inch. By using the tool-reported wall thickness instead of the nominal, Enbridge effectively added another 14 percent to the maximum allowable pressure rating for the pipeline segment. The Enbridge crack management program did not compare the tool-reported wall thickness in the 2004 in-line corrosion inspection, which measured local wall thickness, with the 2005 in-line crack-inspection reported wall thickness. Enbridge also did not apply a nominal wall thickness during the engineering assessment of the 2005 in-line inspection data.

### 2.4.4 Corrosion and Cracking Interactions

In 2005, Enbridge had no procedure that accounted for the interaction between corrosion and cracking and the potential influence on crack depth reporting. The USCD tool Enbridge used in 2005 measured the crack depth from the surface adjacent to the crack; therefore, if the pipe's wall was free of corrosion, then the estimated depth reported by the crack tool closely matched the actual crack depth. However, if corrosion had caused wall loss on the surface adjacent to the crack, then the crack depth measured by the tool was less than the actual depth of the crack relative to the original surface of the outer wall. The 2004 corrosion inspection results and the 2005 crack inspection results showed areas where cracks and corrosion overlapped in regions directly over the ruptured area.

Enbridge did not have a procedure to account for wall loss due to corrosion when it was evaluating the in-line inspection crack-tool-reported data and was preparing the excavation list. Considering interacting threats in addition to individual threats to pipeline integrity provides a more accurate assessment of potential hazards. The practice is also recognized in Federal regulations and industry guidance, which highlight the importance of integrating all available information in an integrity management program. According to API 1160, "The integration of information is a key component for managing system integrity." API 1160 further notes that it is important to integrate all available information from various sources in the decision-making process; in particular, an operator should compare the "coincident occurrence" of suspected high-risk conditions. Title 49 CFR 195.452(f)(3) states that one of the minimum requirements of an integrity management program is "an analysis that integrates all available information about the integrity of the entire pipeline and the consequences of a failure."

### 2.4.5  Crack Growth Rate Not Considered

Enbridge integrity management did not adequately address the effects of a corrosive environment on crack growth rates. In its 2005 USCD engineering assessment, the Enbridge crack management group used a fatigue crack growth model to predict the remaining life of the pipeline to ensure that in-line inspection intervals were selected at a frequency that allowed it to monitor crack growth. Enbridge did not calculate crack growth rates for other potential crack mechanisms (such as SCC or corrosion fatigue). In 2011, an Enbridge consultant conducted a systemwide threat assessment review to examine the pipeline integrity threats. The threat assessment used data from an existing Enbridge leak-report database, which contained data collected from 1984 to 2010. According to the threat assessment, the "environmentally assisted cracking mechanism that is most prevalent along Enbridge's liquid pipeline system is either near-neutral pH SCC or corrosion fatigue." Much of the information used to draw this conclusion was available to the Enbridge crack management group. However, until the time of the Marshall accident, Enbridge's crack management plan focused only on fatigue cracks. The growth rates of environmentally assisted cracks (such as corrosion fatigue cracks) can be an order of magnitude or more greater than nominal fatigue crack growth rates.[117] Because Enbridge did not include crack growth from corrosion fatigue in its analysis, some cracks in the pipeline could grow significantly faster than predicted under the Enbridge engineering assessment. Enbridge's crack management program and reinspection interval selection is inadequate because it fails to consider all potential crack growth mechanisms that are prevalent in its pipeline.

### 2.4.6  Need for Continuous Reassessment

The TSB's investigation of the 2007 rupture of Enbridge's Line 3 in Glenavon, Saskatchewan, identified limitations of in-line inspection tools and of the engineering assessment methods Enbridge used to evaluate pipeline safety based on the inspection reports. The Enbridge USCD tool inspection conducted in 2006 on Line 3 measured the depth of the defect that ultimately failed and reported it within a depth range of 12.5 to 25 percent of estimated wall thickness. Enbridge had conducted an engineering assessment of the crack defect and determined that the predicted failure pressure of the pipeline segment was greater than the hydrostatic test pressure; consequently, the feature was not excavated.

Enbridge changed its process, based on the findings in the 2007 TSB report, to include tool tolerances during an engineering assessment of Line 3. However, the changes implemented

---

[117] W. Chen, *Report on Achieving Maximum Crack Remediation Effect from Optimized Hydrotesting*, prepared by University of Alberta, Department of Chemical and Materials Engineering, Edmonton, Alberta, for the U.S. Department of Transportation, PHMSA, June 15, 2011.

on Line 3 because of the Glenavon accident were never applied retroactively to the 2005 in-line inspection data collected for Line 6B. The Enbridge integrity management program did not incorporate a process of continuous reassessment to all of its pipeline engineering assessments when it neglected to apply the revised crack assessment methods to Line 6B. API Standard 1160, titled "Managing System Integrity for Hazardous Liquid Pipelines," defines pipeline integrity risk assessment as a continuous process and risk analysis as a continuous reassessment process. The standard also states that any applicable information or experience "should be factored into the understanding of system risks."

## 2.4.7  Effect of Integrity Management Deficiencies

To examine the role that some of the deficiencies described above played in Enbridge not identifying the crack-like features as an integrity threat between 2005 and 2010, the NTSB conducted an engineering assessment of the six crack-like features identified in the 2005 in-line inspection of the ruptured segment. Variables such as tool tolerances, nominal wall thickness, and interaction of corrosion and cracking were evaluated, using Enbridge's analysis software and assumptions from 2005, to determine whether the 51.6-inch crack feature would have triggered an excavation of the ruptured segment. The results of the assessment showed any one of the variations used in the predicted failure pressure calculations would have resulted in a calculated failure pressure below the stated Enbridge criteria (that is, hydrostatic test pressure) and required that the rupture feature be placed on an excavation list.

In addition, the NTSB examined the impacts to the engineering assessment when the excavation criteria for cracks were equal to the excavation criteria for corrosion. The predicted failure pressure results of the Enbridge 2005 engineering assessment for the six crack-like features were compared against a threshold of 1.39 times the MOP. The findings show that the 51.6-inch-long crack-like defect that resulted in the rupture had a predicted failure pressure that was less than 1.39 times the MOP but greater than the hydrostatic test pressure.[118] Had Enbridge's crack management program used a margin of safety equivalent to the margin of safety used in the corrosion management program (1.39 times MOP), the crack-like feature that eventually grew to failure would have been identified for excavation.

Enbridge currently includes an allowance for tool tolerance, developed from field excavations, with the crack depth when it is analyzing crack features. By adding the tool tolerance to the crack depth, the crack depth estimates used in the analysis are increased and some uncertainty associated with the in-line inspection tool's sizing of the defects is mitigated. Enbridge now uses the lesser of either the nominal wall thickness or the remaining wall thickness reported in the USWM tool inspection report when performing engineering assessments of crack defects.

Since the accident, Enbridge has added an analysis of SCC to its process for analyzing crack growth in addition to its analysis for fatigue crack growth. However, Enbridge still does not consider corrosion fatigue in its analysis of crack growth. Because corrosion fatigue cracks

---

[118] Crack defects from in-line inspection reports had to have a predicted or calculated failure pressure of less than hydrostatic test pressure to be excavated in 2005.

can grow faster than SCC or fatigue cracks, Enbridge's current analysis of crack growth can still underestimate crack growth rates in areas of corrosion.

Therefore, the NTSB concludes that Enbridge's integrity management program was inadequate because it did not consider the following: a sufficient margin of safety, appropriate wall thickness, tool tolerances, use of a continuous reassessment approach to incorporate lessons learned, the effects of corrosion on crack depth sizing, and accelerated crack growth rates due to corrosion fatigue on corroded pipe with a failed coating.

The NTSB recommends that Enbridge revise its integrity management program to ensure the integrity of its hazardous liquid pipelines as follows: (1) implement, as part of the excavation selection process, a safety margin that conservatively takes into account the uncertainties associated with the sizing of crack defects from in-line inspections; (2) implement procedures that apply a continuous reassessment approach to immediately incorporate any new relevant information as it becomes available and reevaluate the integrity of all pipelines within the program; (3) develop and implement a methodology that includes local corrosion wall loss in addition to the crack depth when performing engineering assessments of crack defects coincident with areas of corrosion; and (4) develop and implement a corrosion fatigue model for pipelines under cyclic loading that estimates growth rates for cracks that coincide with areas of corrosion when determining reinspection intervals.

To ensure that the approach adopted by Enbridge under the integrity management program is consistent with PHMSA's regulations, as recommended in the above safety recommendation, the NTSB believes that it is prudent for the regulator to perform an inspection of the revised Enbridge integrity management program. Therefore, the NTSB recommends that PHMSA conduct a comprehensive inspection of Enbridge's integrity management program after it is revised in accordance with the above safety recommendation.

Typically, different tools, techniques, and vendors are involved in performing various in-line inspections of a pipeline to assess its integrity. The NTSB concludes that to improve pipeline safety, a uniform and systematic approach in evaluating data for various types of in-line inspection tools is necessary to determine the effect of the interaction of various threats to a pipeline. The Pipeline Research Council International has been involved in energy pipelines research programs since 1952; it also works with many trade associations such as the American Gas Association, the Interstate Natural Gas Association of America, and NACE International. The NTSB therefore recommends that the Pipeline Research Council International conduct a review of various in-line inspection tools and technologies—including, but not limited to, tool tolerance, the probability of detection, and the probability of identification—and provide a model with detailed step-by-step procedures to pipeline operators for evaluating the effect of interacting corrosion and crack threats on the integrity of pipelines.

It is NTSB's expectation that the safety recommendation to PHMSA to revise 49 CFR 195.452 would require all hazardous liquid pipeline operators to correct deficiencies in their integrity management programs. However, the NTSB recognizes the effort and the time required to make these revisions. The NTSB concludes that pipeline operators should not wait until PHMSA promulgates revisions to 49 CFR 195.452 before taking action to improve pipeline safety. Therefore, the NTSB recommends that PHMSA issue an advisory bulletin to all hazardous liquid and natural gas pipeline operators describing the circumstances of the accident in Marshall, Michigan—including the deficiencies observed in Enbridge's integrity management program—and ask them to take appropriate action to eliminate similar deficiencies.

## 2.5 Mischaracterization of the Crack Feature

According to PII, a "crack-like" characterization was indicative of a single linear crack whereas a "crack-field" characterization implied that the feature was made up of a cluster of small cracks typically associated with SCC. All six features identified on the ruptured segment, including the 51.6-inch-long feature that grew to failure, were initially characterized as "crack-field" features by the junior analyst; however, a supervisor changed the final report to read "crack-like" features. When PII identified a feature as a "crack-field," PII also reported the length of the longest individual crack within the cluster. Enbridge used a criterion of 2.5 inches for the longest crack as a trigger for excavation of "crack-field" defects.

After the Marshall accident, PII reexamined the in-line inspection data and determined that the features were misclassified. Based on this examination of the failure defect, the rupture feature would have had a longest indication[119] that measured 3.5 inches. Because this longest indication within the cluster was greater than the Enbridge excavation criteria for "crack-field" features, the 51.6-inch feature would likely have been excavated by Enbridge in 2005.

Therefore, the NTSB concludes that PII's analysis of the 2005 in-line inspection data for the Line 6B segment that ruptured mischaracterized crack defects, which resulted in Enbridge not evaluating them as crack-field defects.

## 2.6 Control Center

For over 17 hours, Enbridge control center staff directly involved with operating Line 6B did not recognize that the pipeline had ruptured. During this time, the control center staff believed that column separation was present in the pipeline and that the pipeline could and should be started. After 17 hours, the control center received a call from a gas utility technician stating that he had found oil on the ground.

The NTSB examined Enbridge's control center operations to understand how the staff failed to detect the rupture. The investigation found that the control center staff's errors—the protracted misinterpretation of the pipeline status and the two pipeline startups (each of which pumped additional crude oil into the environment and exacerbated the damage caused by the rupture)—were influenced by multiple factors. The investigation examined the Enbridge control center staff's team performance and training, preparedness to detect pipeline ruptures, and tolerance for procedural deviance.

---

[119] *Longest indication* refers to the longest crack within the cluster of cracks of a "crack-field" defect.

### 2.6.1  Team Performance

The control center staff involved in pipeline operations consisted of control center operators, terminal operators, MBS analysts, shift leads, and supervisors. Control center operators were given the authority to decide when to terminate pipeline product flow with input from the MBS analysts. That is, operators had the final authority to terminate flow without the fear of repercussion from the company. The control center operators were to use input from the MBS analysts, who were responsible for determining the validity of MBS alarms. When MBS alarms occurred, operators were to consult with MBS analysts and to inform shift leads. If shift leads needed assistance in making operating decisions, they consulted with and obtained approval from higher-level supervisors; an on-call supervisor was available outside of normal business hours. Shift leads were to oversee and facilitate the work of the control center operators.

During shift B, MBS alarms associated with the Line 6B rupture appeared on the operator's SCADA display. Operator B1 notified the MBS analyst, who determined that the alarms were due to column separation. The control center operator and the shift lead's subsequent actions regarding Line 6B were consistent with, and largely influenced by, the MBS analyst's determination of the cause of the MBS alarm and his characterization of the alarm as false. Later, when shift lead B2 discussed with the on-call supervisor the inability to merge the separated oil columns in Line 6B, the on-call supervisor deferred to MBS analyst B's explanation for the column separation and the analyst's suggestion that line pressure be increased to compensate for the inactive Niles PS. The on-call supervisor approved the shift lead's request to authorize starting up the line again.

The transcript of the conversations regarding the Line 6B second startup and the actions and decisions of those involved in operating Line 6B during the time of the accident reveal a control center team that performed ineffectively during the events of this accident. At the time of the accident, the MBS analyst became the de facto team leader because his conclusions provided an explanation for the Line 6B situation that affected the team's perceptions and actions regarding the line. More important, the MBS analyst provided more than an assessment of whether the alarm was valid—he proposed that the alarm was caused by column separation, and he proposed a solution (that is, starting up the line flow with greater pump power than previously had been used). The control center operator and shift lead eventually accepted the MBS analyst's proposed cause and course of action, despite the fact that the MBS analyst was not assigned a team leadership position. The control center operator, shift lead, and supervisor did not seek alternative explanations of the MBS alarm. Given the deference of the team to someone who had exceeded his area of responsibility by providing an explanation for the MBS alarm and a proposed solution, lack of effective team performance was evident. Therefore, the NTSB concludes that the ineffective performance of control center staff led them to misinterpret the rupture as a column separation, which led them to attempt two subsequent startups of the line.

The NTSB has investigated previous accidents in which breakdowns in team performance occurred. In these accidents, team leaders transferred their authority to subordinates who they believed possessed more expertise than they did in the circumstances they were encountering. During restricted visibility conditions at a Detroit airport, the captain of a transport aircraft deferred to his first officer's navigation on the ground.[120] The captain had just been cleared to return to flight operations and had completed his captain recertification process after an extended absence. The first officer unknowingly guided the aircraft onto an active runway. The airplane was then struck by an aircraft that was taking off.

In a recent marine accident,[121] a licensed deck officer (the third mate), who was new to the vessel and on his first watch, deferred the vessel navigation to the helmsman who did not have a mate's license and had been on the vessel for 17 months. The helmsman steered and navigated the vessel onto rocks, and the vessel grounded.

Similarly in the Marshall accident, the assigned leader of the team (the on-call supervisor) deferred his authority to the MBS analyst. The two individuals essentially reversed roles, as was seen in the two previously mentioned accidents.

The ineffective performance of the control center team in this accident is consistent with human factors research on team performance, which has shown that the quality of team performance is influenced by team structure and team leadership. In essence, the effectiveness of the team leader (that is, the person responsible for defining goals, organizing resources to maximize performance, and guiding individuals toward those goals) influences the effectiveness of the team. Further, team coordination in this accident had broken down as well, such that other team members failed to recognize that the MBS analyst had incorrectly interpreted the MBS alarm and consequently had proposed an improper solution to its real cause. In a 2007 study, researchers stated the following:

> ...coordination is the behavioral mechanism team members use to orchestrate their performance requirements. When coordination breakdowns occur, this can lead to errors, missed steps or procedures, and lost time.... For example, if one team member makes an error, this will likely translate to another team member error if it is not caught and corrected.[122]

In this accident, none of the control center team members involved in Line 6B operations recognized that the cause of the alarms was a rupture and that starting the line would only exacerbate, rather than correct, the underlying condition.

Human factors research also has shown that team effectiveness and performance levels are enhanced by team training.[123] Although Enbridge control center staff worked in teams, they

---

[120] *Northwest Airlines, Inc., Flights 1482 and 299, Runway Incursion and Collision, Detroit Metropolitan/Wayne County Airport, Romulus, Michigan, December 3, 1990,* Aviation Accident Report NTSB/AAR-91/05 (Washington, D.C.: National Transportation Safety Board, 1991).

[121] *Grounding of U.S. Passenger Vessel* Empress of the North, *Intersection of Lynn Canal and Icy Strait, Southeast Alaska, May 14, 2007,* Marine Accident Report NTSB/MAR-08/02 (Washington, D.C.: National Transportation Safety Board, 2008).

[122] K.A. Wilson and others, "Errors in the Heat of Battle: Taking a Closer Look at Shared Cognition Breakdowns Through Teamwork," *Human Factors*, vol. 49, no. 2 (2007), pp. 243–256.

[123] (a) E. Salas, N.J. Cooke, and M.A. Rosen, (2008) On Teams, Teamwork, and Team Performance: Discoveries and Developments," *Human Factors*, vol. 50, no. 3 (2008), pp. 540–547. (b) E. Salas, N.J. Cooke, and J.C. Gorman, "The Science of Team Performance: Progress And the Need for More . . .," *Human Factors*, vol. 52, no. 2 (2010), pp. 344–346. (c) C.R. Paris, E. Salas, and J.A. Cannon-Bowers, "Teamwork in Multi-Person Systems: A Review and Analysis," *Ergonomics*, vol. 43, no. 8 (2000), pp. 1052–1075.

were not trained to do so, and PHMSA's regulations did not require Enbridge to provide team training. Enbridge trained its operators primarily individually, providing them with the knowledge and the skills needed to operate the pipelines, using simulated operational scenarios with instructors playing the roles of other control center staff. Control center operators, MBS analysts, shift leads, and supervisors did not train together. Therefore, the NTSB concludes that Enbridge failed to train control center staff in team performance, thereby inadequately preparing the control center staff to perform effectively as a team when effective team performance was most needed.

Further, the ineffective team performance noted in this accident was similar to the inadequacies of the SCADA control center staff the NTSB noted in its investigation of the September 9, 2010, gas pipeline rupture and fire in San Bruno, California. In that accident, the NTSB found "that it was evident from the communications between the SCADA center staff, the dispatch center, and various other PG&E employees that the roles and responsibilities for dealing with such emergencies were poorly defined" and that "PG&E's response to the Line 132 break lacked a command structure with defined leadership and support responsibilities within the SCADA center."[124]

Given the team performance deficiencies noted in both the San Bruno and the Marshall accidents and the pivotal roles these deficiencies played in control center staff errors, there is a clear need for pipeline companies to address team performance in their operator training. In 14 CFR 121.404, the FAA requires airline pilots to be trained in team performance, which is referred to as crew resource management (CRM) in aviation, and provides guidance to airlines on developing, implementing, reinforcing, and assessing team performance (in the January 22, 2004, FAA Advisory Circular 120-51e, "Crew Resource Management Training"). Team training prepares people to work efficiently and effectively as members of a group. CRM in commercial aviation seeks to reduce human errors in the cockpit by improving interpersonal communications, leadership skills, and human decision-making. The essential elements of CRM training include the following:

- Learning to function as members of teams, not as a collection of technically competent individuals.

- Instructing how to behave in ways that foster crew effectiveness.

- Providing opportunities to practice the skills necessary to be effective team leaders and team followers.

- Training on effective team behaviors during normal, routine operations.

CRM programs have been developed in several transportation areas. For passenger flight operations, 14 CFR 121.419, 121.421, and 121.422, require pilots, flight attendants, and dispatchers to participate in CRM training. In marine transportation, the Coast Guard requires licensed mariners on internationally operating vessels to participate in bridge resource management (BRM) training. In railroad transportation, the Federal Railroad Administration has sponsored research to develop rail CRM programs. Additionally, there has been substantial

---

[124] NTSB/PAR-11/01, p. 98.

research on the effectiveness of CRM programs.[125] There have been considerable materials published on the objectives and basic curriculum of team training through CRM, and similar curricula is available in several transportation modes that prepare individuals in team practice sessions to work together as teams. Therefore, the NTSB recommends that PHMSA develop requirements for team training of control center staff involved in pipeline operations similar to those used in other transportation modes.

## 2.6.2 Training

Few of the Enbridge control center operators or shift leads who were involved in Line 6B operations had experienced a pipeline rupture before this accident. The majority of operators the NTSB interviewed indicated that their primary exposure to leaks occurred during regularly scheduled annual simulated exercises. Control center operators commented on the relative frequency of the column separations they had experienced, particularly in areas of changing elevation (not a factor in this accident) and at times during line startups and shutdowns (a factor in this accident). Moreover, some control center operators stated that MBS alarms sometimes occurred during transient conditions, such as pipeline startups or shutdowns, and often were explained by the MBS analysts as being related to pressure transmitter problems or column separations. API RP 1130 discusses control center operator complacency and leak detection credibility due to an increased frequency of leak detection alarms and stresses the importance of control center operator training on leak detection systems. Given the infrequency of actual ruptures and the relatively high frequency of MBS alarms encountered during line startups and shutdowns, it was natural for control center staff to assume the MBS alarms for Line 6B had been caused by column separation. Consequently, the MBS analysts' incorrect interpretation of the MBS alarms as resulting from column separation was readily accepted by operators, shift leads, and on-call supervisors without additional analysis. The evidence suggests that the control center staff's repeated experiences with MBS alarms caused by column separation rather than a rupture affected their ability to interpret the alarms correctly.

In accordance with PHMSA regulations, Enbridge control center operators were given extensive training in pipeline operations, which included regular testing of their knowledge and skills. After becoming operators, they were required to demonstrate continued operating knowledge and skills through triennial operator requalification. By contrast, shift leads, MBS analysts, and supervisors were not required to demonstrate continued proficiency. The transcript of control center conversation following the first startup revealed that the on-call supervisor did not have the knowledge and technical skills necessary to properly advise shift lead B2 and question MBS analyst B about pipeline operating matters. Although consistent with PHMSA requirements, Enbridge's practice of requiring only some of the decision-makers involved in pipeline operations to demonstrate their knowledge and skills through operator qualifications is counter to safe operating principles. Therefore, the NTSB concludes that Enbridge failed to ensure that all control center staff had adequate knowledge, skills, and abilities to recognize and

---

[125] For example, (a) E. Salas and others, "Does Crew Resource Management Training Work? An Update, an Extension, and Some Critical Needs," *Human Factors*, vol. 48, no. 2 (2006), pp. 392-412. (b) P. O'Connor and others, "Crew Resource Management Training Effectiveness: A Meta-Analysis and Some Critical Needs," *International Journal of Aviation Psychology*, vol. 184, no. 4. (2008), pp. 353-368.

address pipeline leaks, and their limited exposure to meaningful leak recognition training diminished their ability to correctly identify the cause of the MBS alarms.

Consequently, the NTSB recommends that Enbridge establish a program to train control center staff as teams, semiannually, in the recognition of and response to emergency and unexpected conditions that includes SCADA system indications and MBS software.

The NTSB is also concerned that other pipeline operating companies may have a similarly inconsistent standard for maintaining proficiency among all staff involved in pipeline operational decisions. Therefore, the NTSB recommends that PHMSA extend operator qualification requirements in 49 CFR Part 195 Subpart G to all hazardous liquid and gas transmission control center staff involved in pipeline operational decisions.

### 2.6.3  Procedures

Failure to use available leak indications, the use of incomplete procedures, and the influence of the MBS analyst were evident in an examination of shifts A and B during the accident. At the time of the shutdown, on July 25, operators A1 and A2 received a series of nearly simultaneous SCADA pressure-related alarms near the Marshall PS indicative of a rupture. These initial alarms were followed by a 5-minute MBS alarm (a severe leak alarm) 3 minutes later. The sudden drop in pressure at the Marshall PS, a SCADA alarm of a local shutdown of the Marshall PS, and the MBS alarm were all leak triggers identified under the *Leak Triggers from SCADA Data* procedure. The occurrence of one or two leak triggers mandated that the control center operator execute the *Suspected Leak Trigger* procedure requiring that a leak be ruled out within 10 minutes or the pipeline be shut down. Three or more leak triggers required that the control center operator shut down the pipeline immediately and the shift lead make emergency notifications.

However, due to the pressure transients generated at the time of the shutdown and rupture, many of the low-pressure alarms appeared multiple times and cleared shortly after alarming. In addition, the 5-minute MBS alarm cleared on its own as the pipeline flows approached zero following the shutdown.

Nonetheless, the Line 6B SCADA console display highlighted the low pressures at the Marshall PS that remained below minimum suction pressure and indicated an abnormal operating condition. Because the pressure alarms that initially appeared at the SCADA console had cleared, the control center operator attributed them to the shutdown. When MBS analyst A explained to operator A1 that the leak detection alarm was due to column separation at the Marshall PS, operator A1 assumed that the low pressure and remaining alarm indications were also symptoms of a column separation condition. The supervisor of the MBS group stated that it was commonly understood that leak detection alarms clear following a shutdown; however, this was not documented in either the control center procedure or the MBS analysts' procedure.

During the two startups on shift B, there were several SCADA indications of a leak, including zero pressure at the Marshall PS, the lack of pressure downstream of the Marshall PS when the line had been operated for 10 minutes, and the volume differences (between the amount of oil pumped into Line 6B and the amounts received at the delivery locations). Additionally repeated, active 5-minute, 20-minute, and 2-hour MBS alarms were received during the course of the two start attempts. Active MBS alarms were identified under the control center *Leak Triggers from SCADA Data* procedure; however, the inability to increase pressure downstream of the last PS and the excessive volume differences were not in that procedure. The *Suspected Column Separation* procedure required the control center operator to shut Line 6B down within 10 minutes, but because shift lead B1 decided to use an unapproved draft version of the *Starting Up Into Known Column Separation* procedure, the 10-minute limitation was exceeded.

During the shutdown on shift A and the startups on shift B, both MBS analysts had declared the presence of column separation in the pipeline, and, in both instances, the control center operators did not first examine elevation profiles on SCADA, historical SCADA trends of pressures and flows, or historical alarm logs to rule out a leak. Elevation profiles revealed that the Marshall area was not conducive to column separation, and historical alarm records showed that MBS alarms on Line 6B were rare. Adding to the confusion were control center procedures for MBS indications that were not fully integrated with the MBS procedures. The procedures were developed by different groups and used inconsistent language to describe MBS alarms and to explain how to determine whether the alarms were "valid" or "false." The inconsistent language contributed to confused roles and responsibilities when control center staff analyzed leak alarms. Although column separation and ruptures have similar SCADA indications, a rupture has far greater consequences. The Enbridge procedures did not ensure that leaks were ruled out first, under all circumstances.

Therefore, the NTSB concludes that the Enbridge control center and MBS procedures for leak detection alarms and identification did not fully address the potential for leaks during shutdown and startup, and Enbridge management did not prohibit control center staff from using unapproved procedures.

The MBS reported flow imbalances in the pipeline; to do so, the software relied on real-time SCADA pipeline pressures and flows to calculate these imbalances. Differences between the configuration of the MBS system and the actual pipeline result in either false MBS alarms or additional indications of column separation erroneously generated. To generate credible leak detection alarms, the MBS software and the SCADA system must use identical pipeline pressures and flows. MBS analyst B realized the actual pipeline configuration and pressures did not match that of the leak detection software during the first startup. The MBS analyst had to override the pressure values in the MBS software to represent the valve closure at the Niles PS. This action was completed about the time Line 6B was shut down following the first startup. The difference in pressure readings contributed to a reduced credibility of Enbridge's MBS alarms during the first startup because it resulted in additional column separation indications on Line 6B.

The MBS analyst on shift B informed the on-call supervisor, at the shift lead's request, that the MBS alarms following the first startup of Line 6B were "false alarms" because column separation was present in the pipeline. MBS analyst B based his characterization of the alarm on a known limitation of pressure transient leak detection models, which is that column separations can render the MBS unreliable and reduce the credibility of the leak detection alarms. The API recognizes that a CPM alarm is probably the most complex alarm that a control center operator will experience. To correctly recognize and respond to this type of alarm, the API believes that an operator needs specific training and appropriate reference material. MBS analyst B told NTSB investigators about this alarm's complexity; however, the analyst's actions on July 26 did not reflect a valid understanding of the alarm.

Therefore, the NTSB concludes that Enbridge's control center staff placed a greater emphasis on the MBS analyst's flawed interpretation of the leak detection system's alarms than it did on reliable indications of a leak, such as zero pressure, despite known limitations of the leak detection system.

In addition to the issues of credibility, Enbridge was confident that pipeline ruptures occurring in remote or difficult-to-access areas would have limited consequences because of its 10-minute restriction on continued pipeline operations in uncertain situations. According to Enbridge procedures, the pipeline would be shut down after 10 minutes if operational alarms remained unresolved. The control center staff, to some extent, and the Chicago regional manager believed that unintended product releases would be reported by outside sources (that is, either affected citizens or community officials). This belief was evident in the conversation between the shift lead and the Chicago regional manager during shift C. For example, at 10:16 a.m., on July 26, the Chicago regional manager said to shift lead C2, "… right now … I'm not convinced. We haven't had any phone calls. I mean, it's … perfect weather out here. Someone—if it's a rupture, someone's going to notice that, you know, and smell it." The visual confirmation of the leak did not occur until 11:17 a.m. on July 26. In the absence of that confirmation from a person located in Marshall, control center personnel discounted the possibility of a leak, largely because no external confirmation of a leak was present. Thus, the absence of information on a leak led to the belief that there was no leak, and that some other phenomenon, yet unrecognized, was causing the column separation.

Moreover, there was no evidence that any member of the control center staff sought to obtain information from anyone in the Marshall vicinity to verify the presence of a leak. Rather than actively soliciting information from sources in the Marshall area, the control center staff continued their erroneous decision-making by misinterpreting the absence of notifications from the Marshall community as actual information that there was no leak. In contrast, the first responders to the scene at Marshall, who were dispatched with knowledge of possible gas odors, actively sought information about a gas leak. Upon finding none, they believed that there was no leak, despite the fact that they detected but could not identify the type of strong odors present in the area. Their error of responding only to a gas leak and not considering other possibilities differs from the control center staff's error of using the lack of external notifications as support for a belief that Line 6B was experiencing a column separation.

Therefore, the NTSB concludes that Enbridge control center staff misinterpreted the absence of external notifications as evidence that Line 6B had not ruptured.

The combination of procedural gaps, the failure to use available leak indications, and the misinterpretation of the lack of external notifications added to the control center staff's inability to recognize the rupture. Therefore, the NTSB recommends that Enbridge incorporate changes to its leak detection processes to ensure that accurate leak detection coverage is maintained during transient operations, including pipeline shutdown, pipeline startup, and column separation.

## 2.6.4  Tolerance for Procedural Deviance

Before this accident, Enbridge managers were confident that any pipeline leak that occurred would have limited consequences because the company had restricted pipeline operations to no more than 10 minutes when MBS alarms could not be resolved. This restriction derived from the company's experience in the 1991 Grand Rapids, Minnesota, accident and its determination that even with a pipeline rupture, 10 minutes of operating time would limit the product flow to controllable amounts.

However, control center staff did not comply with the 10-minute restriction twice on July 26, as shown by the two startups. One Enbridge control center operator told NTSB investigators that staff had become accustomed to exceeding the 10-minute restriction. Because the MBS alarms often were attributed to column separation, an operator could attempt to pump additional oil into the pipeline to restore pressure and bring the columns together, even if the process exceeded 10 minutes.

Research into the Space Shuttle Challenger accident demonstrated that, in complex systems, technical personnel can allow a "culture of deviance" to develop.[126] A researcher observed in that accident that an early decision to continue shuttle operations in violation of requirements cultivated an operating culture in which not adhering to requirements became the norm. Decisions made thereafter made it easier for shuttle personnel to avoid adhering to other requirements, thus "normalizing" the deviation from technical requirements. Ultimately, a culture of deviance from technical requirements became the operating culture of shuttle personnel.

A similar culture of deviance appears to have developed in the Enbridge control center as control center operators, shift leads, and their supervisors believed that it was acceptable to not adhere to the 10-minute restriction when given the "right" circumstances. No system can operate safely when a culture of deviance from procedural adherence has become the norm, as the evidence suggests occurred in the Enbridge control center. Therefore, the NTSB concludes that although Enbridge had procedures that required a pipeline shutdown after 10 minutes of uncertain operational status, Enbridge control center staff had developed a culture that accepted not adhering to the procedures.

## 2.6.5  Alcohol and Drug Testing

Enbridge did not act in accordance with 49 CFR 199.225(2)(i), which places an 8-hour time limit on postaccident alcohol testing. Specifically, specimens for alcohol testing were collected for shifts A, B, and C on the morning of July 27 and about noon on July 28; however, the specimens should have been collected in accordance with PHMSA's regulation of 8 hours by the evening of July 26 following the confirmation of the pipeline rupture. Enbridge did not provide PHMSA with an explanation for its noncompliance, but a control center supervisor told NTSB investigators that the delay occurred because the rupture was not confirmed and because staff had left the control center after their duty assignment. The NTSB believes that Enbridge had

---

[126] D. Vaughan, *The Challenger Launch Decision: Risky Technology, Culture, and Deviance at NASA* (Chicago: The University of Chicago Press, 1996).

adequate knowledge of the rupture and time to collect the specimens. Further, the NTSB believes that Enbridge ignored key personnel for testing, such as MBS analysts and on-call supervisors, who played critical roles in the Line 6B operations during the accident. Enbridge's postaccident drug testing, however, was in accordance with PHMSA's regulation of 32 hours. The results of the drug tests were negative. Therefore, the NTSB concludes that insufficient information was available from the postaccident alcohol testing; however, the postaccident drug testing showed that use of illegal drugs was not a factor in the accident.

In its investigation of the 2010 San Bruno pipeline accident, the NTSB learned that PG&E did not conduct postaccident alcohol testing within the required time limit and failed to provide PHMSA with an explanation for its actions. As a result, the NTSB issued two recommendations to PHMSA. The first, Safety Recommendation P-11-12, urged PHMSA to amend 49 CFR 199.105 and 49 CFR 199.225 to eliminate operator discretion with regard to testing of covered employees. The revised regulation should require drug and alcohol testing of each employee whose performance either contributed to the accident or cannot be completely discounted as a contributing factor to the accident. The second, Safety Recommendation P-11-13, urged PHMSA to issue guidance to pipeline operating companies regarding postaccident alcohol and drug testing.

In an April 24, 2012, letter addressing PHMSA's actions in response to these safety recommendations, the NTSB stated that it understood that PHSMA was reviewing its legal authority and policy to clarify the regulatory language identified in 49 CFR 199.105(b) and 199.225(a)(1). After it completes its discussions with the U.S. Secretary of Transportation, PHSMA will clarify the regulations as needed. Pending receipt of PHSMA's intended course of action, Safety Recommendation P-11-12 was classified "Open—Acceptable Response." Because PHMSA issued Advisory Bulletin 2012-02 on February 23, 2012, which provided immediate guidance on the need for postaccident drug and alcohol testing and listed the employees covered by the rule, Safety Recommendation P-11-13 was classified "Closed—Acceptable Action." Because there is still pending action by PHMSA, no recommendation is required to correct Enbridge's deficiencies in alcohol and drug testing.

### 2.6.6 Work/Sleep/Wake History

The shift leads, MBS analysts, and operators involved in this accident normally worked 12-hour schedules that rotated between the day and the night shifts. That is, they worked 2 days followed by 3 nights, or 3 nights followed by 2 days, with on-duty periods beginning at either 8:00 a.m. or 8:00 p.m.[127] Procedures were in place to prevent someone from switching directly from one shift schedule to another without having at least 24 hours off duty. With such a schedule, staff were assured of 3 to 5 successive days off following completion of the fifth on-duty period. Operator A1 had worked 4 days in a row and was scheduled to work the night shift on July 26. The Line 6B operators, the MBS analyst, and the shift leads on duty during shift B had maintained a regular night schedule since at least July 23.

---

[127] These times are expressed in eastern daylight time for the report; 8:00 a.m. and 8:00 p.m. eastern daylight time are 6:00 a.m. and 6:00 p.m. local Edmonton time, respectively.

Thus, with the exception of MBS analyst A, who had been off duty the 4 days before the accident, all of the Line 6B control center operators, MBS analysts, and shift leads had maintained regular work schedules for at least the 2 days or nights prior to the accident. However, detailed information regarding their actual sleep and wake times, as well as non-work activities, was not available.

## 2.7  Pipeline Public Awareness

Firefighters were dispatched to investigate an outdoor odor in response to a 911 call received on the evening of July 25. The caller to 911 said that there was a strong odor of either natural gas or crude oil near the airport along 17 Mile Road. Firefighters searched the area with combustible gas indicators and examined nearby industrial business areas and two natural gas facilities on Division Drive. The firefighters were unfamiliar with the odors associated with crude oil and were unable to identify the source. Over the course of the 14 hours following the first call to report the outdoor odor, seven more calls to 911 reported strong natural gas or petroleum odors in the same area. The 911 operators repeatedly informed the callers that the fire department had been dispatched to investigate the issue, but the 911 operators did not contact the pipeline operator or advise the public of health and safety risks. The 911 operators never dispatched the fire department in response to the subsequent calls even though these calls occurred over several hours, indicating an ongoing problem. The actions of both the first responders and the 911 operators are consistent with a phenomenon known as confirmation bias,[128] in which decision makers search for evidence consistent with their theories or decisions, while discounting contradictory evidence. Although there was evidence available to the first responders that something other than natural gas was causing noticeable odors in the Marshall area, they discounted that evidence, largely because it contradicted their own findings of no natural gas in the area. Similarly, the 911 operators, with the evidence from the first responders of no natural gas in the area, discounted subsequent calls regarding the strong odors in the Marshall area. Those calls were inconsistent with their own views that the problem causing the odors was either nonexistent or had been resolved. Although Enbridge had provided training to emergency responders in the Marshall area in February 2010, the firefighters' actions showed a lack of awareness of the nearby crude oil pipeline: they did not search along the Line 6B right-of-way, and they did not call Enbridge. The NTSB concludes that had the firefighters discovered the ruptured segment of Line 6B and called Enbridge, the two startups of the pipeline might not have occurred and the additional volume might not have been pumped.

The NTSB reviewed Enbridge's PAP, which was intended to inform the affected public, emergency officials, and public officials about pipelines and facilitate their ability to recognize and respond to a pipeline rupture. Although RP 1162 requires operators to communicate with audiences every 1 to 3 years, Enbridge mailed its public awareness materials to all audiences annually. However, even with more frequent mailings, this accident showed that emergency officials and the public lacked actionable knowledge.

---

[128] R.S. Nickerson, "Confirmation Bias; A Ubiquitous Phenomenon in Many Guises," *Review of General Psychology*, vol. 2, no. 2, (1998), pp. 175-220.

Public knowledge of pipeline locations and the hazards associated with the materials transported is critical for successful recognition and reporting of releases, as well as the safe response to pipeline ruptures. The transportation of hazardous materials by pipeline is unlike hazardous materials transportation by railroad or highway because a pipeline is a permanent fixture. A pipeline presents a unique challenge to awareness because it is often buried. When pipeline releases occur, a properly educated public can be the first to recognize and report the emergency.

The NTSB found that Enbridge conducted annual informal assessments and participated in the PAPERS survey every 2 years. A review of the 2009 PAPERS survey responses showed that of those who responded only 23 percent of the affected public and 47 percent of emergency officials responded that they were "very well informed" about pipelines in their community. Although the Enbridge program plan stated that effectiveness reviews were to be conducted, no specific guidelines or measurements for the evaluations were defined. Enbridge's failure to have a process for using these survey results for improvements demonstrated a lack of commitment to improving the quality of its program. Therefore, the NTSB concludes that Enbridge's review of its PAP was ineffective in identifying and correcting deficiencies. The NTSB further concludes that had Enbridge operated an effective PAP, local emergency response agencies would have been better prepared to respond to early indications of the rupture and may have been able to locate the crude oil and notify Enbridge before control center staff tried to start the line.

In May 2011, Enbridge revised its public awareness plan and created a public awareness committee that includes a performance metrics subcommittee. According to the committee charter, the committee meets four times a year and is responsible for an annual review of the PAP and the program performance measures.

In July 2011, PHMSA conducted an audit of Enbridge's PAP. PHMSA identified several deficiencies in Enbridge's program evaluation and effectiveness reviews and required that Enbridge correct the deficiencies.

Although Enbridge and PHMSA have taken these actions, the NTSB is concerned that pipeline operators do not provide emergency officials with specific information about their pipeline systems. The brochures that Enbridge mailed did not identify its pipeline's location. Instead, the brochures directed the audiences to pipeline markers and to PHMSA's National Pipeline Mapping System. In the NTSB's 2011 report of the natural gas transmission pipeline rupture and fire in San Bruno, California, the NTSB made the following safety recommendation to PHMSA:

> Require operators of natural gas transmission and distribution pipelines and hazardous liquid pipelines to provide system-specific information about their pipeline systems to the emergency response agencies of the communities and jurisdictions in which those pipelines are located. This information should include pipe diameter, operating pressure, product transported, and potential impact radius. (P-11-8)

In its response letter to the NTSB, PHMSA stated that it had an emergency responder forum to identify pipeline emergencies for which emergency responders need to know how to adequately prepare and respond. This safety recommendation was classified "Open—Acceptable Response." Although PHMSA has held the emergency responder forum, no rulemaking has been initiated. Therefore, the NTSB reiterates Safety Recommendation P-11-8 to PHMSA. Because system-specific pipeline information is critical to the safe response to pipeline incidents, the NTSB is also concerned about the emergency officials' lack of awareness of Enbridge's pipeline. Therefore, the NTSB recommends that the International Association of Fire Chiefs and the National Emergency Number Association inform their members about the circumstances of the Marshall, Michigan, pipeline accident and urge their members to aggressively and diligently gather from pipeline operators system-specific information about the pipeline systems in their communities and jurisdictions.

## 2.8  Environmental Response

### 2.8.1  Effectiveness of the Emergency Response to this Accident

First responders' initial containment efforts and tactics proved ineffective in preventing substantial quantities of oil from spreading and traveling miles downstream of the rupture. Enbridge's first responders arrived on the scene just as oil was reaching the Kalamazoo River. Much of Enbridge's initial efforts were concerned with the placement of oil containment measures downriver of the advancing oil sheen. These oil containment measures were placed many miles from the release site; these measures could have been put to better use on Talmadge Creek, which was much closer to the release.[129] Minimizing the release of oil from the source area would have reduced both the exposure risk to citizens living downriver and the severity of the environmental pollution resulting from this accident. The large volume of oil that escaped the source area also contributed greatly to the estimated $767 million cleanup for this accident. Nearly 2 years after the accident, crews are still removing submerged oil and contaminated soils miles from the release site.

During interviews, first responders said that they were unaware of the scale of the oil release; this lack of knowledge contributed to their poor decision-making. The Enbridge crossing coordinator, whose crew of four individuals served as the entire team involved in Enbridge's first response effort, told NTSB investigators that the first action the crew took upon locating the pipeline rupture site was to travel about 0.25 mile north to the Division Drive crossing where fire trucks were stationed. The crossing coordinator saw a large amount of oil flowing on the water and decided to follow the creek downstream about 1 to 1 1/2 miles to find the point where there was no oil and to install first containment measures there. He said the crew saw a very light oil sheen beginning as they placed sorbent boom across the swiftly flowing stream in an attempt to funnel oil to a collection point for a vacuum truck. Describing his rationale for installing the sorbent boom downriver, he told NTSB investigators that the crew at that time had no idea how much oil was released or whether oil would ultimately discharge that far downstream, and he suggested that the sorbent booming was a token effort given the few responders that were available on scene and the response time for additional personnel.

---

[129] *Characteristics of Response Strategies: A Guide for Spill Response Planning in Marine Environments.*

About 1 hour after the crossing coordinator confirmed the oil spill, the first arriving PLM supervisor from Bay City, who acted as the interim Enbridge incident commander, also observed the thickly oiled creek at Division Drive. Although the supervisor was aware that the bulk of the oil was still upstream near the source area and he observed oil actively flowing through the unprotected culvert, he nonetheless focused all of his attention on placement of the majority of oil spill response resources about 8.9 miles downstream on the Kalamazoo River ahead of the discharge at Heritage Park.

The decision to ignore the pool of oil upstream of the Division Drive culvert in favor of placing containment measures much farther downstream demonstrates a lack of awareness and knowledge of the dynamics and consequences of major oil releases and the need for more training. Although the first responders did not have the NRC's estimate of the amount of released oil during the initial phase of the response, they observed heavy amounts of oil flowing through the culvert pipe. Rather than attempting to stop the oil at the culvert pipe, which was within 0.25 mile of the source, they decided instead to try to stop the oil at the leading edge of the spill downstream.

The first responders were not alone in failing to recognize better opportunities to contain the oil spill. The Federal, state, and local response personnel, and the Enbridge supervisors, who arrived later, observed heavy amounts of oil discharging into the creek, yet, building a more effective underflow containment dam near the source area was the last strategy attempted on the first day of the response. The Bay City PLM supervisor who acted as the interim Enbridge incident commander told NTSB investigators that under normal weather conditions, he would have ordered the Division Drive culvert pipe completely plugged with earth; however, he considered the flow of water to be too great to attempt this action. An underflow dam at the culvert pipe would have solved this problem by facilitating a continuous flow of water while at the same time retaining much of the oil.

Regardless of the recent rainfall, opportunities to reduce the downstream impact of the oil spill were missed. Even if the volume of oil released was unknown, a more effective approach to mitigating the effects of the oil spill with limited resources would have been to focus on containing the bulk of the oil as close to the point of release as possible.[130] As a primary response, attempting to contain the advancing oil sheen miles downstream of the pipeline rupture site— while enormous quantities of oil were flowing through culvert pipes near the source area—was not an effective strategy. According to Enbridge's facility response plan, source containment should have been the primary concern of first responders. An operating-and-maintenance procedure referenced in the plan states that an attempt must be made to confine the product as close to the release source as possible to prevent it from entering a major river.

During the 10 years prior to this accident, Enbridge had participated in 2 of the 26 government-initiated oil spill response drills (in 2003 and 2004) under the National Preparedness for Response Exercise Program. PHMSA also participated in these two drills. Although the program requires pipeline operators to participate in at least one

---

[130] *Region 5 Regional Contingency Plan/Area Contingency Plan*, Section 3.2 Discharge/Release Control (U.S. Environmental Protection Agency and U.S. Coast Guard, November 2009).

government-initiated drill within a 36-month period, PHMSA has not frequently conducted exercises even though it has committed to conducting not more than 20 unannounced government-initiated exercises annually. Key Enbridge personnel who participated as first responders during the Marshall accident had received training that focused on oil-boom deployment and boat-handling for responses in large rivers and creeks. The training did not sufficiently address techniques that are appropriate for wetland environments, high water, or small creeks with swift moving water.

Therefore, the NTSB concludes that although Enbridge quickly isolated the ruptured segment of Line 6B after receiving a telephone call about the release, Enbridge's emergency response actions during the initial hours following the release were not sufficiently focused on source control and demonstrated a lack of awareness and training in the use of effective containment methods.

Workers with spill response duties need to be adequately trained to deploy and operate equipment they will actually use in a response and must be able to demonstrate knowledge of procedures for mitigating or preventing an oil discharge.[131] Therefore, the NTSB recommends that Enbridge provide additional training to first responders to ensure that they (1) are aware of the best response practices and the potential consequences of oil releases and (2) receive practical training in the use of appropriate oil-containment and -recovery methods for all potential environmental conditions in the response zones.

Enbridge crews primarily deployed sorbent booms in the fast-flowing Talmadge Creek, which, according to industry and Federal guidance, is an ineffective method of containing oil except in stagnant waters. Sorbent booms are generally used for small spills or as a polishing technique to capture sheen escaping from skirted oil booms, not as a principal containment method for a large release. Had more effective containment measures been placed at strategic locations along Talmadge Creek—such as installing plywood sheet underflow dams over the seven culvert pipe stream crossings located between the release site and the Kalamazoo River—less oil might have entered the Kalamazoo River. NTSB investigators observed that the equipment used to construct underflow structures was not part of Enbridge's response equipment inventory. By chance, several pieces of surplus pipe and earth-moving equipment, which had been stored at the Marshall PLM shop for another purpose, were available for constructing an earthen underflow dam in the source area. Installing the first earthen underflow dam was a difficult and slow process that took all afternoon to complete. Nevertheless, first responders told NTSB investigators that using underflow dams was one of the major successes in the response to this accident.

Underflow dams constructed of plywood or other suitable material are easily and quickly installed over culvert pipe and would have been a more effective containment strategy to minimize the consequences of the release. The Bay City PLM supervisor recognized in retrospect that blocking the culvert pipes would likely have proven effective. An EPA training exercise held just 2 years earlier in Wood River, Nebraska, involved EPA personnel who

---

[131] *Training Reference for Oil Spill Response* (U.S. Department of Transportation, U.S. Environmental Protection Agency, U.S. Department of the Interior, joint publication, August, 1994).

observed the deployment of culvert underflow structures.[132] The NTSB postaccident photograph of the interior of the culvert pipe at Division Drive shows a thick black band of oil stain several inches thick about one-third the height of the pipe, which suggests that conditions would have been ideal to install an underflow dam at that location.

Although culvert pipe underflow dams are recognized as an effective method in these conditions, no emergency responders took the initiative to implement this method. Instead, crews attempted to contain oil in front of the culverts with skirted oil boom backed up with sorbent boom, even after creek water levels had returned to normal. By then, the water level was too shallow for skirted oil containment boom to be effective. The skirted oil booms that Enbridge had available on its spill response trailers are more suitable for open water response in slow flowing and deeper rivers and are less effective in small streams like Talmadge Creek.[133] Even the Enbridge facility response plan acknowledges that the use of booms is ineffective in fast current, shallow water, and steep bank environments. Nonetheless, Enbridge first responders were not provided with tools to construct underflow dams or with alternative oil containment methods appropriate for the environmental conditions that existed on the day of this accident.

Therefore, the NTSB concludes that had Enbridge implemented effective oil containment measures for fast-flowing waters, the amount of oil that reached Talmadge Creek and the Kalamazoo River could have been reduced.

Enbridge PLM supervisors stated that, as a result of this accident, they have recognized the value of having supplies on hand that are not necessarily immediately available elsewhere during an emergency. Such supplies might include corrugated metal pipe, plastic pipe, plywood, and stone for constructing underflow dams. The environment surrounding each segment of pipeline may present different challenges for containing oil in the event of an accident. A thorough assessment of potential oil release routes in conjunction with applicable best practices should help to identify equipment needs for those areas.

Therefore, the NTSB recommends that Enbridge review and update its oil pipeline emergency response procedures and equipment resources to ensure that appropriate containment equipment and methods are available to respond to all environments and at all locations along the pipeline to minimize the spread of oil from a pipeline rupture.

### 2.8.2 Facility Response Planning

A facility response plan is supposed to help the pipeline operator develop a response organization and ensure the availability of resources needed to respond to an oil release. The plan should also identify the response resources that are available in a timely manner, thereby reducing the severity and impact of the discharge.

---

[132] *Shallow Water Spill Containment and Boom Deployment Training (A Case Study), Platte River Whooping Crane Maintenance Trust, Wood River, Nebraska* (U.S. Environmental Protection Agency Region 7) August 27–28, 2008 <http://www.epa.gov/oem/docs/oil/fss/fss09/campbell.pdf>.

[133] *Oil Spill Response in Fast Moving Currents, a Field Guide* (Groton, Connecticut: U.S. Coast Guard Research and Development Center, October 2001.)

## 2.8.2.1 Regulatory Requirements for Facility Response Planning

Title 49 CFR 194.115 requires pipeline operators to identify response resources and ensure that, either by a contract or other approved means, these resources will be available to mitigate a worst-case discharge under the three-tier response criteria. The regulation stops short of providing specific guidance for the amount of resources that must arrive at the scene of a discharge. In its February 23, 2005, final rule on response plans for onshore transportation-related pipelines, PHMSA stated it does not believe that it is necessary to specify the amount of response resources; PHMSA allows operators to determine the amount and to demonstrate that sufficient response resources are provided for their facility response plans.[134] Consequently, pipeline operators are left with vague three-tier response criteria that allow them to subjectively define what resources are adequate and that provide no measure for regulators to evaluate the sufficiency of spill response planning.

Enbridge has chosen to interpret the Tier 1 requirement as meaning the company resources that are stationed at the local PLM facility, while Tier 2 refers to the company resources throughout the company's Chicago region. The amount of company-owned response resources provided in the facility response plan is not identified with any basis in capability to recover a particular quantity of discharge. According to Enbridge's interpretation of the regulation, its Tier 3 resources, which consisted of two contracted oil spill response organizations that are identified as Coast Guard-classified oil spill removal organizations[135] for response to a worst-case discharge, would not be deployed to the scene until 60 hours after a discharge. Other pipeline operators may have any number of different interpretations of what constitutes resources necessary to remove a worst-case discharge.

The current PHMSA facility response planning regulation allows operators to interpret the requirements, rendering it improbable that PHMSA would be able to perform an adequate review of facility response plans or enforce Federal requirements that pipeline operators identify and ensure that adequate response resources are available to respond to worst-case discharges. In contrast, regulatory requirements for oil spill response capability planning that are administered by the Coast Guard[136] and by the EPA[137] provide specific response capability standards. For instance, both the Coast Guard and EPA regulations provide a matrix for identifying necessary resources for facility response planning. These regulations require that resources identified in the response plan for meeting the applicable worst-case discharge planning volume must be located such that they can arrive on scene within the times specified for the applicable response planning tiers. Had the Enbridge pipeline facilities been subject to the EPA or Coast Guard regulations, the company would have been required to plan for an on-water recovery of a worst-case discharge by ensuring the availability of the resources shown in table 7.

---

[134] *Federal Register*, vol. 70, no. 35 (February 23, 2005), p. 8734.

[135] The Coast Guard created the voluntary oil spill removal organization classification program so that plan holders could list oil spill removal organizations in response plans in lieu of providing extensive detailed lists of response resources if the organization has been classified by the Coast Guard and its capacity has been determined to equal or exceed the response capability needed by the plan holder.

[136] Title 33 CFR Part 154, Appendix C.

[137] Title 40 CFR Part 112, Appendix E.

**Table 7.** Response resources for on-water recovery that Enbridge would have been required to identify in its facility response plan and have available by contract or other means, had its facilities been regulated by the Coast Guard or the EPA.

|                                                    | Tier 1      | Tier 2      | Tier 3      |
|----------------------------------------------------|-------------|-------------|-------------|
| Time                                               | 12 hours    | 36 hours    | 60 hours    |
| Effective daily recovery capacity (gallons/day)    | 78,750[a]   | 119,994     | 180,012     |

[a] For river and canal operating environments, Appendix C caps the Tier 1 response capability at 78,750 gallons per day.

To determine whether an operator has sufficient equipment capacity identified in its facility response plan to meet the applicable planning criteria listed in table 5, the Coast Guard and EPA regulations require operators to report oil recovery equipment by manufacturer, model, and effective daily recovery capacity.[138] Although pipeline facilities are not required to conduct any similar exercise to determine the capacity of their resources to recover oil, PHMSA references Coast Guard regulations at 33 CFR Part 154, Appendix C and other regulatory agency sources of nonmandatory guidance to assist operators in preparing response plans. No indication exists in the Enbridge response plan that the company utilized any such guidance. The NTSB concludes that PHMSA's regulatory requirements for response capability planning do not ensure a high level of preparedness equivalent to the more stringent requirements of the Coast Guard and the EPA.

When accidents occur, the risk of environmental damage can be greater for pipelines than for fixed facilities and shipping terminals because pipelines can travel for hundreds of miles and response resources may be required at locations that are difficult to predict and can be hard to reach. Nonetheless, the Oil Pollution Act of 1990 mandates an equivalent level of response for all facilities and vessels that handle oil and petroleum products: the capability to remove a worst-case discharge to the maximum extent practicable and to mitigate or prevent a substantial threat of a worst-case discharge. PHMSA's regulations for oil pipeline response planning are clearly inferior when compared to similar Coast Guard and EPA requirements.

The NTSB concludes that without specific Federal spill response preparedness standards, pipeline operators do not have response planning guidance for a worst-case discharge.

Because the current PHMSA regulation provides no assurance that oil pipeline operators will develop adequate facility response plans to provide for response to worst-case discharges, the NTSB recommends that PHMSA amend 49 CFR Part 194 to harmonize onshore oil pipeline response planning requirements with those of the Coast Guard and the EPA for facilities that handle and transport oil and petroleum products to ensure that pipeline operators have adequate resources available to respond to worst-case discharges.

---

[138] Coast Guard and EPA regulations provide a formula for calculating effective daily recovery capacity that considers potential limitations of oil recovery equipment due to available daylight, weather, sea state, and percentage of emulsified oil in the recovered material.

Until specific response planning requirements are included in 49 CFR Part 194, the NTSB recommends that PHMSA issue an advisory bulletin to notify pipeline operators (1) of the circumstances of the Marshall, Michigan, pipeline accident, and (2) of the need to identify deficiencies in facility response plans and to update these plans as necessary to conform with the nonmandatory guidance for determining and evaluating required response resources as provided in Appendix A of 49 CFR Part 194, "Guidelines for the Preparation of Response Plans."

## 2.8.2.2 Adequacy of Enbridge Facility Response Plan

Enbridge stated that it relied on company-owned resources for Tier 1 and Tier 2 responses. The facility response plan did not provide any description of the effective daily recovery capability of the response equipment in Enbridge's inventory, leaving a plan reviewer unable to determine whether the equipment was adequate for the job. Under both Coast Guard and EPA regulations, Enbridge would have been required to quantify its equipment recovery capacities to determine whether they were adequate against the three-tier planning criteria. It is doubtful that the recovery equipment identified in Enbridge's facility response plan would have been sufficient to satisfy the requirements of either the Tier 1 or the Tier 2 level of Coast Guard and EPA oil spill response regulations.

The EPA reported that Enbridge did not have adequate resources on site to deal with the magnitude of the spill and experienced significant difficulty locating necessary resources. The facility response plan identified two oil spill response organizations, but neither organization had the capability to respond to Marshall, Michigan, in a timely manner. More than 4 hours after it became aware of the oil release, Enbridge first contacted Bay West, which launched its resources to Marshall more than 5 hours after notification. Bay West finally arrived on scene on July 27, after a 10- to 11-hour drive. The other oil spill response organization, Garner Environmental Services, Inc. arrived on scene on July 29, 3 days after the spill was reported. By then, it was too late for either spill response contractor to mitigate the spread of the oil release.

The EPA also reported that available local contractors were not used until the EPA provided the contact information for local contractors who could respond quickly. Once on scene, the Bay City PLM supervisor spent considerable time calling local contractors not identified in the facility response plan. In addition, the facility response plan did not indicate that prior agreements were in place to ensure that contractors other than Bay West and Garner Environmental Services, Inc. had crews and equipment available during an emergency.

In accordance with 49 CFR 194.115(a),[139] pipeline operating companies and response contractors or organizations must have a contract or an agreement to identify and ensure the availability of specified personnel and equipment within stipulated response times for a specified geographic area. Enbridge should have been prepared with local resources on standby to respond to an accident because Bay West and Garner Environmental Services, Inc. had told Enbridge that they would be unable to respond quickly unless they could use local contractors. If the facility response plan had identified sufficient contractor resources near Marshall, Michigan, and these

---

[139] Title 49 CFR 194.115(a) states, "Each operator shall identify and ensure, by contract or other approved means, the resources necessary to remove, to the maximum extent practicable, a worst case discharge and to mitigate or prevent a substantial threat of a worst case discharge."

contractor resources had been under contract, the response to the oil spill would have been more timely and, therefore, more effective.

Further, the equipment identified by Enbridge's facility response plan was more suited to ideal weather conditions than to the river conditions that existed in this accident. No provisions existed for equipment to construct underflow dams, which were the most effective means of containment in this accident.[140]

In summary, the spill response was hampered by inadequate resources on site; lack of spill response organizations under contract near Marshall, Michigan; and use of spill response equipment that was not appropriate for the environment and weather conditions. These deficiencies were all a result of poor response planning.

PHMSA issued its June 23, 2010, facility response plan advisory bulletin to notify pipeline companies of the need to review and update their plans to ensure adequate resources are available to comply with emergency response requirements. Enbridge responded that, 5 days before the Marshall accident, it had concluded that its plan was complete and appropriate for responding to a worst-case discharge. However, Enbridge's actions following the discovery of the oil in Marshall revealed that the plan had not considered all possible operating environments and appropriate response methods. PHMSA stated that it plans to include a review of lessons learned when it reviews the Enbridge facility response plan due for renewal in 2015 or when Enbridge next amends its plan.

The NTSB concludes that the Enbridge facility response plan did not identify and ensure sufficient resources were available for the response to the pipeline release in this accident.

Therefore, the NTSB recommends that Enbridge update its facility response plan to identify adequate resources to respond to and mitigate a worst-case discharge for all weather conditions and for all its pipeline locations before the required resubmittal in 2015.

### 2.8.2.3 PHMSA Oversight of Facility Response Plans

PHMSA has a small staff to review and oversee facility response plans when compared to other agencies that review plans that are required under the Oil Pollution Act of 1990. PHMSA receives on average about two facility response plans per week to review for renewal.[141] PHMSA has 1.5 full-time employees managing about 450 response plans, which is far fewer than EPA Region 6, which has 27 employees and contractors reviewing 1,700 plans, or the Coast Guard Sector Boston, which assigns 7 or 8 inspectors and trainees to review 45 plans. Therefore, PHMSA has dedicated significantly fewer resources to facility response plan review as compared to other Federal agencies, which calls into question PHMSA's ability to conduct adequate assessments.

---

[140] As noted earlier, crews found surplus pipe and equipment and took the initiative to construct underflow dams, although too late, to contain much of the oil that was released.

[141] A Volpe draft report indicates that 450 pipeline facility response plans must be reviewed and renewed every 5 years. PHMSA's website at <http://phmsa.dot.gov/pipeline/initiatives/opa> reports that 1,500 facility response plans have been submitted to PHMSA.

Within 2 weeks of receiving the Enbridge facility response plan, PHMSA had approved it. With this short turnaround time, only a cursory review of the plan was likely conducted. Because no specific regulatory guidance exists to measure the adequacy of the plan for response capability, it could be approved only based on the judgment of PHMSA staff. The review of the Enbridge facility response plan included a company-submitted, 16-element self-assessment affirming the adequacy of the plan. PHMSA's environmental planning officer was assigned to review the questionnaire and the facility response plan to determine whether it met appropriate regulatory requirements. The environmental planning officer approved the plan without requiring supplemental information or citing any deficiencies in the plan.

Essentially, the regulations allow the pipeline industry to dictate the requirements of an adequate spill response and to determine whether those requirements have been met. The NTSB noted that there were no metrics for what was required within a tier and no such activities were identified in the plan. Further, neither the regulations nor the plan defined what constitutes "enough trained personnel."

PHMSA did not perform on-site audits to verify the content and adequacy of plans before approving them. In contrast, both the Coast Guard and the EPA conduct on-site audits and plan reviews after the initial review and approval of the submitted plan.

The NTSB concludes that if PHMSA had dedicated the resources necessary and conducted a thorough review of the Enbridge facility response plan, it would have disapproved the plan because it did not adequately provide for response to a worst-case discharge.

The Oil Spill Liability Trust Fund, create by Congress in 1986, is currently funded to $1 billion from sources such as the Barrel Tax,[142] transfers from other pollution funds, cost recoveries, and penalty collection. PHMSA and other Federal agencies receive annual appropriations to cover administrative, operational, personnel, enforcement, and research and development costs related to Oil Pollution Act activities. Such activities include regulation and enforcement of facility operations and response planning and cooperative relationships with oil industry stakeholders, which include periodic drills and implementation of changes to national and area contingency plans.

At the time of this accident, PHMSA received an $18.9 million appropriation annually[143] from the Oil Spill Liability Trust Fund for various expenses necessary to conduct the functions of its pipeline safety program, including the facility response planning preparedness program, which consists of 1.5 full-time positions. In 2008, PHMSA received about $1.5 million more from the fund than the EPA,[144] yet the EPA operates a significantly more robust facility response plan program that includes on-site audits and exercises.

---

[142] Section 405(a) of the Energy Improvement and Extension Act of 2008, Public Law 110-343, div. B, extended the per-barrel excise tax of $0.08 a barrel for petroleum products produced or imported into the United States through 2017.

[143] *Pipeline and Hazardous Materials Safety Administration Budget Estimates, Fiscal Year 2012*, p. 50.

[144] *Oil Spill Liability Trust Fund Annual Report Fiscal Year 2004–Fiscal Year 2008*, National Pollution Funds Center, U.S. Department of Homeland Security, U.S. Coast Guard.

Therefore, the NTSB recommends that the U.S. Secretary of Transportation audit PHMSA's onshore pipeline facility response plan program's business practices, including reviews of response plans and drill programs, and take appropriate action to correct deficiencies. The NTSB further recommends that the U.S. Secretary of Transportation allocate sufficient resources as necessary to ensure that PHMSA's onshore pipeline facility response plan program meets all of the requirements of the Oil Pollution Act of 1990.

## 2.9  Summary of Enbridge Organizational Deficiencies

To evaluate the role of Enbridge in this accident, the NTSB's investigation focused primarily on the Line 6B operations before, during, and after the rupture. During the investigation, major deficiencies of the company emerged, as discussed in previous sections of this report. These deficiencies led to the rupture, exacerbated its results, and then failed to mitigate its effects. These deficiencies include the following:

- Enbridge's integrity management program had numerous deficiencies that resulted in Enbridge not repairing a detected feature on a pipeline susceptible to corrosion and cracking because of its failed coating.

- Enbridge's PAP failed to effectively inform the affected public, which included citizens and emergency response agencies, about the location of its pipeline, of the key indicators of unintended product releases from the pipeline, and how to report suspected product releases.

- Despite the availability of the information necessary for a correct interpretation, Enbridge's control center staff misinterpreted the rupture and started the pipeline twice during the 17 hours it took to identify the rupture.

- Enbridge's postaccident response failed to either slow or stop the flow of the released oil into a major waterway.

Although these deficiencies involved different elements of Enbridge's operations, and may appear unrelated, taken together they suggest a systemic deficiency in the company's approach to safety. Each of the following identified deficiencies, either individually or together, played a part in the accident:

- Enbridge's response to past integrity management related accidents focused only on the proximate cause, without a systematic examination of company actions, policies, and procedures that may have been involved.

- An integrity management program that, in the absence of clear regulatory guidelines, consistently chose a less-than-conservative approach to pipeline safety margins for crack features.

- A period of rapid growth in control center activities and personnel occurred without an objective assessment of the safety implications of the growth.

- A leak-detection process that was prone to misinterpretation and differing expectations of control center analysts and operators.

Taken together, the evidence suggests that the Marshall accident was the result not of isolated deficiencies in the company's integrity management system, its control center oversight, its PAP, or its postaccident emergency response activities, but rather of an approach to safety that did not adequately address the combined risks. By focusing on only the immediate cause of each incident, the company failed to look for and to determine patterns or underlying factors. Some of the underlying factors in this accident began many years earlier and converged with more recent changes only at the time of rupture.

Enbridge became increasingly tolerant of the procedural violations designed to minimize the adverse consequences of a rupture. Finally, Enbridge's emergency response to this accident was ineffective because it failed to stop hundreds of thousands of gallons of oil from entering the Kalamazoo River.

Enbridge insufficiently assessed pipeline defects for excavation and remediation to prevent flaws from becoming cracks that resulted in a rupture, inadequately prepared its control center staff to identify the ruptured pipeline, and inadequately prepared communities adjacent to pipelines to contain leaks that occurred in the lines. Enbridge also inadequately prepared its first responders to contain a major spill.

Therefore, the NTSB concludes that Enbridge's failure to exercise effective oversight of pipeline integrity and control center operations, implement an effective PAP, and implement an adequate postaccident response were organizational failures that resulted in the accident and increased its severity.

Although Enbridge met PHMSA regulations in its pipeline operations, the evidence indicates that the company had multiple opportunities to identify and to address safety hazards before this accident occurred, but it failed to do so. Even the response to a safety culture assessment conducted following the Clearbrook, Minnesota, accident in 2007,[145] which resulted in the creation of the position of director of safety culture, was insufficient. This director was tasked only with examining field safety of pipeline operations. Although Enbridge had implemented what it referred to as a health and safety management system, the system only partially met the standards of an SMS. For example, it addressed only on-site safety, not pipeline operations. Control center errors were identified as employee-caused and were not considered system deficiencies, contrary to SMS guidelines. Had the company implemented and maintained a comprehensive SMS, it would have focused not only on field operations safety, but also would have incorporated control center operations, pipeline integrity management, and postaccident response plans and a comprehensive continuous examination of the safety of pipeline operations.

Enbridge's safety program focused on the welfare of individuals in the work environment, but it did not consider the safety of operational processes, such as control center operations and integrity management. Previous accidents in other industries and transportation modes have revealed this organizational deficiency—that is, instituting safety programs that

---

[145] *Enbridge Energy Partners, L.P. 34"-Line No. 3, Milepost 912; Clearwater County, Minnesota, November 28, 2007,* Accident Report, prepared by the Pipeline and Hazardous Materials Safety Administration, Office of Pipeline Safety, Central Region Office and the Minnesota Department of Public Safety, Fire Marshall's Office, Office of Pipeline Safety. The NTSB delegated this accident investigation; the pipeline accident number is DCA-08-FP-003.

address only personal safety, not operational system safety. For example, in its investigation of the March 23, 2005, explosion and fire in a chemical refinery, which killed 15 people and injured 80, the U.S. Chemical Safety and Hazard Investigation Board noted that British Petroleum had focused on the personal safety of employees and not on the process safety of its operations. The investigation report[146] stated, "As personal injury safety statistics improved, [British Petroleum] Group executives stated that they thought safety performance was headed in the right direction. At the same time, process safety performance continued to decline at Texas City."

Also, in its investigation of the June 22, 2009, collision of two Washington Metropolitan Area Transit Authority trains, where 9 people were killed and 52 injured, the NTSB observed a deficient organizational safety culture, stating in its report,[147] "The NTSB is concerned that [Washington Metropolitan Area Transit Authority] senior management may have placed too much emphasis on investigating events such as station and escalator injuries to the exclusion of passenger safety during transit."

In recent years, several transportation modes have implemented SMSs to enhance the safety of their operations, and the NTSB has consistently supported these activities. The NTSB has advocated the implementation of SMSs in transportation systems by elevating SMSs to its Most Wanted List. However, the NTSB has not called for an SMS in pipeline operations. This Marshall accident and the 2010 pipeline accident in San Bruno, California, indicate that SMSs are needed to enhance the safety of pipeline operations.

Both the San Bruno accident and the Marshall accident involved errors at the management and operator levels in both pipeline integrity and control center operations. The delays in recognizing and responding to the pipeline rupture and the deficiencies in control center team performance were prominent aspects of both accidents.

SMSs continuously identify, address, and monitor threats to the safety of company operations by doing the following:

- Proactively addressing safety issues before they become incidents or accidents.
- Documenting safety procedures and requiring strict adherence to the procedures by safety personnel.
- Treating operator errors as system deficiencies and not as reasons to punish and intimidate operators.
- Requiring senior company management to commit to operational safety.
- Identifying personnel responsible for safety initiatives and oversight.
- Implementing a nonpunitive method for employees to report safety hazards.

---

[146] *Refinery Fire and Explosion, BP, Texas City, Texas, March 23, 2005*, Report No. 2005-04-I-TX (Washington, D.C.: U.S. Chemical Safety and Hazard Investigation Board, 2007), p. 144.

[147] *Collision of Two Washington Metropolitan Area Transit Authority Metrorail Trains Near Fort Totten Station, Washington, D.C., June 22, 2009*, Railroad Accident Report NTSB/RAR-10/02 (Washington, D.C.: National Transportation Safety Board, 2010).

- Continuously identifying and addressing risks in all safety-critical aspects of operations.

- Providing safety assurance by regularly evaluating (or auditing) operations to identify and address risks.

The evidence from this accident and from the San Bruno accident indicates that company oversight of pipeline control center management and operator performance was deficient. In both cases, pipeline ruptures were inadequately identified and delays in identifying and responding to the leaks exacerbated the consequences of the initial pipeline ruptures.

Therefore, the NTSB concludes that pipeline safety would be enhanced if pipeline companies implemented SMSs.

The API facilitates the development and maintenance of national consensus standards for the petroleum and petrochemical industry, including liquid and gas pipelines. In 1990, the API published API RP 750, *Management of Process Hazards*, which is an SMS for the refining and chemical industries.

Because of the improvements to safety that accrue from the use of a comprehensive SMS, the NTSB recommends that the API facilitate the development of an SMS standard specific to the pipeline industry that is similar in scope to the API's RP 750, *Management of Process Hazards*. The development should follow established American National Standards Institute requirements for standard development.

# 3 Conclusions

## 3.1 Findings

1. The following were not factors in this accident: cathodic protection, microbial corrosion, internal corrosion, transportation-induced metal fatigue, third-party damage, and pipe manufacturing defects.

2. Insufficient information was available from the postaccident alcohol testing; however, the postaccident drug testing showed that use of illegal drugs was not a factor in the accident.

3. The Line 6B segment ruptured under normal operating pressure due to corrosion fatigue cracks that grew and coalesced from multiple stress corrosion cracks, which had initiated in areas of external corrosion beneath the disbonded polyethylene tape coating.

4. Title 49 *Code of Federal Regulations* (CFR) 195.452(h) does not provide clear requirements regarding when to repair and when to remediate pipeline defects and inadequately defines the requirements for assessing the effect on pipeline integrity when either crack defects or cracks and corrosion are simultaneously present in the pipeline.

5. The Pipeline and Hazardous Materials Safety Administration (PHMSA) failed to pursue findings from previous inspections and did not require Enbridge Incorporated (Enbridge) to excavate pipe segments with injurious crack defects.

6. Enbridge's delayed reporting of the "discovery of condition" by more than 460 days indicates that Enbridge's interpretation of the current regulation delayed the repair of the pipeline.

7. Enbridge's integrity management program was inadequate because it did not consider the following: a sufficient margin of safety, appropriate wall thickness, tool tolerances, use of a continuous reassessment approach to incorporate lessons learned, the effects of corrosion on crack depth sizing, and accelerated crack growth rates due to corrosion fatigue on corroded pipe with a failed coating.

8. To improve pipeline safety, a uniform and systematic approach in evaluating data for various types of in-line inspection tools is necessary to determine the effect of the interaction of various threats to a pipeline.

9. Pipeline operators should not wait until PHMSA promulgates revisions to 49 CFR 195.452 before taking action to improve pipeline safety.

10. PII Pipeline Solutions' analysis of the 2005 in-line inspection data for the Line 6B segment that ruptured mischaracterized crack defects, which resulted in Enbridge not evaluating them as crack-field defects.

11. The ineffective performance of control center staff led them to misinterpret the rupture as a column separation, which led them to attempt two subsequent startups of the line.

12. Enbridge failed to train control center staff in team performance, thereby inadequately preparing the control center staff to perform effectively as a team when effective team performance was most needed.

13. Enbridge failed to ensure that all control center staff had adequate knowledge, skills, and abilities to recognize and address pipeline leaks, and their limited exposure to meaningful leak recognition training diminished their ability to correctly identify the cause of the Material Balance System (MBS) alarms.

14. The Enbridge control center and MBS procedures for leak detection alarms and identification did not fully address the potential for leaks during shutdown and startup, and Enbridge management did not prohibit control center staff from using unapproved procedures.

15. Enbridge's control center staff placed a greater emphasis on the MBS analyst's flawed interpretation of the leak detection system's alarms than it did on reliable indications of a leak, such as zero pressure, despite known limitations of the leak detection system.

16. Enbridge control center staff misinterpreted the absence of external notifications as evidence that Line 6B had not ruptured.

17. Although Enbridge had procedures that required a pipeline shutdown after 10 minutes of uncertain operational status, Enbridge control center staff had developed a culture that accepted not adhering to the procedures.

18. Enbridge's review of its public awareness program was ineffective in identifying and correcting deficiencies.

19. Had Enbridge operated an effective public awareness program, local emergency response agencies would have been better prepared to respond to early indications of the rupture and may have been able to locate the crude oil and notify Enbridge before control center staff tried to start the line.

20. Had the firefighters discovered the ruptured segment of Line 6B and called Enbridge, the two startups of the pipeline might not have occurred and the additional volume might not have been pumped.

21. Although Enbridge quickly isolated the ruptured segment of Line 6B after receiving a telephone call about the release, Enbridge's emergency response actions during the initial hours following the release were not sufficiently focused on source control and demonstrated a lack of awareness and training in the use of effective containment methods.

22. Had Enbridge implemented effective oil containment measures for fast-flowing waters, the amount of oil that reached Talmadge Creek and the Kalamazoo River could have been reduced.

23. PHMSA's regulatory requirements for response capability planning do not ensure a high level of preparedness equivalent to the more stringent requirements of the U.S. Coast Guard and the U.S. Environmental Protection Agency.

24. Without specific Federal spill response preparedness standards, pipeline operators do not have response planning guidance for a worst-case discharge.

25. The Enbridge facility response plan did not identify and ensure sufficient resources were available for the response to the pipeline release in this accident.

26. If PHMSA had dedicated the resources necessary and conducted a thorough review of the Enbridge facility response plan, it would have disapproved the plan because it did not adequately provide for response to a worst-case discharge.

27. Enbridge's failure to exercise effective oversight of pipeline integrity and control center operations, implement an effective public awareness program, and implement an adequate postaccident response were organizational failures that resulted in the accident and increased its severity.

28. Pipeline safety would be enhanced if pipeline companies implemented safety management systems.

## 3.2  Probable Cause

The National Transportation Safety Board (NTSB) determines that the probable cause of the pipeline rupture was corrosion fatigue cracks that grew and coalesced from crack and corrosion defects under disbonded polyethylene tape coating, producing a substantial crude oil release that went undetected by the control center for over 17 hours. The rupture and prolonged release were made possible by pervasive organizational failures at Enbridge Incorporated (Enbridge) that included the following:

- Deficient integrity management procedures, which allowed well-documented crack defects in corroded areas to propagate until the pipeline failed.

- Inadequate training of control center personnel, which allowed the rupture to remain undetected for 17 hours and through two startups of the pipeline.

- Insufficient public awareness and education, which allowed the release to continue for nearly 14 hours after the first notification of an odor to local emergency response agencies.

Contributing to the accident was the Pipeline and Hazardous Materials Safety Administration's (PHMSA) weak regulation for assessing and repairing crack indications, as well as PHMSA's ineffective oversight of pipeline integrity management programs, control center procedures, and public awareness.

Contributing to the severity of the environmental consequences were (1) Enbridge's failure to identify and ensure the availability of well-trained emergency responders with sufficient response resources, (2) PHMSA's lack of regulatory guidance for pipeline facility response planning, and (3) PHMSA's limited oversight of pipeline emergency preparedness that led to the approval of a deficient facility response plan.

# 4 Recommendations

## 4.1 New Recommendations

**To the U.S. Secretary of Transportation:**

Audit the Pipeline and Hazardous Materials Safety Administration's onshore pipeline facility response plan program's business practices, including reviews of response plans and drill programs, and take appropriate action to correct deficiencies. (P-12-1)

Allocate sufficient resources as necessary to ensure that the Pipeline and Hazardous Materials Safety Administration's onshore pipeline facility response plan program meets all of the requirements of the Oil Pollution Act of 1990. (P-12-2)

**To the Pipeline and Hazardous Materials Safety Administration:**

Revise Title 49 *Code of Federal Regulations* 195.452 to clearly state (1) when an engineering assessment of crack defects, including environmentally assisted cracks, must be performed; (2) the acceptable methods for performing these engineering assessments, including the assessment of cracks coinciding with corrosion with a safety factor that considers the uncertainties associated with sizing of crack defects; (3) criteria for determining when a probable crack defect in a pipeline segment must be excavated and time limits for completing those excavations; (4) pressure restriction limits for crack defects that are not excavated by the required date; and (5) acceptable methods for determining crack growth for any cracks allowed to remain in the pipe, including growth caused by fatigue, corrosion fatigue, or stress corrosion cracking as applicable. (P-12-3)

Revise Title 49 *Code of Federal Regulations* 195.452(h)(2), the "discovery of condition," to require, in cases where a determination about pipeline threats has not been obtained within 180 days following the date of inspection, that pipeline operators notify the Pipeline and Hazardous Materials Safety Administration and provide an expected date when adequate information will become available. (P-12-4)

Conduct a comprehensive inspection of Enbridge Incorporated's integrity management program after it is revised in accordance with Safety Recommendation P-12-11. (P-12-5)

Issue an advisory bulletin to all hazardous liquid and natural gas pipeline operators describing the circumstances of the accident in Marshall, Michigan—including the deficiencies observed in Enbridge Incorporated's integrity management program—and ask them to take appropriate action to eliminate similar deficiencies. (P-12-6)

Develop requirements for team training of control center staff involved in pipeline operations similar to those used in other transportation modes. (P-12-7)

Extend operator qualification requirements in Title 49 *Code of Federal Regulations* Part 195 Subpart G to all hazardous liquid and gas transmission control center staff involved in pipeline operational decisions. (P-12-8)

Amend Title 49 *Code of Federal Regulations* Part 194 to harmonize onshore oil pipeline response planning requirements with those of the U.S. Coast Guard and the U.S. Environmental Protection Agency for facilities that handle and transport oil and petroleum products to ensure that pipeline operators have adequate resources available to respond to worst-case discharges. (P-12-9)

Issue an advisory bulletin to notify pipeline operators (1) of the circumstances of the Marshall, Michigan, pipeline accident, and (2) of the need to identify deficiencies in facility response plans and to update these plans as necessary to conform with the nonmandatory guidance for determining and evaluating required response resources as provided in Appendix A of Title 49 *Code of Federal Regulations* Part 194, "Guidelines for the Preparation of Response Plans." (P-12-10)

## To Enbridge Incorporated:

Revise your integrity management program to ensure the integrity of your hazardous liquid pipelines as follows: (1) implement, as part of the excavation selection process, a safety margin that conservatively takes into account the uncertainties associated with the sizing of crack defects from in-line inspections; (2) implement procedures that apply a continuous reassessment approach to immediately incorporate any new relevant information as it becomes available and reevaluate the integrity of all pipelines within the program; (3) develop and implement a methodology that includes local corrosion wall loss in addition to the crack depth when performing engineering assessments of crack defects coincident with areas of corrosion; and (4) develop and implement a corrosion fatigue model for pipelines under cyclic loading that estimates growth rates for cracks that coincide with areas of corrosion when determining reinspection intervals. (P-12-11)

Establish a program to train control center staff as teams, semiannually, in the recognition of and response to emergency and unexpected conditions that includes supervisory control and data acquisition system indications and Material Balance System software. (P-12-12)

Incorporate changes to your leak detection processes to ensure that accurate leak detection coverage is maintained during transient operations, including pipeline shutdown, pipeline startup, and column separation. (P-12-13)

Provide additional training to first responders to ensure that they (1) are aware of the best response practices and the potential consequences of oil releases and (2) receive practical training in the use of appropriate oil-containment and -recovery methods for all potential environmental conditions in the response zones. (P-12-14)

Review and update your oil pipeline emergency response procedures and equipment resources to ensure that appropriate containment equipment and methods are available to respond to all environments and at all locations along the pipeline to minimize the spread of oil from a pipeline rupture. (P-12-15)

Update your facility response plan to identify adequate resources to respond to and mitigate a worst-case discharge for all weather conditions and for all your pipeline locations before the required resubmittal in 2015. (P-12-16)

**To the American Petroleum Institute:**

Facilitate the development of a safety management system standard specific to the pipeline industry that is similar in scope to your Recommended Practice 750, *Management of Process Hazards*. The development should follow established American National Standards Institute requirements for standard development. (P-12-17)

**To the Pipeline Research Council International:**

Conduct a review of various in-line inspection tools and technologies—including, but not limited to, tool tolerance, the probability of detection, and the probability of identification—and provide a model with detailed step-by-step procedures to pipeline operators for evaluating the effect of interacting corrosion and crack threats on the integrity of pipelines. (P-12-18)

**To the International Association of Fire Chiefs and the National Emergency Number Association:**

Inform your members about the circumstances of the Marshall, Michigan, pipeline accident and urge your members to aggressively and diligently gather from pipeline operators system-specific information about the pipeline systems in their communities and jurisdictions. (P-12-19)

## 4.2  Reiterated Recommendation

As a result of this accident investigation, the National Transportation Safety Board reiterates the following previously issued safety recommendation:

Require operators of natural gas transmission and distribution pipelines and hazardous liquid pipelines to provide system-specific information about their pipeline systems to the emergency response agencies of the communities and jurisdictions in which those pipelines are located. This information should include pipe diameter, operating pressure, product transported, and potential impact radius. (P-11-8)

## BY THE NATIONAL TRANSPORTATION SAFETY BOARD

**DEBORAH A.P. HERSMAN**
Chairman

**ROBERT L. SUMWALT**
Member

**CHRISTOPHER A. HART**
Vice Chairman

**MARK R. ROSEKIND**
Member

**EARL F. WEENER**
Member

**Adopted: July 10, 2012**

# 5 Appendixes

## 5.1 Appendix A: Investigation

The National Response Center was notified about the Enbridge Incorporated (Enbridge) Line 6B rupture and release of crude oil in Marshall, Michigan, on July 26, 2010, at 1:33 p.m. The Pipeline and Hazardous Materials Safety Administration (PHMSA) notified the National Transportation Safety Board (NTSB) about the accident about 8:30 a.m., eastern daylight time, on July 27, 2010. The investigator-in-charge and other investigative team members were launched from the NTSB's Washington, D.C., headquarters office to Marshall, Michigan; another investigator was launched to the Enbridge control center in Edmonton, Alberta, Canada. Due to the severity of the accident, additional investigators were sent to Marshall from headquarters; another team member was launched from Jacksonville, Florida, to assist with the environmental response investigation. Chairman Deborah A.P. Hersman was the Board Member on scene. Investigative groups were formed to study integrity management, materials, control center operations, environmental response, emergency response, and human performance issues.

Parties to the investigation were PHMSA, Enbridge, PII Pipeline Solutions, and the U.S. Environmental Protection Agency.

## 5.2  Appendix B: Enbridge's MBS and Control Center Operations Procedures

*MBS Procedure for Examining MBS Alarms*

Enbridge Responses to IR No. 108
Page 2 of 17

1) Using the flow chart to respond to a 5-min MBS alarm related to column separation.

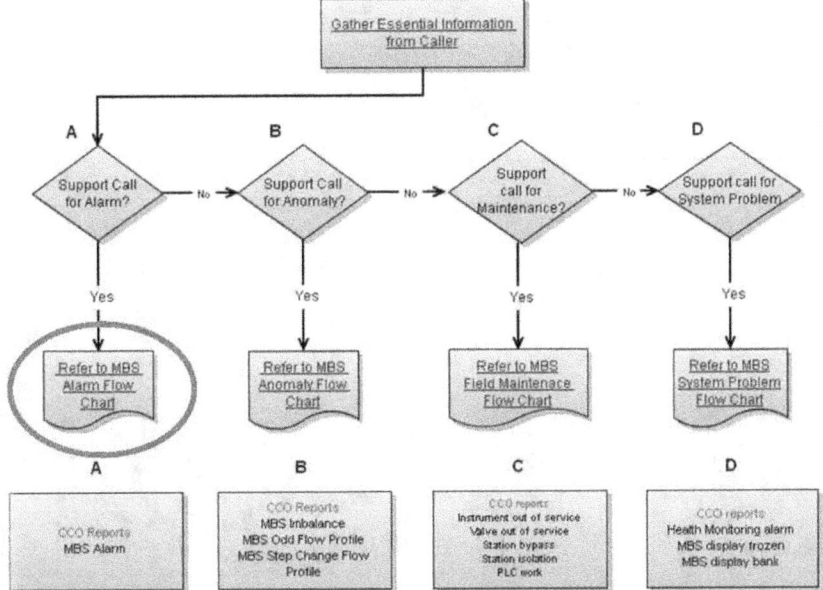

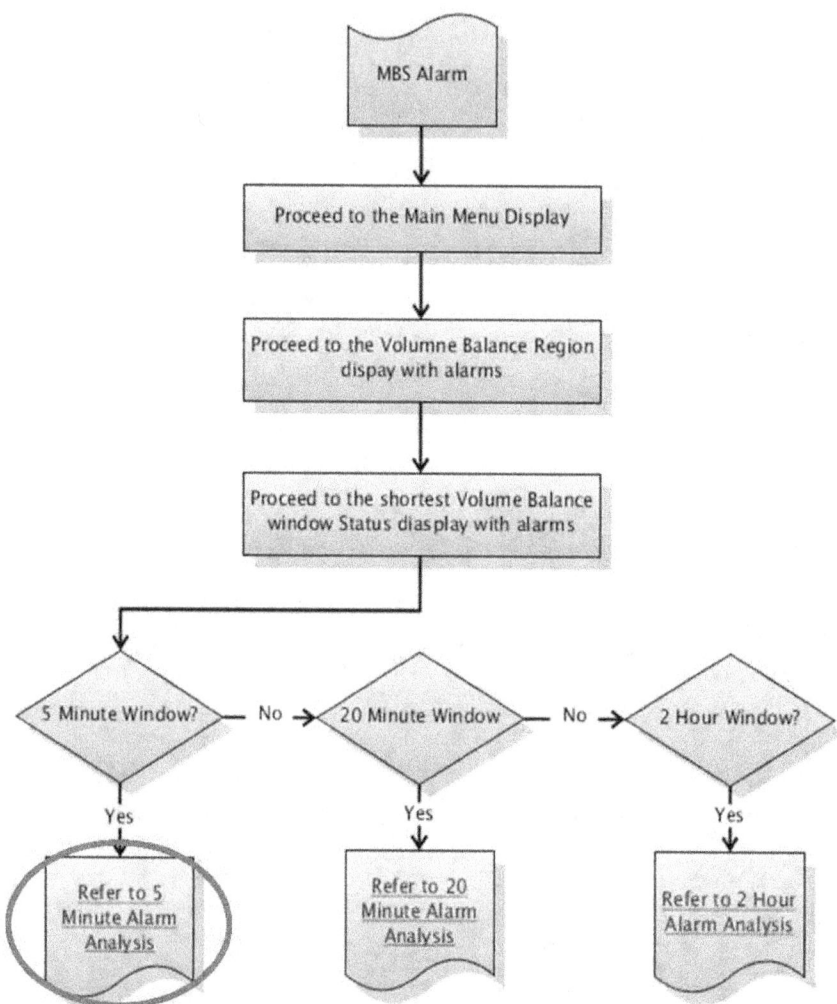

**Enbridge Responses to IR No. 108**
**Page 4 of 17**

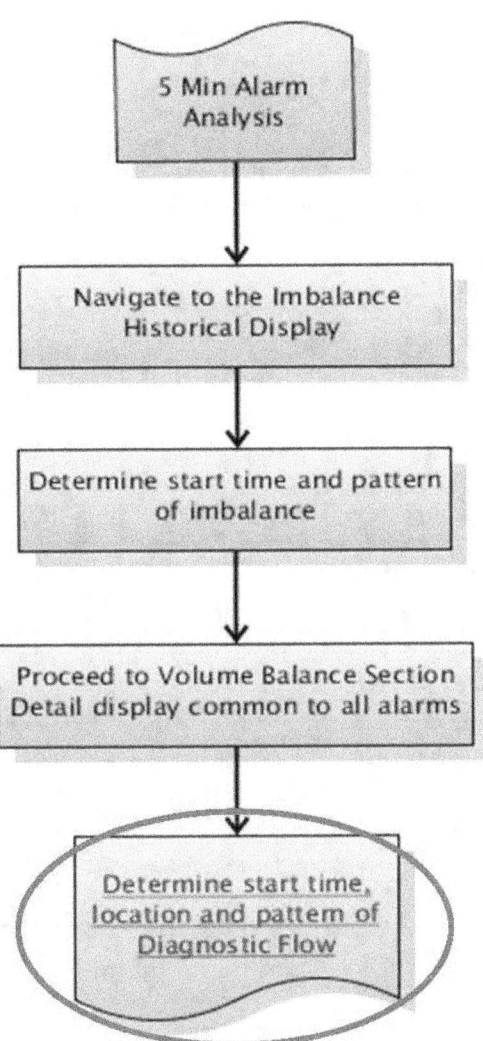

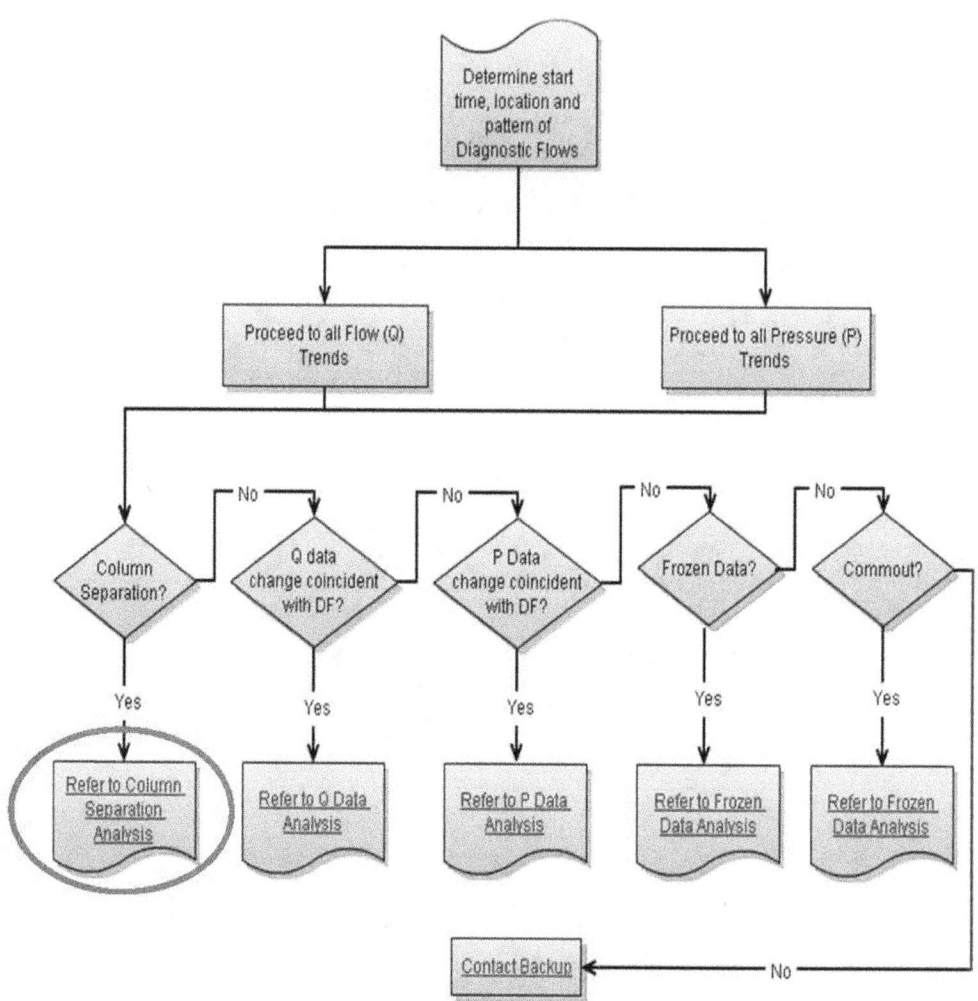

Final Step

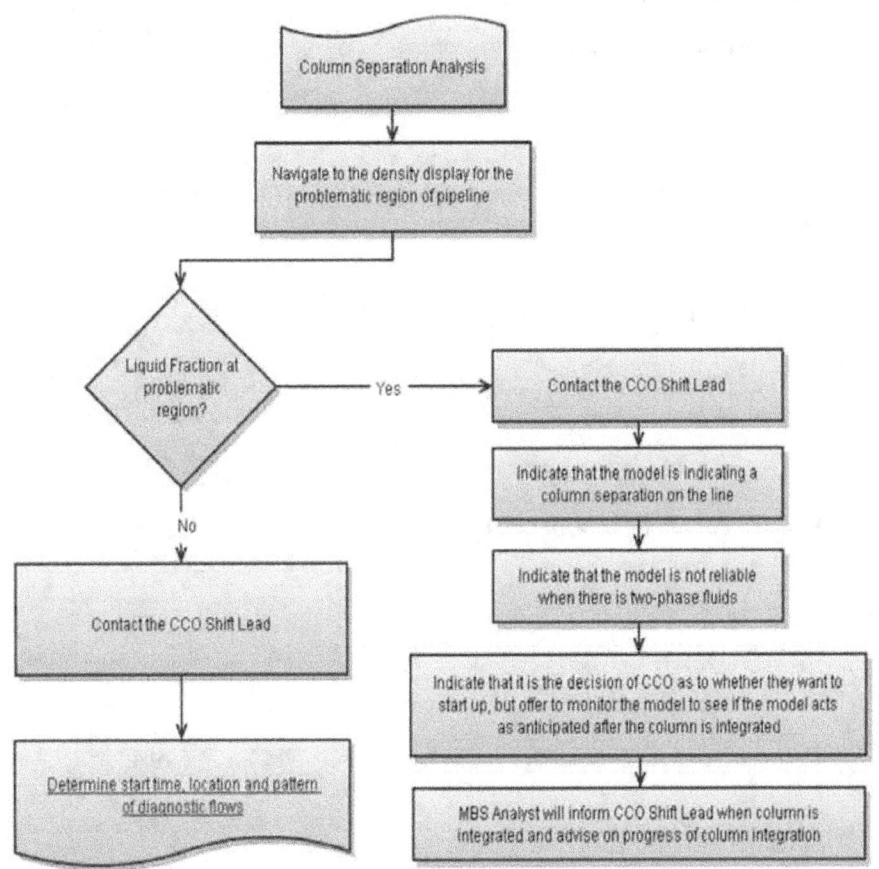

Control Center Procedure for *Suspected Column Separation*

**@DBTitle -**

Δ Emergency Procedures-1. Emergency Response - Pipeline

*e*ENBRIDGE

## k) Suspected Column Separation

In the event of a suspected column separation:

Pipeline Operator:

1. Notify Shift Lead

If a column separation is suspected from incoming SCADA data and the column cannot be restored within 10 minutes:

Pipeline Operator:

1. Notify Shift Lead

2. Shut down the specific line.

3. Sectionalize

4. Isolate

5. Execute the Abnormal Operations Condition Reporting procedure

Shift Lead:

1. Execute the Emergency Notification procedure

If field personnel locate a leak:

1. Initiate the Confirmed Leak - Field Personnel Verification procedure.

If field personnel do not locate a leak:

- permission to restart the line may be granted only by the Pipeline Control on-call designate

Related Topics:
Line 52 Suspected Column Separation

This document is valid only for the date shown: 12/14/2010

Control Center Procedure for *Column Separation–Draft Procedure Used on July 26, 2010*

## Main Topic

**Author:**   Melissa Marshall/CNPL/Enbridge      **Date Composed:**   05/03/2010 09:52 AM
**Subject:**   Suspected Column Separation
**Category:** Suspended Procedure Modification

**Originator:** Jason Ridley

**Justification/Reason for Change:** There are times where we have a suspected column separation and given the drained volume, cannot restore the column in 10 minutes, requiring an additional shutdown. These changes will bring our suspected column separation procedures in line with best practices.

**Reviewers:** CCO On-Shift Staff, Training, Technical Services, Engineering,

**Primary Approver:** CCO Management (Ian Melligan)

**Review Period:** 14 days

**Procedure Section and Name(s):** Section A, k) Suspected Column Separation

**Notes:**

- Formatted procedures have been placed in the Control Centre Operations Forum

Please provide feedback in the Control Centre Operations Forum by **May 17th.**

## k) Suspected Column Separation

In the event of a suspected column separation:

Pipeline Operator:

1. Notify Shift Lead.

If a column separation is suspected from incoming SCADA data and the column cannot be restored within 10 minutes:

Pipeline Operator:

1.  Notify Shift Lead.

2.  Shut down the specific line.

3.  Sectionalize☐.

4.  Isolate☐.

5.  Execute the Abnormal Operations Condition Reporting☐ procedure.

Shift Lead:

1.  Execute the Emergency Notification☐ procedure.

If field personnel locate a leak:
  - Initiate the Confirmed Leak - Field Personnel Verification procedure

If field personnel do not locate a leak:
  - permission to restart the line may be granted only by the Pipeline Control on-call designate

If a starting up into a known column separation:

Pipeline Operator:

1.  Notify Shift Lead

2.  Calculate the amount of volume drained (from CMT, tank levels, etc)

3.  Calculate a restoration time to restore the column separation (volume drained/ flow rate) = time

Shift Lead:

1.  Confirm calculated restoration time with Pipeline Operator

2.  Request Operator to start up the line into the column separation starting the 10 minute rule when the calculated restoration time expires.

If the column cannot be restored under the above conditions:
  - request operator to shutdown, sectionalize and isolate

3.  Execute the Emergency Notification☐ procedure.

Control Center Procedure for *MBS Leak Alarm*

@DBTitle -                                        <u>IR 63: EMERGENCY PROCEDURES</u>

A Emergency Procedures-1. Emergency Response - Pipeline

### c) MBS Leak Alarm

If a leak detection alarm occurs:

Pipeline Operator:

1. Notify Shift lead
2. Record AOC in FACMAN

Shift Lead:

1. Assess the alarm

If any of the following conditions occur:
- A 2 hour alarm is received by itself and not in conjunction with a 5 or 20 minute alarm.
- The green line on the alarm assessment screen remains below the red alarm line for 5 minutes
- The green line drops below the red line again anytime within 20 minutes of the initial alarm
- There is any doubt about the reliability of the model

1. Execute the MBS Alarm - Analysis by MBS Support procedure

If none of the above conditions occur:

1. Execute the MBS Alarm - Temporary Alarm procedure

Related Topics:
Abnormal Operations Reporting Requirements
MBS System Malfunction

This document is valid only for the date shown: 08/01/2010

Control Center Procedure for *MBS Leak Alarm–Analysis by MBS Support*

Δ Emergency Procedures-1. Emergency Response - Pipeline

*ENBRIDGE*

## MBS Leak Alarm - Analysis by MBS Support

If the Shift Lead determines that an MBS Alarm requires analysis by MBS Support:

- Notify MBS Support.

If after 10 minutes, an analysis of the alarm is not complete:

- Shut down the pipeline and standby for analysis.

If MBS Support advise the alarm is valid:

- Execute the MBS Valid Alarm⧉ procedure

If MBS Support advise the alarm is false:

- Execute the MBS Temporary Alarm⧉ procedure

This document is valid only for the date shown: 08/01/2010

Control Center Procedure for *MBS Leak Alarm–Temporary Alarm*

<u>IR 63: EMERGENCY PROCEDURES</u>

A. Emergency Procedures-1. Emergency Response - Pipeline

## MBS Leak Alarm - Temporary Alarm

If the Shift Lead or MBS Support determines that an MBS alarm is temporary:

Pipeline Operator:

1. Continue normal operations
   - No pipeline shutdown is required, or
   - If pipeline was shutdown, resume normal operations

Related Topics
☐ Abnormal Operations Reporting Requirements

This document is valid only for the date shown: 08/01/2010

Control Center Procedure for *MBS Leak Alarm–Valid Alarm*

A. Emergency Procedures-1. Emergency Response - Pipeline

### MBS Leak Alarm - Valid Alarm

If the MBS Support determines that the MBS alarm is valid:

Pipeline Operator:

1. Shut down the alarming pipeline
2. Sectionalize
3. Isolate

Shift Lead:

1. Request MBS support to provide the following information:
   - station to station estimate of the potential leak location
   - total imbalance
   - synopsis of pressure trends near the potential leak location

2. Contact the police.
   - For Norman Wells Pipeline, contact police if the emergency is within a 5 kilometre radius of Norman Wells, Tulita, Wrigley or Ft. Simpson.

3. Contact Regional/District Management and :
   - indicate that the line is shut down for a Material Balance System (MBS) alarm **only**
   - identify the potential leak location between the two identified adjacent stations

4. Contact the CCO Admin On-Call or Deisgnate

**Note:** Permission to restart the pipeline may only be granted by Control Centre Operations on-call designate in agreement with Regional Management

Related Topics
Abnormal Operations Reporting Requirements

This document is valid only for the date shown: 08/01/2010

Control Center Procedure for *Leak Triggers From SCADA Data*

A. Emergency Procedures-4. Incident Analysis

## Leak Triggers - From SCADA Data

Leak triggers are unexplained, abnormal operating conditions or events that indicate a leak:

From Pipeline SCADA Data:
### Upstream of Suspected Leak Site:
- sudden drop in upstream discharge pressure
- sudden change in upstream control valve throttling or pump speed
- one or more upstream units shut down (or lock out) in combination with a sudden drop in upstream discharge pressure and/or sudden change in upstream control valve throttling or percentage VFD control
- sudden increase in upstream flow rate

### Downstream of Suspected Leak Site:
- sudden drop in downstream suction pressure
- sudden change in downstream control valve throttling or pump speed
- one or more downstream units shut down (or lock out) in combination with a sudden drop in downstream suction pressure and/or sudden change in downstream control valve throttling or percentage VFD control
- sudden drop in holding pressure at a delivery location
- sudden decrease in downstream flow rate

From the Material Balance System (MBS):
- An MBS alarm is active

From Terminal SCADA Data:
### Injection Terminals
- sudden increase in flow rate
- sudden decrease in pressure
- one or more booster pumps shut down (or lock out) in combination with a sudden decrease in pressure

### Delivery/Landing Terminals
- sudden decrease in flow rate
- sudden decrease in pressure
- PCV closing

If **one or two** leak triggers occur, execute the Suspected Leak▯ procedure.
If **three or more** triggers occur, execute the Confirmed Leak▯ procedure.

Related Topics
▯MBS Leak Alarm
▯Abnormal Operations Condition Reporting Requirements

This document is valid only for the date shown: 08/01/2010

Control Center Procedure for *Suspected Leak–Pipeline–From SCADA Data*

### Suspected Leak - Pipeline - From SCADA Data

If a leak is suspected as a result of 1 or 2 leak triggers from SCADA data:

Pipeline Operator:

1. Notify Shift Lead

2. Establish the initial time of the anomaly from historical data.

   - In the event of 3 or more Leak Triggers, execute the Confirmed Leak - SCADA or CMT Data <Link> procedure

If a leak cannot be ruled out within 10 minutes or less from the initial time of the anomaly:

Pipeline Operator:

1. Shut down the specific line.

2. Sectionalize <Link>

3. Isolate <Link>

Shift Lead:

1. Continue investigation if necessary to confirm leak triggers.

2. Execute the Emergency Notification <Link> procedure

If field personnel locate a leak:

1. Execute the Confirmed Leak - Field Personnel Verification <Link> procedure.

If field personnel do not locate a leak:

   - permission to restart the pipeline may only be granted by Control Centre Operations on-call designate in agreement with Regional Management

Related Topics:
Leak Triggers
Abnormal Operations Reporting Requirements

Control Center Procedure for *Confirmed Leak–Pipeline–SCADA or CMT Data*

### Confirmed Leak - Pipeline - SCADA or CMT Data

In the event of a confirmed leak from SCADA or CMT data:

Pipeline Operator:

1. Immediately shut down the specific line using the Stop Line <Link> command

    - Notify Shift Lead

2. Sectionalize <Link>

3. Isolate <Link>

4. Execute the Abnormal Operations Condition Reporting <Link> procedure

Shift Lead:

1. Execute the Emergency Notification Procedure <Link>

2. Complete the Reported Incident Information Receiving Form.

Related Topics:
Leak Triggers

Control Center Procedure for *Abnormal Operating Conditions*

## a) Abnormal Operating Conditions

An Abnormal Operating Condition (AOC) is a condition that may indicate a malfunction of a component or deviation from normal operation that may:
- Indicate a condition exceeding design limits, or
- Result in a hazard(s) to persons, property or the environment

The following are identified as AOCs for Control Centre Operations. Additional conditions that could constitute an AOC according to the above definition must be reported to CCO Management.

**Pipeline Obstruction**
Obstruction Triggers – Pipeline  <Link>
Obstruction Triggers – Terminal  <Link>
Pipeline Obstruction  <Link>

**Station Lockout**
Station Lockout  <Link>

**Suspected Leak**
Suspected Leak - Pipeline - From SCADA Data  <Link>
Building Leak Detected  <Link>
Densitometer Trouble or Densitometer Leak  <Link>
Station Trouble (those that state "bldg leak")  <Link>
Leak Triggers - From CMT Data  <Link>
Leak Triggers - From SCADA Data  <Link>

**MBS Alarm**
MBS Alarm  <Link>
MBS System Malfunction  <Link>

**Suspected Column Separation**
Suspected Column Separation  <Link>

**Communications Failure**
Communications Failure – Pipeline  <Link>
Communications Failure – Terminal  <Link>

**SCADA Field Equipment Malfunction**
PLC Outage – Station  <Link>
PLC Failure  - Frozen Data  <Link>
Pressure Readback Outage – Station  <Link>

**Confirmed Leak**
Confirmed Leak - Pipeline - SCADA or CMT Data  <Link>

**Valve Malfunction**

Control Center Procedure for *Unknown Alarm or Non Defined Procedure to an Alarm*

- IR 6.1 CCO MANEUVERS

C. Maneuvers-3. Operating Standards

ENBRIDGE

## b) General Operating Standards - Unknown Alarm or Non-defined Procedure to an Alarm

In the event of an unknown SCADA alarm or a SCADA alarm without a defined procedure; Control Centre actions are based on alarm severity:

**S2 Informational:**
- No action required

**S4 Warning:**
- Discretionary Operator response to alarm dependant on operating conditions
- Notify the Shift Lead if unsure of response
- If multiple S4 alarms are active for a related issue, the response and severity may be raised
- FACMAN creation may be required
- Advise on-site/on-call personnel if required

**S6 Severe:**
- Notify Shift Lead
- Advise on-site/on-call personnel
- Create a FACMAN

**S8 Critical:**
- Notify Shift Lead
- Immediately notify on-site personnel
- Immediately call out field personnel if site is unmanned
- Create a FACMAN

Create a SCADA problem report for all unknown Control Centre alarms

This document is valid only for the date shown: 08/01/2010

Control Center Procedure for *Suspected Leak–Pipeline from CMT Volume Difference*

A. Emergency Procedures-1. Emergency Response - Pipeline

ENBRIDGE

## Suspected Leak - Pipeline - From CMT Volume Difference

In the event of a Leak Trigger☐ from the Commodity Movement Tracking (CMT) linefill report:

- Verify that the volumes at both the pumping and receiving stations are correct.

If the volumes are correct and exceed the Volume Balance Threshold☐ for the pipeline:

1. Initiate a 10 minute volume check at both the pumping and receiving stations.

2. Analyze PCS historical data
    - Verify that the negative volume imbalance was accompanied by a corresponding increase in pipeline pressures

3. Compare the volumes from the 10 minute volume check

If the difference between the pumped volume and the landed volume from the 10 minute volume check is more than 10%, or if the negative volume imbalance was not accompanied by a corresponding increase in pipeline pressures:

- Execute the Confirmed Leak - Pipeline - SCADA or CMT Data☐ procedure.

Related Topic:
☐Abnormal Operations Condition Reporting Requirements

This document is valid only for the date shown: 08/01/2010

Control Center Procedure for *Leak and Obstruction Triggers–On Pipeline Startup from SCADA Data*

A. Emergency Procedures-4. Incident Analysis

## Leak and Obstruction Triggers - On Pipeline Startup - From SCADA Data

In addition to other Leak Triggers and Obstruction Triggers on a flowing pipeline, the following trigg

In the event that pressure changes do not propagate throughout a pipeline segment within the expected Wave Travel Time:

If the event is accompanied by an unexplained, abnormal increase in pressure:

- execute the Suspected Pipeline Obstruction procedure

If the pipeline was shut down with sufficient pressure to maintain Minimum Holding Pressure in the pipeline segment:

- execute the Confirmed Leak procedure

If the pipeline was shut down with insufficient pressure to maintain Minimum Holding Pressure in the pipeline segment:

- execute the Suspected Column Separation procedure

Related Topic:

*Sample Estimated Wave Travel Time (Miles):*

| Segment Length (mi) | Wave Travel Time |
|---|---|
| 30 | 45 sec |
| 40 | 1 minute |
| 60 | 90 sec |
| 80 | 2 minutes |

*Sample Estimated Wave Travel Time (Kilometers):*

| Segment Length (km) | Wave Travel Time |
|---|---|
| 40 | 40 sec |
| 60 | 1 minute |
| 100 | 100 sec |
| 300 | 5 minutes |

This document is valid only for the date shown: 08/01/2010

## 5.3   Appendix C: Supervisory Control and Data Acquisition Plots

SCADA Discharge Pressure Recorded at the Time of Rupture

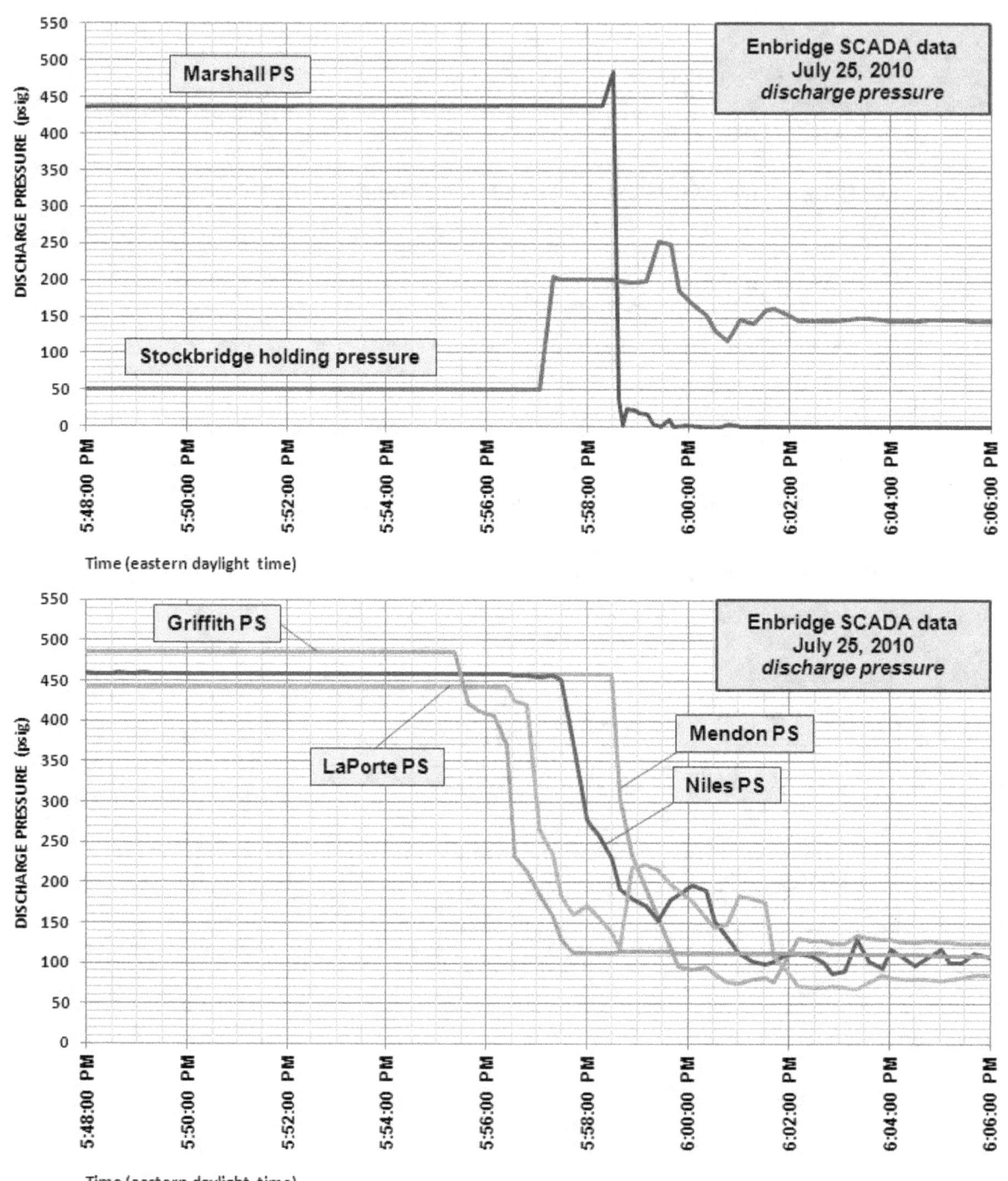

SCADA Suction Pressure Recorded at the Time of Rupture

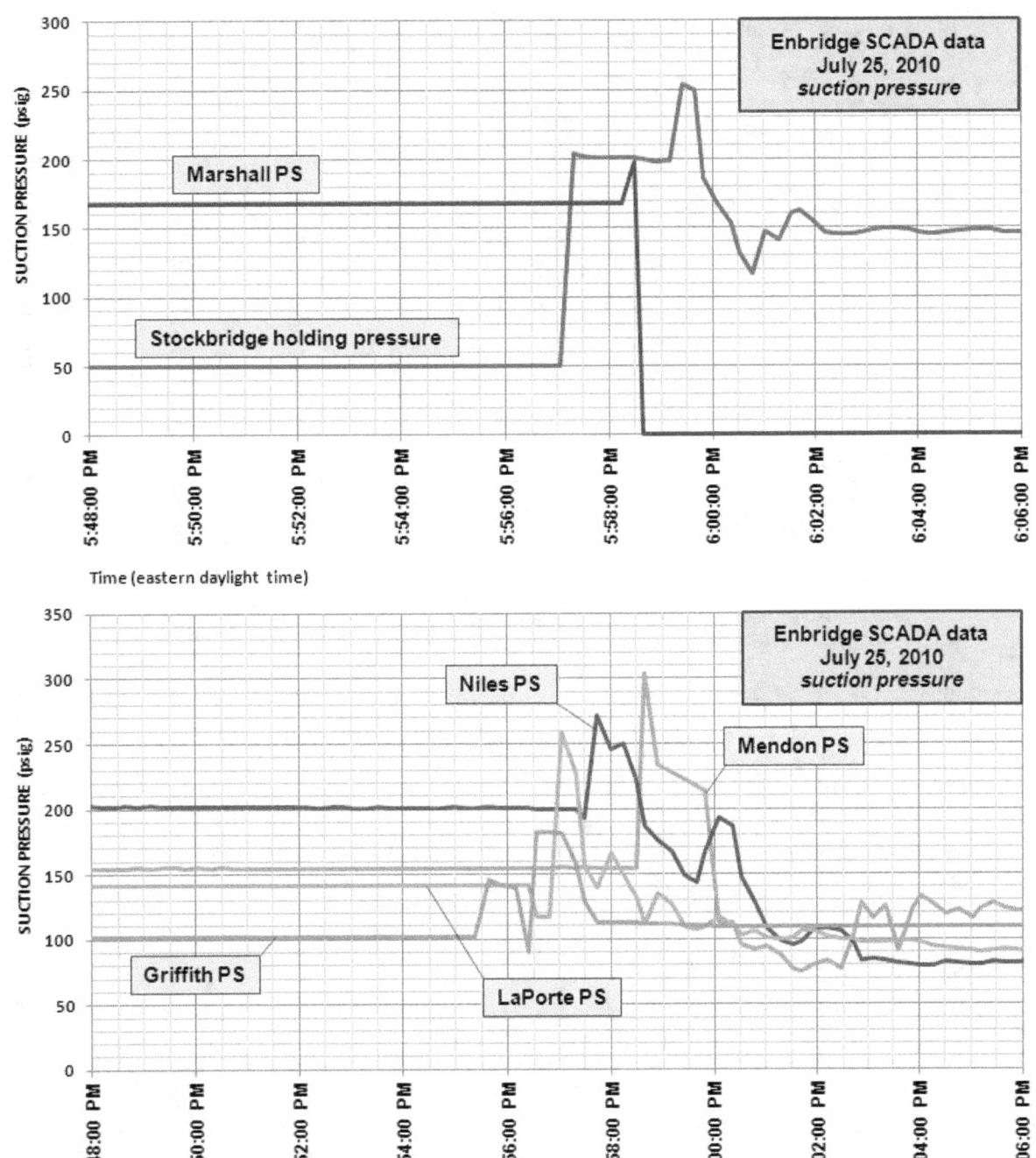

SCADA Pressure and Volumes Pumped—Startup One

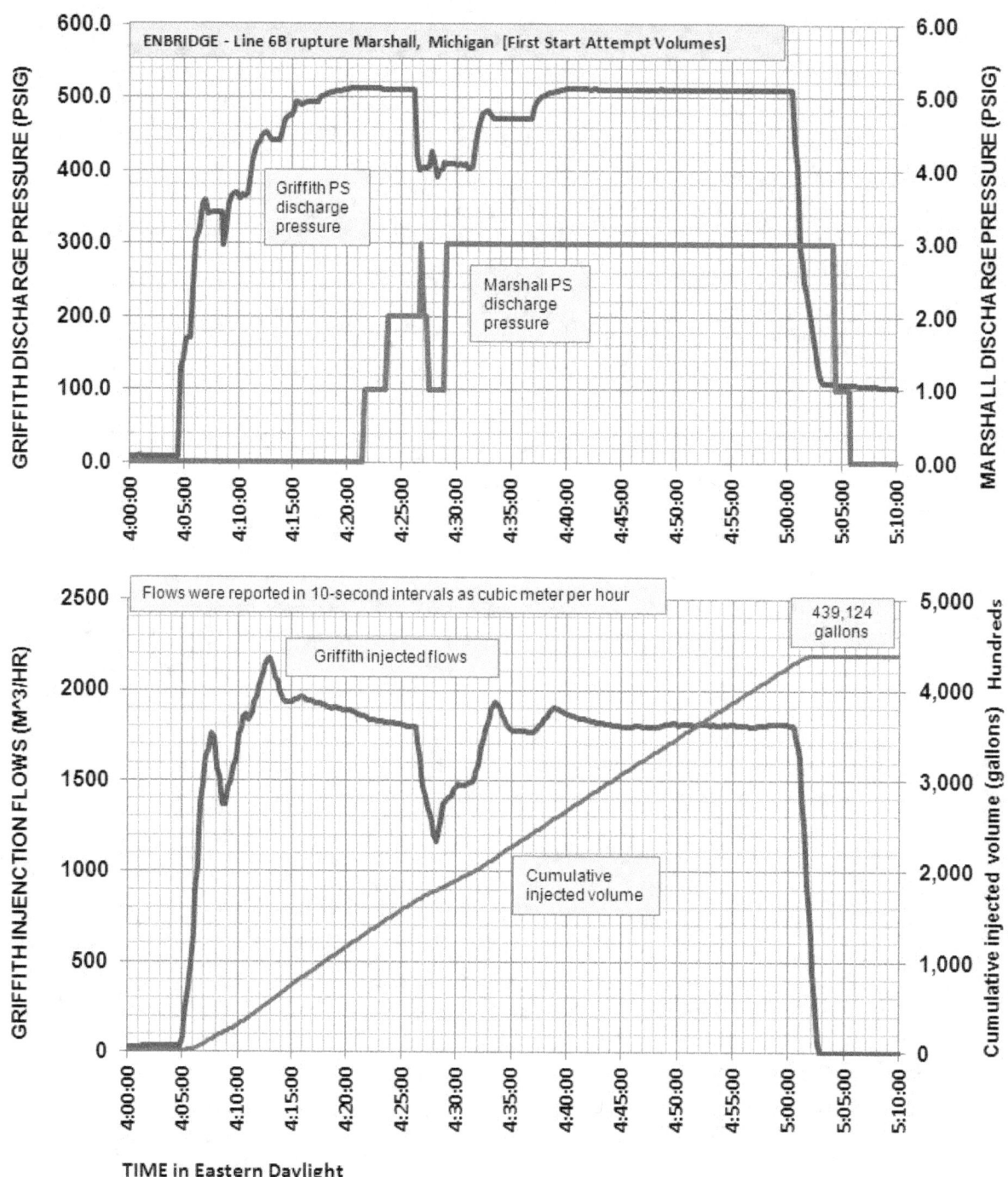

SCADA Pressure and Volumes Pumped—Startup Two

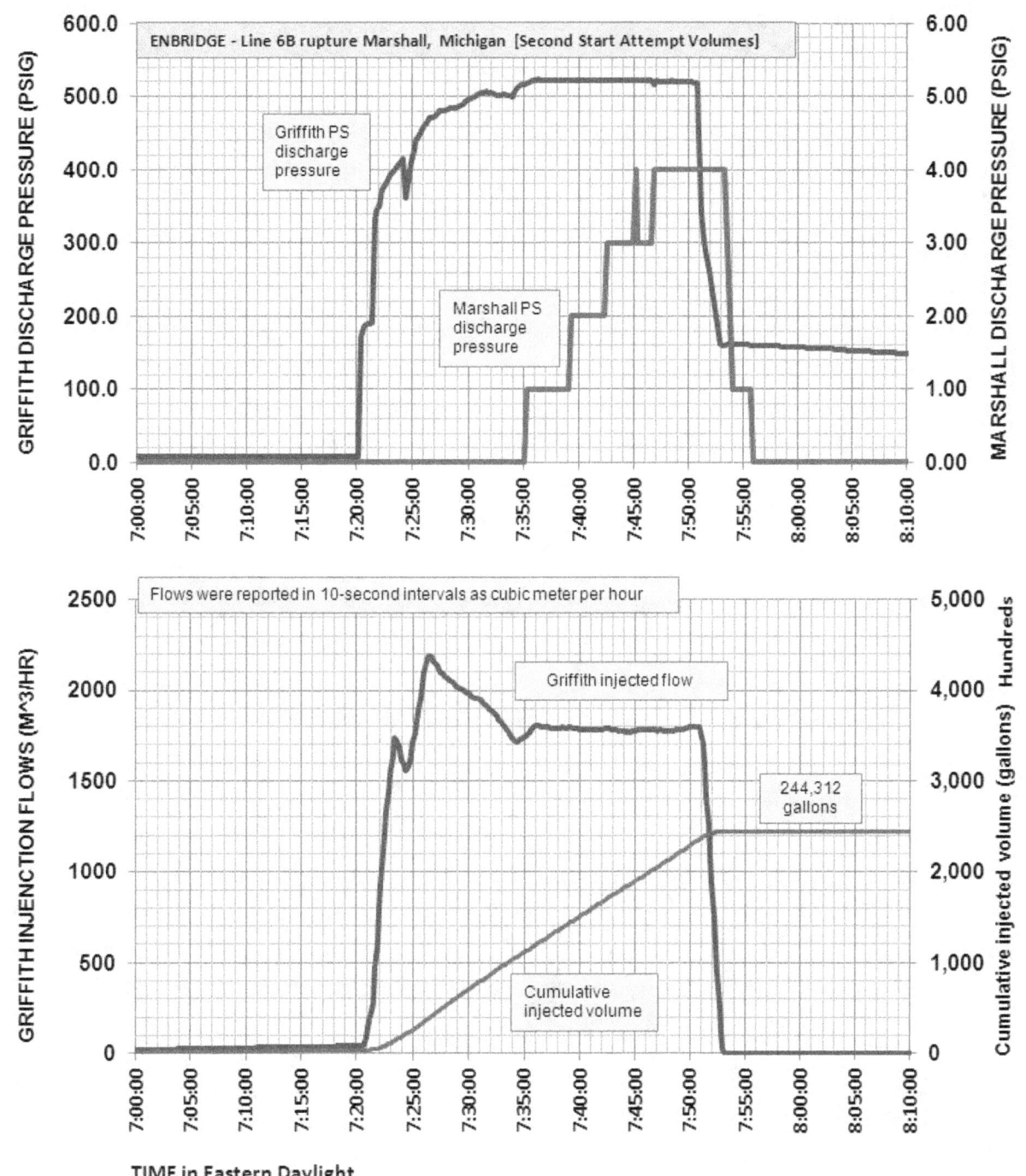

TIME in Eastern Daylight